CW00961349

Isn't It About Time?

How to stop
putting things off
and get on with your life

Andrea Perry

Worth Publishing
www.worthpublishing.com

First published by Worth Publishing Ltd, 2002
6 Lauderdale Parade, London W9 1LU
www.worthpublishing.com

ISBN 1-903269-03-2

Typeset by G&E 2000 Digital Media Group, Peterborough, UK
Printed and bound in Great Britain by Bath Press, Bath, UK

Cover and text design by Tracey Weeks for G&E 2000
© Worth Publishing.

Contents

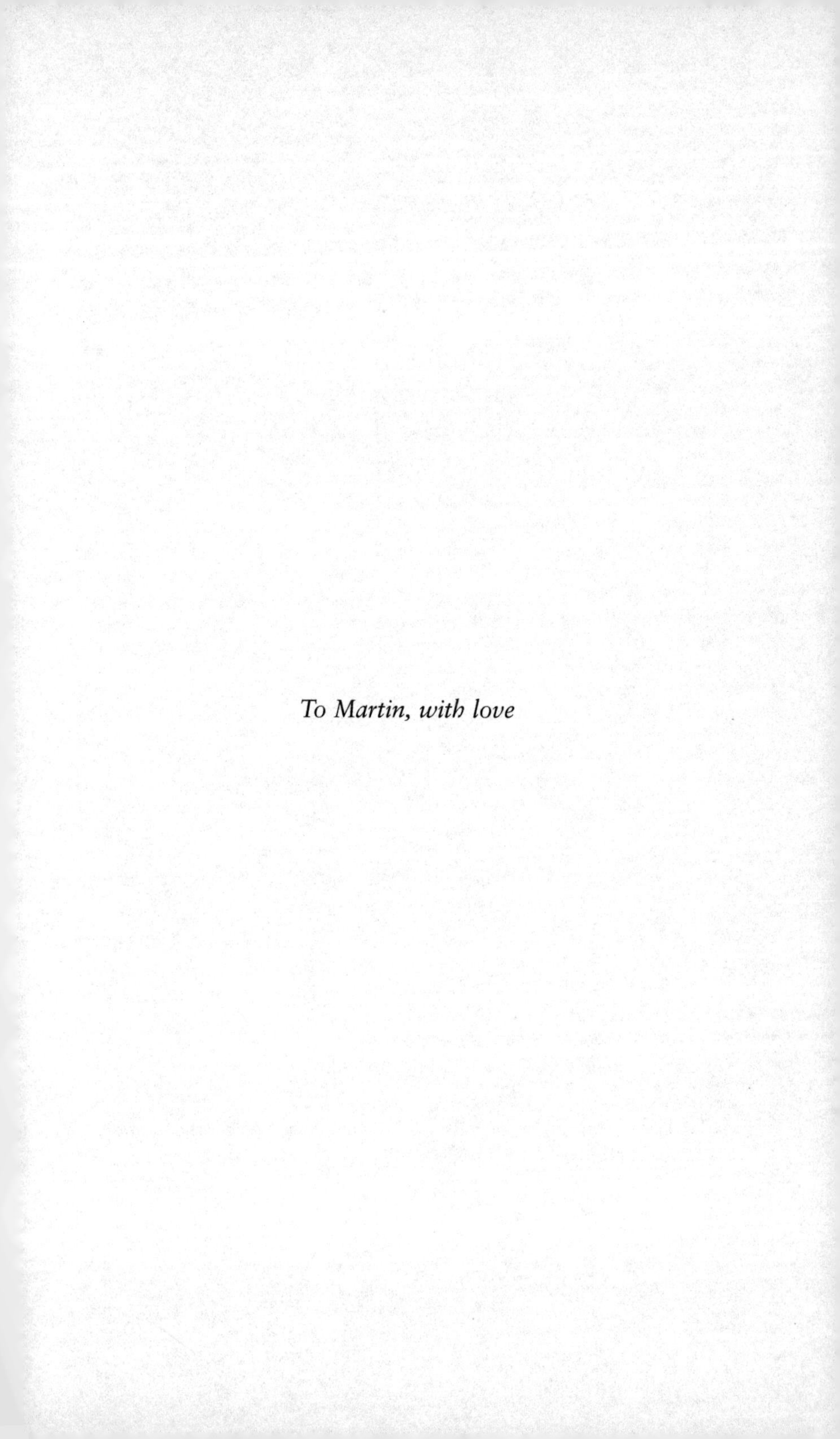

To Martin, with love

Acknowledgements

Many people have contributed, to the writing and completion of this book, and I feel very fortunate to have benefitted from their encouragement, skill and inspiration.

Firstly, I would like to thank and appreciate the people who shared their paths to overcoming procrastination in therapy with me, or in workshops. So much of what I have learnt comes from their courage and insight, and the changes they made. I'd like to thank the staff of Chapel Orchard, Merton, and Kingston College who gave me support, encouragement and a rich diversity of opportunities over the years to become aware, experiment, grow professionally and personally – and to laugh a lot. The process was generously facilitated by my supervisors, especially Alida Gersie, Parizad Bathai, Gordon Waller and Marina Jenkyns, to whom my thanks; and above all to T, whose wisdom, kindness and sheer tenacity contributed so much to my capacity to thrive.

I would like to thank Sarah Thayer, who was the first person to believe in the book, and to whose advice I have often referred; and the other students at Kingston College who made teaching there such a pleasure. I would like to thank Joel Mischon for his cartoons, and for completing them even when I was procrastinating about finishing the manuscript!: Louize Petch for her love, support and thoughtful advice on Part 2: Jenny Stacey for her feedback, comments and capacity to produce champagne at opportune moments: Catherine Pestano for her "tough love" approach and for her constant stream of encouragement and inspiring ideas: Anne Crump for her design feedback: Jane Wood for her sharp perception, wit, and lessons in reliability: Clifton Fearon, trainer at Courtney's gym at the Paddington Recreation Centre, for his help with *It's time to move your body*: Bruce Currie for his bountiful support and for sharing the creative process: Brian Swinson of G&E 2000, who took on the project of designing *Isn't It About Time?* with friendly confidence: Tracey Weeks, also of G&E 2000, for her constant warmth, imagination and much needed patience when asked to amend "just one more thing".

I would like to thank the staff of Worth Publishing for their whole-hearted enthusiasm for the project. Nell Crowdey, for promoting the book at every opportunity well before it was finished; Petra Howard-Wuerz, for her energy and sense of fun, and for her professionalism and advice on representing the book.

Most of all to Martin Wood, husband, and fellow garden-maker, without whose consistent love, support, good sense, and willingness to produce cups of tea at any time of the day or night, this book would not have been created – my love, as always, and gratitude.

Isn't It About Time?

Do you put things off?

Do you tell yourself – *I'll do it later* – or tomorrow, another time – even when you know you probably could – or should – do the Thing today? You're not alone. Nearly everyone procrastinates now and again – me included, of course! It can be an irritating habit, or a real difficulty, and if you live with someone else who puts things off a lot, it can drive you up the wall. Have a look at the **Questionnaire** at the end of Part 1, and count the number of "True" responses you make. The total will give you a quick indication of how large a part procrastination currently plays in your life.

As I've been writing and talking to people about this book, I've heard the same old "joke" from friends as well as strangers ... *I bet you'll never finish it!* Hmm. For years one of my favourite phrases was – *I'll do it tomorrow*. Sometimes clients and colleagues remarked that they saw me as confident, decisive and effective – and they were right, of course, I could be. But I often had a sinking sense of – *if only they knew...!* – because I *also* had a pile of put-off commitments, half-finished projects and long-avoided decisions lying in wait for me outside the consulting room. So I had the advantage of knowing first-hand about the struggles the people I worked with experienced, when they attempted to start, stay committed to or complete what they genuinely wanted to do. They felt frustrated and trapped by their seeming inability to just *get on with it!*, just as I did.

I'd like to say that one day, one of us stumbled over a magic, catch-all, universally applicable solution – but that's not what happened. Between us, over time, through trial and error, we discovered many different ways to overcome procrastination, and as many individual journeys to stop putting things off and to becoming as effective and creative as you want to be. So ***Isn't It About Time?*** offers you an understanding of how procrastination develops as a habit in the first place, and many, many strategies for moving forward which worked for me and the people I've met in therapy and in business. They, and the friends and families we've had the great good fortune to be loved by in the process, join me in celebrating the completion this book represents.

And it's well worth celebrating, because the good news is that no matter how entrenched your habit, *you can learn to stop putting off your life.* You can free yourself and your energies for *much* more enjoyable and satisfying ways of living. You can unblock your systems, and get your show back on the road again, no matter how stuck you may feel right now. Even if you automatically put things off when you could or should be getting going, you have the capacity to be effective and you can develop it hugely.

Which can be a very exciting process, from Day One. Because when you start to do things differently, you'll find that hidden inside the often irritating and bewildering habit of procrastination is a secret source of great value and delight, which you will be able to draw on. If you're someone who procrastinates a great deal, then you have vast stores of unexplored treasure to unlock and to benefit from.

I hope ***Isn't It About Time?*** helps you find your own key.

Part 1
I'll do it tomorrow...

JUST ANOTHER
5 MINUTES

Procrastination – thief of time

To procrastinate is to create delay. It's to put off the "Thing" you need or want to do until later, maybe until tomorrow, (given the literal meaning of the word). But as anyone who has ever procrastinated knows, it's unlikely that tomorrow *really* means doing the Thing the next day. *I'll do it tomorrow* in true procrastination-speak means this year, next year, sometime, never. Which is why it's not the same as postponement.

When you postpone a task, a decision, a conversation, you know that when the time comes, you'll do what you've said you'll do. When you say – "later", it feels different, if you're confident you can trust yourself to follow through, no matter how hard or difficult the Thing is. When you or I procrastinate, on the other hand, we're trying to avoid something; to notice what we need or want, for example, to make plans, see the task through, or to finish it off – or even to rest afterwards. All our actions, everything we do, make, create, say, more towards or away from, follow these stages.

We move through the stages as if we're following a spiral. It's not a closed cycle, because each time you complete an action, you move forward in time – you are no longer who, what or where you were. Your body, mind, heart and soul have more experience of life – and you're older!

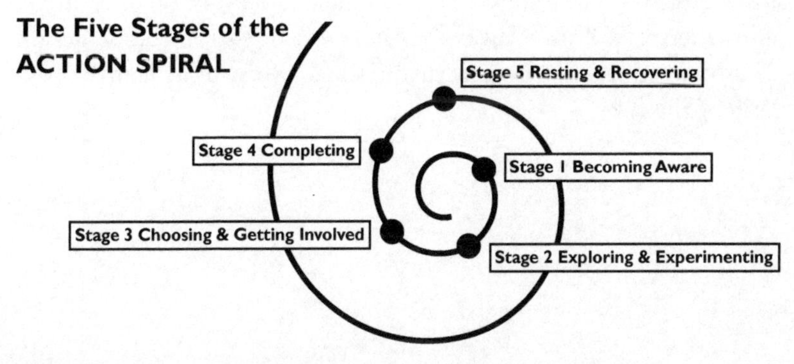

Stage 1: Becoming aware of
what you need or want to do

Stage 2: Exploring and experimenting;
planning: getting ready

***Stage 3: Choosing** what you're going to do*
*and **Getting Involved** in doing it*

***Stage 4: Completing** what you set out to do*

Stage 5: Pausing,
withdrawing from action, taking a break, reflecting on what you've done

You'll find the image of the **Action Spiral** throughout this book, because –

You can procrastinate at any stage in the spiral - and some of us do!

Understanding the **Action Spiral** shows you how you let yourself move ahead with your life, and how you get stuck. We learn to navigate our journey through these stages from the moment we're born. We get lessons in how to go about doing things from the first adults in our lives, by watching what they do and by being given permission (or not) to do things for ourselves. You can learn to be effective and follow your own logic and intuition in creative, constructive and joyful ways. Or you can learn to block action and forward motion by procrastinating. Most of us learn a mixture of the two.

~

This section, **Part 1**, is all about how procrastination can seriously affect your life, who does it and who doesn't, and how overcoming the habit will bring you huge benefits.

To help you identify your own particular way of putting things off, in the next section, **Part 2**, I'll first describe *How We Learn To Do Things* as we develop as babies and small children, and how we acquire the important permission to build our resources and gain the satisfaction of being effective. I'll then explain *How Procrastination Develops*, and how we acquire the habit of blocking forward movement through each – or every! – stage of the Action Spiral.

You may, on the other hand, want to go straight to the "solutions" section! **Part 3**, *Ways Forward*, is full of ideas and suggestions for allowing the effective part of yourself to develop and become more active and creative, and for letting the part of you that puts things off retire. The suggestions are often grouped according to which stage of the Spiral you feel you get blocked, so once you know which one is most challenging for you, you can focus on that and sail through the rest!

In **Part 4** *If Someone You Know Procrastinates*, you'll find thoughts on what you can do to help if your partner, child, colleague, boss or anyone else is procrastinating – and what can be more of a hindrance! And finally, **Part 5** *A New Way of Living* addresses how life can be when your old habit of procrastination has moved on to better things....

So you can read straight on from here, or you can dip in and out. The most important thing is that you enjoy the ride.

If you think you procrastinate,
and you want to do something about it,
you're reading the right book.

Procrastination is a way to resist the forward-going motion of the **Action Spiral**, by bidding for time. There's usually a lot of verbal activity going on, in our heads or out loud; we come up with phrases like these –

> *I'll do it soon*
> *I'll have another coffee and then I'll call the doctor*
> *I'll call the plumber when I get back from holiday*
> *I'll tell him about the money when he's in a better mood*
> *I'll ask her about the promotion when I've finished this work*
> *I'll spend some time with the kids when I've got more energy*
> *I'll send some money to that charity when I've got a stamp*
> *I'll do it later, after I've read my e-mail, done the ironing, lost 3 stone*, dusted the top of the curtains*, climbed that mountain, made my first (or second) million, sailed around the world**

Amazing what starts looking interesting and important when you want to avoid something else!!!

Sound familiar? Perhaps you've noticed a phrase you use yourself ? (I'm glad I'm not the only one!) Procrastination is just one strategy in the whole repertoire of human behaviours, so it's likely that most of us do it at some time or other.

Becoming aware.

It's pretty unlikely that you procrastinate over every aspect of your life. But if you know you do it sometimes, and you want to understand what's going on in order to do things differently, increasing your awareness of when you do and when you don't procrastinate is a good starting place on the way to making positive changes.

Close your eyes, or stare into space, and remember the last time you put something off
(It might have been over something you wanted or needed to do, or something someone else wanted or needed you to do)

Get as clear a picture as you can, filling in all the little details in your mind's eye

What was the Thing ?
Did you want to Do it or not ?
What phrases went through your mind ?
How did you feel as you thought about Doing the Thing ?
How did you feel after you had decided to put off doing it?
What happened next ?
If you eventually Did the Thing, how did you feel then ?

NEXT ....

Remember the last time you thought of something you wanted or needed to do,
(or that someone else wanted or needed you to do) - which you then did.
(Again, find as clear and as detailed an image as you can)

What was the Thing ?
Did you want to Do it or not ?
What phrases went through your mind ?
How did you feel as you thought about Doing the Thing ?
How did you feel as you Did the Thing ? and afterwards ?

~

By doing the simple exercise above, you've given yourself some extremely useful information. In ***Isn't It About Time?*** you'll find a lot about how and why we procrastinate, as well as suggestions and ideas as to how to change that behaviour. But it's very important at the outset to remember that you can be decisive, committed and effective, in order to build on your success. And to celebrate this. Because simply focusing on habits you want to change is not enough. This book is written to help you develop your strengths, not necessarily to chop off weaknesses! We'll come back to using these strengths in **Part 3**, after understanding more about procrastination.

Life on Hold

Procrastination is known as the thief of time, but it's worse than that. No matter what it is that you want to do, if you procrastinate, you put your life on hold, you stop moving along the spiral.

> Say you have to do your tax return. You remember you need to do it, set aside a time; maybe you groan a bit if anyone will listen (or is this just me?). Then you move into action, hunt for all the relevant papers, make a coffee and sit down to do it. It's done. You find a stamp and send it off, probably feeling virtuous and relieved. You pause to watch some TV, and then you get on with the next thing.

When you're acting in accord with your thoughts, feelings and intentions, it can be as simple as that. Real feelings come and go, thoughts come and go, and they both contain energy that can be converted and expressed through action. The results of your action give you real-world experience, at thinking, feeling and bodily levels, which you can use for the future and help you improve your choices and decisions. Once you've rested, you become ready once again to notice and pay attention to the next thing, with all your energy available to you.

But if you procrastinate, you hold back. The tax return stays behind the clock on the mantelpiece. You may "go through the motions" of the **Action Spiral** in fantasy, have all kind of feeling responses or new ideas, but you haven't moved a muscle in the real world. You know you'll feel better when it's done, but there is no flow between your thoughts, feeling and movement, no real-world release. You don't think beyond whatever objection has arisen to moving on – you've become selective in following your own logic. So all that energy is still in your system – you can't relax, knowing the "Thing" is still lurking around, waiting for you to tackle it. Your intentions are in conflict, and this can be very uncomfortable.

If you procrastinate, you may experience some - or all! - of the following

- minor grumbling and fretting over what needs to be done
- self-criticism, guilt
- depression
- restlessness, or tiredness, especially in the mornings
- irritability and bad temper; provoking arguments
- tearfulness and being whiny
- swearing, shouting and being hostile
- obsessive and circular thinking, irrationality
- agitated movements
- accumulating chaos
- tension
- raised blood-pressure
- staring into space, immobilisation
- high oral-sensitivity and "mouth hunger": over-eating, drinking, or smoking

Not a lot of fun!

Imagine a car being repeatedly revved outside your window early on a Sunday morning. Procrastinating, or being around a person procrastinating, who is not engaging their internal " gears" to move forward, can be just as disruptive. If procrastinating becomes a habit, even in one area of your life, then sooner or later the ideas and half-started projects, unfulfilled promises and never-tested-out dreams will clutter up your ability to move forward. You get stuck in the moment: your energy gets taken up, as much as files in your computer consume energy even when you don't open them, as much as too many things in your handbag means it takes you ages to find your purse.

Perhaps you tell yourself it doesn't matter that much? But storing an image of *How Much Better Life Will Be when I .....* in the file marked *Things I'll Do Tomorrow* can mean you amble along with lowered expectations of now. You don't get particularly excited anymore, but you just think it's because you're getting older. Procrastination puts your life on hold, in a time-warp, and words like *curious, fascinated, passionate, thrilled, delighted, refreshed,* and *let's do it again tomorrow!* ...gradually lose their meaning.

It's like being a boat, and barnacles being allowed to grow on the sides of your hull. Smaller sea creatures begin to make homes on the sides of the barnacles. Then weed begins to be caught and to grow between the rough edges of the shells, floating out in a green halo around you as you float in the gloomy shallows, aching to glide out into fresher waters. Then old boots and paper and twigs and unimaginable and unmentionable flotsam and jetsam begin to be trapped in the weed (it's definitely getting worse). Eventually any progress you try to make through the water is seriously hampered. Everything takes so much more effort than necessary. All those *I'll get around to it one day's.....* drag you back as you try to move ahead.

If your mind and feelings and spirit are clogged up and sluggish, it's harder to act spontaneously, harder even to notice a lifting of curiosity and excitement that might take you in the direction of something you'd enjoy. Attitudes harden when fresh new ideas aren't allowed in and through, and your whole system gets more rigid if you don't have flow.

Our bodies carry natural metaphors for being creative, productive and giving ourselves permission to take action – and the opposite.

Imagine you're a tube, or a system of tubes.
Your pipes get furred up!
Your arteries get blocked!
Your back gets creaky and your muscles get stiff!

In **Part 2**, I'll describe how different physical problems can arise through the repeated tension of holding ourselves back, when we put off moving through the different stages of the **Action Spiral**. And in **Part 3**, you'll find various kinds of activity which can help release that tension and strengthen your ability to get going again, to re-discover the state of relaxed readiness from which you can respond to whatever inspires your interest, curiosity and passion. And isn't that how we'd all like to live?

Procrastination and Trust

It may not seem like much - but each time you say to yourself –

> *I'll do that Thing – start it – finish it – after the News – first thing in the morning – at the weekend – tomorrow – next week – later – soon ...*

and then, when it comes to the time, you *don't* do the thing and put it off yet again - basically, you're breaking a promise to yourself. Your self-belief and sense of self-worth plummets, and your anxiety about whatever you need to do increases. Whether we can trust ourselves, and how the different aspects of our personalities negotiate with each other plays a big part in being self-confident, happy and creative. Imagine the organising, planning part of yourself and the one that does things in the real world.

> *Do they get on? Do they trust each other? Does the one know that the other will follow through? Do they negotiate, wheedle, bully or rebel? Or does the part of you that does things feel burdened by the expectations of the planner, or unsupported once things don't go according to plan?*

Perhaps they're both stuck, and looking for a mediator. The simplest example of internal conversations is the classic of trying to get out of bed in the morning, when the dialogue probably goes something like this:

Scene: A warm bed, 7.00 am on a Monday morning.
You have decided this is going to be the first day of a new week of healthy living.

Working self:	*I've got to get up if I'm going to have a proper breakfast and walk to work*
Snuggling self:	*But I don't want to leave my lovely bed*
Working self:	*If I don't get up soon, I'll be late*
Snuggling self:	*Yes but if I stay here another just another 10 minutes, I'll still be able to get ready in time. I'm so comfortable and I'm sure I need the rest*

<u>10 minutes pass</u>

Working self:	*If I don't get up now I'll get indigestion when I walk,*
Snuggling self:	*Ah but if I skip breakfast, I'll still be on time for work. No breakfast is a good way to start a new eating pattern. I'll just stay here until quarter past*

<u>10 minutes pass</u>

Working self:	*It's twenty past and I'll definitely miss my train now even if I skip breakfast*
Snuggling self:	*If I take the car, I'll still catch the train. I'll start the walking programme tomorrow. If I get a good rest today, which I obviously need, I'll be more ready*

When you say you'll do something and then do it, you feel secure, and your confidence increases. You know you're trustworthy, you know you're going to do what you say you're going to do. And that builds hope. But you introduce doubt and lose self-trust by not keeping your promises to yourself, or by exciting yourself with hopes and dreams but then not following through. You tell yourself you'll travel along the **Action Spiral**, but you jump off. If someone else kept making promises to you that they didn't keep, you'd soon stop listening, or you'd listen knowing that the words were pretty empty. Who wants to be teased? Who wouldn't become cynical? Why on earth would any of us want to disappoint ourselves in this way?

There's no point in blaming yourself for doing this, but it is worth noticing and beginning to understand. It seems strange – but we all do it, at some time or another.

Try this on your own or with a good friend in a private space or a big park

Part 1. Imagine that you have just achieved something you have always wanted.

Walk about with the thought that life is now full of everything you always wanted, and will remain so. Think of all the things you can look forward to, love and joy and happiness. Enjoy the feelings and any body changes that follow, including how you are breathing. Notice (or ask your friend to notice) how you move, how you hold your body, in which direction you look, anything different to usual.

Part 2. Now imagine that someone you care about has just let you down for the umpteenth time.

Walk about with the thought that life is just as it has always been, that what you hoped for will not happen, that all the promises were empty. Notice the feelings and any body changes that follow, including how you are breathing. Notice (or ask your friend to notice) how you move, how you hold your body, in which direction you look, anything that is different.

Then give yourself a big shake, jump up and down and shout "Never again!! " - or anything else that might amuse you or break you out of the gloom.

Part 3. Repeat Part I as often as you like.

~

What do we procrastinate about ?

ANYTHING. Absolutely anything. Throughout the book you'll find examples of people procrastinating at each stage of the **Action Spiral** – and overcoming the habit and moving on! The interesting thing is that different people put off different things. And you can procrastinate today over the kind of thing that you did easily a year ago; or, conversely, simply get on with something today which used to be incredibly difficult.

This should give us all hope. *At any stage in life* it is possible to learn how to stop procrastinating, and get on with living the kind of life you want. Have a look at the list below of the kinds of things that people procrastinate about. In each category some of the items are about goals and tasks, and some of them are about taking care of what we already have. Notice whether you tend to put off more of one kind than the other. That may give you useful information about your preferences.

**Noticing what you like and don't like
can help you stop procrastinating**

(For more on preferences and choices, see Part 3)

You can put off –

PHYSICAL
Getting eyes tested
Getting teeth checked
Going to the doctor with worrying symptoms, e.g. lumps or

passing blood
Checking breasts and genitals for changes
Losing weight
Taking care of your hair, nails and skin
Enjoying yourself sexually
Getting proper birth control
Having safe sex
Stopping smoking
Taking exercise and getting fit
Having enough sleep, rest and relaxation
Enjoying and appreciating having a body and moving in it

WORK
Finding a job you really enjoy or find satisfying
Developing your skills
Developing your working relationships
Initiating, developing and completing projects
Organising your time
Organising your workspace
Negotiating for more money
Writing and responding to letters, faxes and e-mail
Enjoying and appreciating being at work

RELATIONSHIPS
Working out what you want to give to relationships, and what you'd like to receive
Making friends
Finding a partner
Having children, creating a family
Paying attention to your own needs and those of others
Spending time alone, with people and animals you care about
Listening
Saying what needs to be said, even when it's difficult
Having fun
Making and responding to calls, letters, faxes and e-mail
Buying or making, giving and receiving presents
Enjoying and appreciating relationships

LIVING SPACE
Finding a home you really enjoy, or finding ways to enjoy the one you have
Decorating your home in satisfying ways
Cleaning, washing, ironing,
Carrying out repairs and maintenance
Making glorious gardens, beautiful balconies and pretty patios

APPEARANCE
Sorting out clothes
Buying new clothes
Taking old clothes to a charity shop or clothes swap
Enjoying wearing the clothes you like
Finding hair-styles that suit

THINGS
Sorting things out and taking care of them
De-cluttering, throwing or giving things away
Sticking up photo albums
Maintaining cars and bicycles
Enjoying and appreciating the things you like and want to keep

COMMUNITY
Paying attention to where you live, and who lives nearby
Noticing what you might be able to contribute to your area
Participating in the life of your community
Paying attention to the effect of your life on the environment
Identifying causes you believe in and contributing to their work
Writing to an MP or the local council about issues of importance
Enjoying and appreciating where you live and who lives nearby

INTERESTS
Exploring and experimenting to find out what you enjoy and what you might be interested in or good at
Making time to enjoy interests
Improving skills and learning more about interests

RELAXATION
Noticing when you need to stop
Making time to rest and regenerate
Meditating
Sleeping
Doing things you find relaxing

DREAMS
Day-dreaming
Working out what you think is worthwhile or that you'd really enjoy being/doing or having
Working out the steps in that direction
Taking the steps and talking to the people who can help you
Enjoying the journey as much as arriving
Notice when you've fulfilled your dreams
Celebrating success

VALUES
Working out your values
Living by them
Learning from mistakes

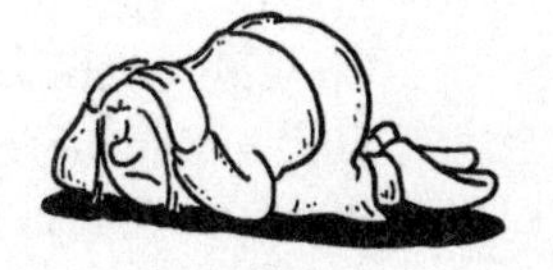

Isn't procrastination useful sometimes ?

This is a very interesting question. All human strategies for coping with life evolve to preserve us, so it must have benefits. Sometimes we really do need to put things off. Taking a break, relaxing, having a snooze, going into idling and musing time and not *doing* all the time is an essential way to stay sane (and is a phase of the **Action Spiral** which people put off at their long-term peril). Rehearsing what you're going to say before you say it can give confidence and avoid unnecessary pitfalls. Avoiding threatening or uncomfortable situations may well keep you safe in a temporary way. Delay may be absolutely the right thing; waiting and watching and allowing space are capacities which could reduce road-rage, for example. But when taking time out, rehearsing, avoiding and delay become habitual, the spontaneous flow of your life is interrupted, and unhelpful and uncomfortable pressure builds up. Procrastination can be such an unconscious, automatic response that it becomes the appendix of life, useful once for digestion, but now pretty much redundant – and just as much a dead end. You don't want to leave it until it requires surgery!

Postponing the Thing can buy you time, at least for a while, which you may need to properly digest or assimilate, plan, think through and so on. So what might look like procrastination could be part of the exploratory, mobilising phase of doing something. My *exploring and experimenting* phase might look like procrastination to you – or even to me! – and vice versa.

> This morning I was trying to find a way into a section of Part 3, and "found myself'" doing all sorts of other bits here and there in Part 2, tidying up grammar, spelling and so on. Once I would have thought that this was Monday morning avoidance of getting down to writing new material. I'd have thought it was purely a distraction from the Real Work (like filling up with crisps rather than having a good meal). But whilst I've been doing it I've been back-burner-ing ideas for Part 3, and now I know how I want to approach it. So was it procrastination, or was it delay with purpose?

Perhaps we can only really tell from the outcome. If you procrastinate, you tend to be left with a sense of incompleteness; you can feel restless, unsatisfied, maybe vaguely guilt, and tired without feeling you've necessarily expended a lot of energy. You know that a part of you is "otherwise engaged" with The Thing you're putting off, and not really available to enjoy and get on with life. When you've done Real Work (physical, mental or emotional) or been involved in Real Play you feel really satisfied. Worn out even, but refreshingly so. And that's the difference. So no, I don't think procrastination is useful. *Consciously* choosing to create delay can be.

Who procrastinates?

So who does it ? Procrastination is a strangely human activity – you don't see cats and dogs doing it! They just go with the flow of doing what they do, as and when they do it. But we humans have developed procrastination as a strategy for coping with complicated lives. Being able to postpone and delay can mean avoiding becoming exhausted, over-burdened, overwhelmed. But it can also all too easily become a way of missing out on excitement, pleasure, responsibility and satisfaction. And it can start to dominate how you approach life, almost without you noticing.

Most people know what it's like to put off this and that, here and there, and realise that we might find more satisfaction in doing things differently. Although some do it more than others, I don't think it's at all helpful to call yourself or anyone else "a procrastinator", and I've avoided doing so in this book. The reason is simple. If I put a label on my whole self, then somewhere inside there develops a sense that *that is who I am*. And maybe even all I am, or could be in the future. Much better to say –

"Sometimes I procrastinate."

In fact even better to say, (even if it's not true),

"Well, I suppose I procrastinate occasionally,
but I'm also very effective, creative and productive"

(For more on constructive self-talk, see Part 3)

Procrastination can stop us living honestly and fulfilling our dreams, but in its worst form, it can bring life to a standstill, or even be life-threatening.

Fatal delay

Forgetting to ask a doctor to check that itchy mole on your face, could diminish your chances of getting adequate treatment for skin cancer. Thinking that tomorrow will be a better day to check your tyres, could lead to a blow-out on the motorway when you or someone in your family is driving fast. Putting off having holidays throughout your working life can mean you have fatal heart attack the day after you retire. Procrastination can lead to serious things going wrong in our lives, or those of others.

Burn-out

You might know someone who is procrastinating in every area of their life, and whose life is being seriously affected as a result. It could be an indication that they are suffering from burn-out, the state beyond ordinary stress which can seriously endanger health and mental stability. They may be feeling mentally and emotionally overwhelmed by the demands of day-to-day living. Life may have lost pleasure and purpose. It's a kind of hell, and the genuine agony is only compounded by other people saying *Well, just do something about it.*

People in this state may need to seek the help of a doctor and take some time out, or find a therapist, counsellor or psychologist who can help them understand what is happening, and offer support.

Fortunately most of us will never experience that terrifying state of immobilisation.

For most people, most of the time, procrastinating is probably just one of the ways in which we cope with busy lives. Some people habitually procrastinate about pretty well everything they do, but it doesn't stop them from having a reasonably successful life. They may have a few disappointments, unfulfilled dreams, regrets, "to do" lists which never get done or don't get done on time, things they wished they'd said, or tried, or experienced etc. – but they and the people around them tolerate this state, moaning now and then, perhaps, but tolerating it. Other people just have one or two areas in their lives in which they procrastinate, or go through a stage of procrastinating for a while only to get back to getting on with things afterwards.

So the short answer to the question *Who procrastinates?* is probably *nearly all of us*, at some time or another.

Who doesn't procrastinate?
Who moves forward?

Even those of us who procrastinate a lot know how to be effective in some areas of our lives. But if we take points along a spectrum, there are people whose general way of living is the opposite of procrastinatory. And how they go about things can be informative – have a look at the clock on the next page.

If you did the second Imaging exercise *(Something you thought about – and then did)*, I imagine that you can recognise yourself in the image on the next page. We are all capable of behaving in ways that respect ourselves, other people and the time we have on the planet. But sometimes we seem to forget, and then we procrastinate.

Isn't It About Time? is about creating the circumstances for yourself in which you can do what you need and want to do – in ways that make you feel proud.

People who move forward...

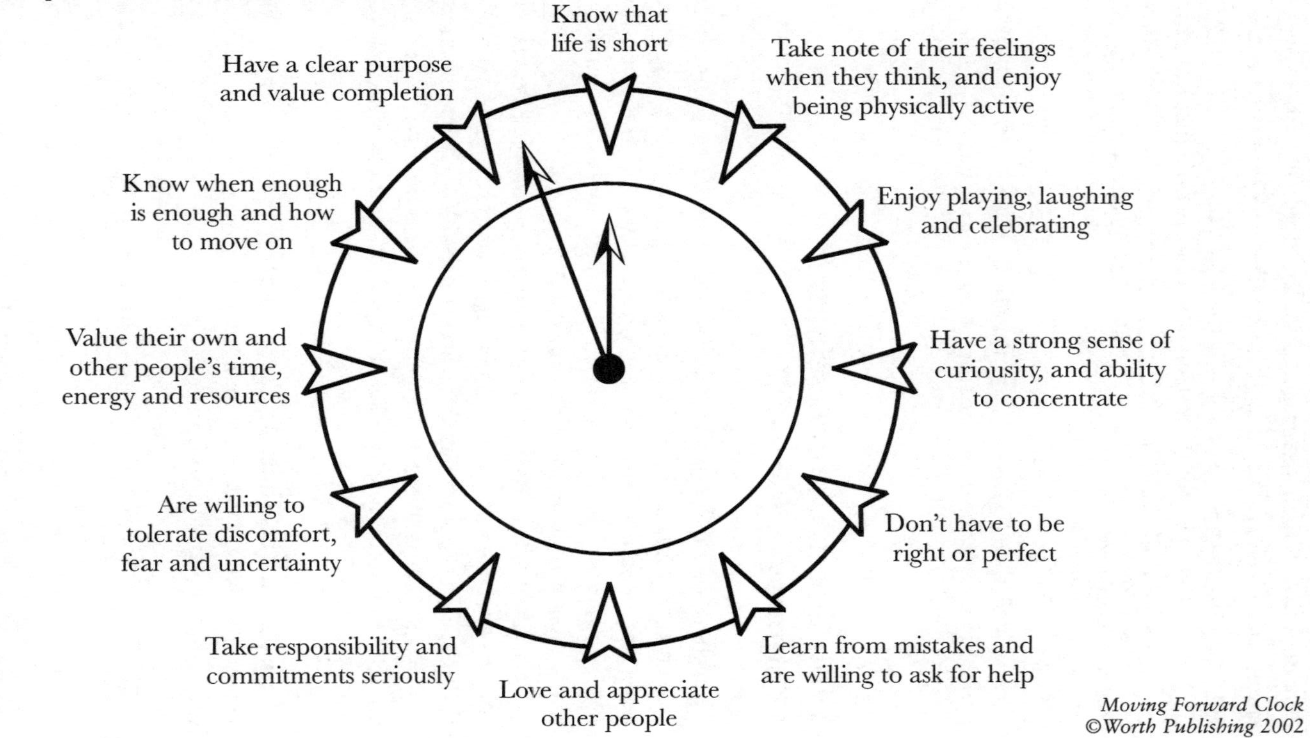

Moving Forward Clock

ARE YOU PUTTING OFF YOUR LIFE?

Answer these questions to get a better idea about you and procrastination.

	TRUE	Neither completely true or false	FALSE
1. You have clothes in your wardrobe which you never wear because they need to go to the dry cleaners, a button is missing, or some stitching has come apart	☐	☐	☐
2. You haven't written your Will, or the one you have written is well out of date	☐	☐	☐
3. You often have rather empty weekends, because you don't get around to planning anything interesting, fun or special	☐	☐	☐
4. If you have to write something, an official letter, report, or essay, or fill in a form, you often leave it until the last minute	☐	☐	☐
5. You rarely finish all the items on your To Do list	☐	☐	☐
6. You can't remember the last time you woke up feeling really refreshed	☐	☐	☐
7. If you have something difficult to say to someone, you wait until the person is in a good mood	☐	☐	☐

	TRUE	Neither completely true or false	FALSE
8. *As a child, you used to use magic words to keep yourself or other people safe*	☐	☐	☐
9. *Your partner, children or employees seem to have problems with procrastination*	☐	☐	☐
10. *You hardly ever open official mail the moment you pick it up off the door mat*	☐	☐	☐
11. *If you won the lottery, you'd change your life completely*	☐	☐	☐
12. *You've been described as "living on another planet"*	☐	☐	☐
13. *You know that you're good at what you do, but you find it very hard to promote yourself*	☐	☐	☐
14. *You often hear of ideas that you've had being developed and made successful by other people*	☐	☐	☐
15. *You feel guilty if you're not on the go all the time*	☐	☐	☐
16. *As a child, you used to sulk*	☐	☐	☐

17. *You find it hard to watch horror or suspense movies, as the images keep you awake or disturbed long after watching them*	☐	☐	☐
18. *You feel bogged down by the amount of paperwork in your life*	☐	☐	☐
19. *You wish you were better informed about world affairs*	☐	☐	☐
20. *If someone saw inside your handbag, briefcase, attic or kitchen drawers right now, you'd be horrified*	☐	☐	☐
21. *You often feel uncertain over whether you should walk away from situations, decisions and people which make you feel uncomfortable, or whether you should stay and try to change things*	☐	☐	☐
22. *You have a burning, possibly secret, ambition, which you never seem to find time to prioritise*	☐	☐	☐
23. *You keep text books from college for years "just in case" you need to refer to them*	☐	☐	☐
24. *You rarely experience whole-hearted satisfaction, because completion is so hard for you*	☐	☐	☐

	TRUE	Neither completely true or false	FALSE
25. *Your New Year Resolutions are pretty much the same every year*	☐	☐	☐
26. *You can't remember the last time you had a holiday*	☐	☐	☐
27. *You often miss people's birthdays, anniversaries, or life-events, and special occasions, or forget what family members have asked you to do*	☐	☐	☐
28. *You have a lot of sports equipment, cassettes for learning foreign languages, diet or recipe books which you've barely used*	☐	☐	☐
29. *There was a lot tension in your first home, and your parents rarely had full-on, air-clearing, love-restoring rows*	☐	☐	☐
30. *Often when you finish something difficult, you wonder why it took you so long*	☐	☐	☐

Total of TRUE responses

1-10 *Congratulations – you are obviously used to completing the Action Spiral and being highly effective. But if you've answered TRUE to questions 3, 6, 15 or 26, please look at the sections in this book on Putting off Pausing, because you may be putting off having a rest.*

11-20 *Although you can be effective, understanding at which stage you block yourself on the Action Spiral will help you identify what you need to move forward. You probably realise how much life you are missing. Find something to help you in this book, make one tiny change today, and build up your resources.*

21-30 *Please read this book now! You deserve to enjoy the time of your life – and find an ally or good friend to support you on the way.*

Part 2
To do or not to do

How Children Learn to do Things

How We Learn to Procrastinate Instead

JUST ONE MORE GAME.
ARMADA HERE

To do or not to do

How Children Learn to do Things

So let's look at the **Action Spiral.** I'll describe each stage of how we learn to do things in the very early stages of life, and the kind of permission we need from our adults to help us to navigate that stage effectively and become productive and creative. Then I'll describe the kind of procrastination you might experience in yourself or someone else who has problems at that point.

Optimistic thought

Of course even procrastinating can be part of learning. Each time you do it, you are inevitably accumulating experience of its negative effects. So even as you put things off and seem to be heading in the opposite direction from where you want to go, or digging yourself deeper and deeper into the same old rut, you may just be going round a bigger loop of the spiral than you had imagined, (or a spiral within a spiral) and be trying to teach yourself how to do things more effectively. So when we come to *Part 3, Ways Forward* – you'll see that one of the things which works for some people is to deliberately procrastinate, even harder! louder! faster! – and more often!

Strange but true. More of this later.

So starting at the beginning ....

Stage 1
Becoming Aware

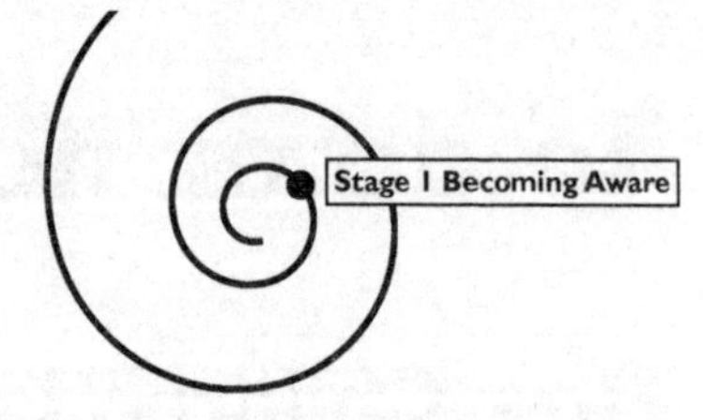

As babies we start "Doing Things" as soon as we can move - even inside the womb, some of us were very busy and active, as your mother may remember, fondly or otherwise. Once we're born, the main things we do as small babies up to about three months are –

- follow the sensitivity of our lips and discover they fit nicely round a nipple or something similar
- give it a good suck once we've found it, and settle into drinking
- look at things, notice sounds
- turn towards what interests us and away from what we don't like
- protest if we're not comfortable
- try to get the attention we need by making noises
- imitate facial expressions of the people who look at us
- wave our arms and legs around a bit

Most of the other things we do are a bit co-incidental to just being alive in the world. We're getting used to sleeping and waking, to being loved, fed, emptying our bladder and bowels whenever, wherever, and being cleaned up.. All the time we are *noticing and absorbing* all the sights and sounds, smells, tastes and touches that come our way. So if one of our thumbs happens to land in our mouths, we might just suck it "because it's there" – it might equally be a foot or a bear's ear, but that's OK. We probably didn't predict that anything would arrive, or go looking for it, but hey, if it's in your mouth, why not? Imagine being pleasantly, amiably, rosily drunk. Things wander in and out of your consciousness, and you have the feeling that the world is presenting itself to you for your amusement. Objects and bits of people take on importance in all sorts of weird ways and at unusual angles. Your mouth goes a bit slack, your aim isn't quite as good but it doesn't seem to matter that much, in fact it's quite nice if things get a bit damp and squelchy. Perhaps it's a bit like that for little people, although their sensitivity, degree of alertness and ability to focus is probably far greater.

Babies and happy tipsy people are responding from moment to moment to the next thing of interest, uncluttered by the thing they were interested in just now. For the vast majority of babies, there is flow between ....

- their interest being caught by something
- responding to it by giving it attention and then
- moving on to the next thing when something else attracts them or their first interest wanes.

This is the first step in the Action Spiral

All through this time the people who are caring for us as babies are giving us messages about who we are, what life is like, who they are, how they feel about us, what they need to do for us, and many other things. Not always in words, but in the way we are touched, handled, looked at, carried and so on.

Messages that might ideally say –

> *"We're so happy you're here, you belong here, we love you. We're glad you are who you are, and it's fine for you to just be here and be taken care of – you don't have to do anything to be loved"* (1)

This is all information that we store – we are learning all the time, even in these early days of our lives. We sleep and lie awake in an atmosphere created by the people we live with, and by us. It may be filled with happy voices, laughter and smiling faces; or tension, raised voices, doors suddenly banging, sighs, tears, and fear. Or a mixture of both. We take it all into our little bodies, along with the milk.

We may be given messages that our attempts to make contact are noticed and welcomed; and we may feel encouraged to have another go. If we are ignored, or completely misread, we might be puzzled or a bit discouraged and not try again for a bit. You might learn that it's fine that your mother can't breast-feed you, or you might pick up a vague sense of depression or reluctance from her when you take a bottle. You may get the idea that pee-ing and poo-ing is just a part of life, and that you'll be dealt with calmly and kindly when you're all mucky. Or you may get the message that there is something "not nice" or quite frankly disgusting going on, and that somehow you're associated with it (and maybe "not quite nice" either).

If as babies we are really hungry, wet, over-tired, or restless on a hot night, we'll express our discomfort in the only way available to us – crying. We may find that the people caring for us quickly learn about our signals and needs, and that the way they have of doing things, the routines they need, and the speed they move at, is pretty compatible with ours. Life is sweet. We feel noticed and understood. But conversely, we might learn that the people caring for us follow their own time-table, and their own thoughts about our needs in ways that leaves us too uncomfortable for far too long. This is hard to bear alone. There is a mismatch, and inevitably, with most of the power on their side (we can still protest), we end up having to do a disproportionate amount of the adjusting, in the interests of survival, away from our basic rhythms, needs and temperament.

Babies need three basic things to support them "just being" in the world.

These are:

1. People taking care of them who are physically and emotionally present a lot of the time
2. Someone who can "read them" well enough to help them to settle down and not get too upset for too long
3. Having some success in their attempts to have an effect on the people taking care of them, at least some of the time.

No adult gets it right all the time. If the baby is responded to in the right-ish kind of way at the right-ish kind of speed (in other words it doesn't have to be exactly right all of the time) then she learns that it is fine for her to notice her own needs and to have them attended to willingly and kindly. This is crucial information. It lays down a template for so much for later on. It's the message we will need to receive time and time again all through our baby and toddler and small-person days, for us to really get the idea that life and people can be trusted. Really knowing this in a deep way means we can adapt to others' needs as well, and gradually find ways to notice and look after our own needs for ourselves. So just being able to be alive, relaxed and aware of our surroundings and to feel good like that is an important gift from our very beginnings. When we have that gift, we can enjoy noticing our amazing world and absorbing with all our senses. Our needs, based in bodily experience, will make themselves known to us from time to time.

Being relaxed, at ease and content, and then becoming aware of something internal or external and giving it our attention, is the first stage in the process of doing things.

But some of us find this basic state of relaxed awareness difficult to find, let alone sustain. You may find it hard to allow yourself to notice information from your body and from the environment, or to give attention to your needs and to what you find interesting. You may accomplish many things, indeed seem extremely productive from the outside, but you have a sense that you are somehow missing out on the richness and subtleties of life that other people seem to enjoy. Or all your achievements are in one area (for example, work); in other aspects of life (relationships, home etc. see the list in Part 1) you feel you're still on the starting blocks. You may have problems with sensation, circulation, difficulties in becoming sexually aroused, skin eruptions or dandruff, or digestive problems.

Difficulties like these may mean that you procrastinate at the AWARENESS stage of the Action Spiral.

Stage 2
Exploring and Experimenting

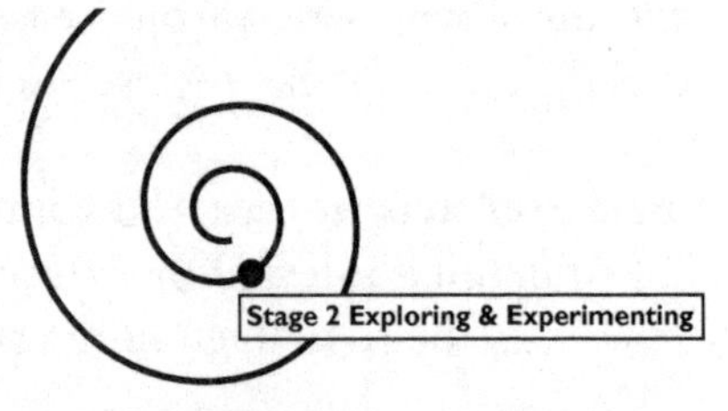

As we get a bit bigger, and a bit stronger, we begin to discover that if we push different bits of ourselves against something firm, something brilliant happens - we can move! And - those weird things we see every day down there (one day we'll call them hands) are connected to us and if we stretch them out we can get that funny furry thing and pull it towards our faces. Yes! We can pull! So now if we like the look of something, we can set about going towards it or getting it for ourselves! And if we don't like it, we can push it away or let it go.

Pushing, pulling, stretching, grabbing, and letting go are wonderful things to be able to do (Imagine if you couldn't anymore - you may have had that experience if you have hurt your back, neck, arm or hand in some way. Incredibly limiting) We are discovering that we can have an impact on the world, that we can express our interests through action, and that we live in a body with lots of different abilities, which are changing and developing every day. We need all kinds of different things to actively explore. We need other children and adults to play with and copy. Then we can find out what this body-thing we've got can experience and can do to and with all those exciting things out there in the world. These are all very big discoveries They set precedents for much else later.

So now let's have an image of a small child of around one year old, in a room with someone who is looking after him. There are lots of interesting things to touch, smell, taste, pull, poke, lift, move into and under, pull himself up on. What will the child do first? It depends. If he is feeling hungry, scared, upset, unwell or tired, he will probably do very little except give signals that he needs food or changing, to cry, be cuddled or sleep.

So adequate rest, good-health and security are important preconditions for beginning to explore what you can do out in the big, wide, colourful world. Children express bags of curiosity and energy when they feel rested, well and secure. When their basic physical and emotional needs are met, they don't want to hang around being rosy-cosy all day. Who would? They want to venture out and explore and experiment and experience being alive in every part of their little bodies. There is a flow and focus in a child's energy when it is fully engaged that is almost luminous. At the awareness stage, the baby simply noticed something, gave it attention and had a reaction. Now the little person wants to grab something in order to put it in his mouth, to see what that's like. His attention flows towards something of interest, and he's there, lifted on a wave of enthusiasm, curiosity and energy towards it. At the same time, the adult with him will be giving him all kinds of messages in the way that he or she responds to the little person's wish to start Doing Things.

Getting our fingers into everything, seeing what things do and how they smell and taste and feel and sound *doesn't mean having to be good at anything*. We're just finding out what the world's like through having lots of experiences. We are *experimenting and exploring*. And to do that we need lots of permission from the people taking care of us, and lots of attention while we find our own strengths and limitations. And of course these are changing and growing all the time, and our interests are developing, so the care we get has to be pretty sophisticated to keep up. Sometimes it'll be a bit restricting, and sometimes it'll be a bit lax. That's inevitable – no adult can get it right all the time.

But over time we need enough permission to feel and to learn that being curious, experimenting and exploring with all our bodily senses alive and active is fine. Children who really receive this kind of message, and are kept safe, have a wonderful start in life, because they are internalising a kind of physical confidence and internal security which they can probably rely on forever. They have good feelings about being physical – they live in their whole body, not just in their heads. If they're interested, curious, or excited about something, they feel it inside their body, and they know it's fine to express it, and fine to follow their interest and curiosity.

Most of us get a mixture of restricting and encouraging messages, starting from when we are tiny and continuing from many years of development. Adults who have managed to give us mostly encouraging messages whilst keeping up with how to keep us safe have done a great job! They've either had lots of positive messages themselves, or they've managed to keep their own anxieties to themselves. Being allowed and encouraged to express our interests in things, to explore and experiment without having to achieve anything or do anything right, also means the adults looking after us need to be able to tolerate MESS. Having a fixed agenda of exactly how things should be or should turn out is unlikely to work without lots of grief on all sides for someone looking after a toddler.

Finding out what crayons do doesn't mean you have to draw a house. Playing with bricks means finding out that knocking things down can be just as much fun as building them up. Especially if someone else has carefully built you a very big tower. You're not being bad, it just may be fun watching the bricks fly and hearing your big brother groan each time. Getting to feed yourself just like your big sister can be fun especially when you use your hands to put the lovely sticky chocolate pudding in your mouth. *Most of it went in the right hole, what's the problem? Bit round the chin and a bit on the cat never hurt anyone. It certainly got a laugh before Mum arrived with her hard wet cloth.* Playing with poo can be great too. It's warm and sticky and smelly, so it's confusing and upsetting how the adults get tense and cross and pick you up and frown and wash you as if you're not loveable. *What did I do? You laughed about the other brown stuff! You confuse me!*

All the time we're experimenting, we're learning a huge amount:

- We're learning about ourselves and our world. We get physical information from our senses (this thing is hard, sharp, hot, sweet, stripey)
- We have a physical response to the thing – it makes us feel comfy, sick, hurt, warm, excited
- We have an emotional response to the thing – it makes us feel happy, sad, angry, scared and surprised
- We notice what we can do, what other people do, what we'd like to do and what we can't do, – and how we feel about all these things
- We're learning about relationships with other people. We notice other people's emotional response to what we're doing – happy, sad, angry, scared, disgusted, disappointed, depressed, frustrated, amused, contented, exhausted, resentful, envious, delighted, excited.....etc.
- We notice that we can have even more of an effect on other people than when we're peacefully lying around or idly toying with our toes
- We notice we have an emotional response to other people's emotions – their happiness can affect us, as can their sadness, anger, fear, disgust and so on.

So much!!!!

What amazing beings people are. It's incredible how much we learn and take in all the time. Initially we're taking it in non-verbally, at a physical and sensory level. Our bodies and emotions remember! So, for example, playing at nine months old with the family pet becomes associated with all these things, so in later life we will be drawing on a huge bank of sensory and emotional information whenever we see, stroke, or avoid a cat. Body and feeling memories are working long before we understand what is said to us, or before we can use words to speak to others or to ourselves in our thoughts (see below); it's been noted that even tiny babies who have been taught sign language can communicate very clear wishes. And the permission to explore and experiment needs to continue as we move forward in our development. It's not as if we leave any stage behind; it's more as if we add the next one on. Like the rings of a tree. So then at any age, we can follow our curiosity when something intrigues us, and we'll find freshness and new information through our senses. (Or we can re-learn to – it's never too late to re-awaken the powerful capacities for excitement and absorption that we were born with).

Expressing our interest by getting closer to something, physically following our intent to explore and experiment and getting feedback through all our senses from that experience, is the next step in doing things. *(2)*

Some of us may have problems feeling that it is really all right to enjoy what we pick up with our senses, to follow what we find interesting and curiosity-and-pleasant-sensation-provoking. You may find it difficult to be physical, or to try new things. You may have health problems such as backache, arthritis (especially in the hands, joints – particularly knees – or lower back, all associated with restricting the action of moving towards and feeling safe to express curiosity): muscular tension, hearing difficulties, poor sight or sense of smell. You may feel tense sexually, and you may have difficulties with balance, co-ordination or rhythm. You may have forgotten how to play.

Difficulties like these may mean that you procrastinate at the EXPLORING and EXPERIMENTING stage of the Action Spiral.

Stage 3
Choosing and Getting Involved

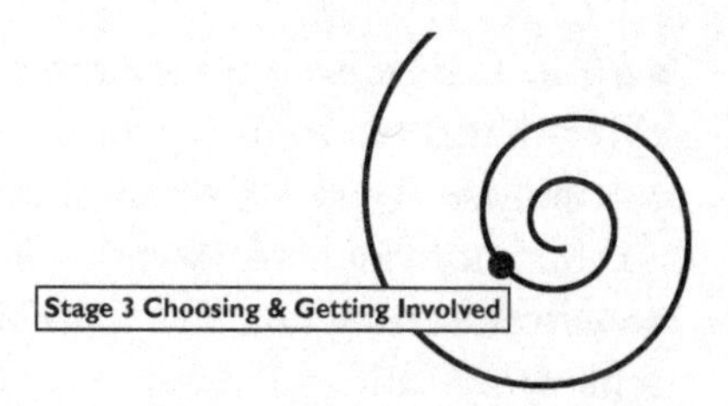

I don't suppose it's any co-incidence that the next stage of developing our Doing skills happens at the same time as we graduate to more solid foods and develop our teeth. *Getting your teeth into something* means choosing what you really want to get involved with. Biting is pro-active. It says *I'll have this bit, but not that.* It separates. It prioritises and excludes. It defines what we are going to concentrate on, at least for a while. A boundary is established, made complete by closing your mouth around what you've bitten off and now start chewing (once you've learnt to!). And just as you have to break eggs to make an omelette, you have to be destructive – in biting and chewing up your food – before you can be constructive – in growing a healthy body.

Having crisp and hard things to bite on rather than soggy or mushy stuff, is exciting. It is an extension of the pushing that I talked about earlier. Biting into a really delicious apple (as I'm doing right now) is much more refreshing than eating porridge or pureed carrot and turnip. Energy is mobilised and released through your muscles in the effort of stretching, biting and crunching. You need to pit your strength against the apple; you win (most of the time!) and you get rewarded with a fresh, juicy, satisfyingly resistant mouthful to chomp on. Once the food is in your mouth you still need to work at it to get anywhere. Biting once is not enough – you now need to exert effort to accomplish what you want by crunching and chewing. We're beginning to have a more sophisticated sense of the challenges and satisfactions of the beginning, middle and end in the process of following what we want to do.

Separating things out, making choices and getting involved in a process is the next stage in the **Action Spiral.** It's not just a question of – *I wonder what will happen if I put this in my mouth* – now we can inter-relate with something and *go through a process* *with it*, maybe even transform the thing. In other words we discover that there is an outcome which is only arrived at after several stages. There's a sense of getting somewhere new – the view is different from here. So now there's even more me around, being powerful, *getting involved with the world because I choose to,* and achieving results.

As tiny babies, everything was interesting and distracting. But once you start experimenting and exploring, giving yourself lots of real-world feedback, you begin to find things that are seriously important, interesting and enjoyable to *you.* Maybe to no-one else. Even if people think *you're just like your Dad*, or Gran, or someone way back in the family tree, *you* are expressing a unique combination of needs, interests, likes and dislikes. Naturally we want to spend time and energy on things we like best, to follow up the things that fulfil our needs and give us the nicest feelings, inspire and excite us. And we probably want to avoid and exclude things we don't like, or which provoked a feeling which was uncomfortable either because of our own reactions or *someone else's.* We've stored the information from our senses and our feelings and we're drawing on it. *We're beginning to have things we know.* And the knowledge and the memories inform our intentions. We are following our tastes as they develop, physically, emotionally and mentally.

So what do we need from the adults looking after us ? We need them to let us get absorbed. To do that they have to let us follow our needs, our excitement and energy, and keep us safe while we can go through our own little process of choosing to start something, and then carrying on to a deeper involvement. Constantly being distracted with other things which the adult thinks are more suitable, or more interesting (for the adult but not to us), is not going to help.

This is such a basic need we have, to be protected whilst we concentrate. It's not unique to humans. When a whole flock of birds is eating in a field, at any given time, a percentage of them is looking up to see if any predator is around. That means the others have the chance to get seriously involved in tugging worms out of the ground (presumably the worms don't have such a good system). Last year I drove with my family through Bushey Park in South London, and we saw a huge stag literally shepherding the sixty or so does and fawns in his herd across the road like a lollipop man. Long traffic queues formed in both directions, as driver after driver switched off engines to watch this beautiful and awe-inspiring creature caring for his family. An unforgettable moment. The deer passed almost soundlessly under the long line of ancient trees, the leaves licked with the golden light of late-autumn sun – just the clip and crack of hooves on the path and soft breathing. The herd cropped the grass as they crossed the road, nuzzled one another; two young bucks were play-fighting until the stag stopped them, mildly but firmly - you could almost hear him saying – *Come on you lads – stop mucking about and cross the road!* The herd was pretty nonchalant, really. The deer could afford to be; no-one was going to mess with the stag. His strength and attentiveness gave them security

Our adults need a good capacity to keep an eye on us while we're doing what we're doing, *and be able to look after themselves* – so that we don't have to! We need to be allowed to be separate from our adults and focus on our own little world. We also need our adults to respect the fact that we want and need to make our own choices. We need support in *excluding* what we don't want and pursuing what we do like. Once again, this has to be within the bounds of safety, and other things like learning to be sociable, gentle, to share, and so on.

Of course, there's been endless debate lasting decades over how much a child should be allowed to follow his or her own feelings, interests, at whose pace and so on, and how much should be imposed and controlled. These are major questions of power, will, culture, and whose needs are given importance. Most problems probably arise from the extremes, either the child being given no power at all, or complete power over everything and everybody. I believe neither is helpful. Each family and each little person's balance point is going to be different, and be changing constantly as we all grow. We need our adults to do their best to respect us as choice-makers, but not to stop making healthy and self-respecting choices for themselves and for other children and adults around us. We need a boundary set around what we can and can't do, to push against in developing our strength, so that we know where we stop and start. But we also need to know we can have an effect on where's it's set and how it changes, so that it's –

neither a straight-jacket *(Whatever you're doing, Don't),*
nor a biscuit cutter *(You have to grow into this shape which we have preordained for you)*
nor a flimsy bit of cloud that melts if you huff on it *(There is no-one here who's stronger than you)*

Help!!

In the womb we had a perfect container which grew as we grew, stretched (to some extent) as we stretched, but that also held us securely. And when it was too small, one way or another, it – as part of our mother! – co-operated with us to let us out. As we're getting bigger, stronger, and more ready to take risks, we need our adults to make a new container with similar features, where muscle walls can be replaced with love, strong arms, clear thinking, respect and consistency. And a *huge* sense of humour.

So whilst we're learning about choosing and getting involved, we need people who ....

- Are quite happy about being ignored whilst we pursue our own interests (i.e. don't need us to depend completely on them)
- Are pretty good at choosing and following through their own interests and can protect their space (even from us)
- Will be interested in what we're up to, and give a hand when we need them to, but not impose their ways or choices or "know" our feelings or experiences for us all the time.
- Are not threatened if our choices are very different from theirs, or if we have a wider choice than they were ever allowed
- Are relaxed about not getting things right first time
- Can let us know in an easy way that Rome wasn't built in a day

- Can get deeply involved and immersed in what they're doing, and can resist our attempts to distract them (we'll want to copy them later),
- Show us by their support and how they live that not everything arrives in instantly swallow-able form, but that real satisfaction can come from "chewing through" something; that some things have to be done many, many times before we achieve what we want, and that some things have to be given up on
- See unexpected obstacles, surprises or even discomfort as a challenge, not necessarily as a reason to stop, and help us learn to tolerate feelings of frustration, exasperation, or wanting to give up when we can't see a way forward.
- Can help us learn that our time, and that of other people, is precious.

So imagine a child at the seaside, who is allowed to be boisterous and adventurous. Rushing in and out of the waves, having a good dig, splashing and being splashed, wet and sandy and roaring with laughter. Maybe she'll have a few bumps along the way to getting strong this summer, maybe she'll get the odd mouthful of salty water, but she's in full contact with her physicality, exuberance and enthusiasm. Next moment, imagine her carefully placing tiny shells all round the edge of her sand castle, breathing heavily and oblivious to the sea coming in and wetting her bikini bottom. Totally absorbed.

Imagine that she's with adults who are enjoying what they're doing as well, and who love watching her playing about and initiating things. They revel in her joy and surprise and her capacity for full-bodied, hearty involvement in everything she's doing. They are available sometimes to join her play when she wants them to, but stay out of it (but near enough) if she wants to do something herself. They initiate things too, things they enjoy and would like to share with her. And they make sure she's safe. Idealistic perhaps, but we've probably all had times like that somewhere along the line. And there's no reason for it to stop as we get bigger if the permission to really get absorbed remains.

But now, conversely, imagine the little girl I once saw, dressed in an immaculate white frock on a beach. Her wrist was connected to her mother's by a long lead like a little dog. She could hardly move without being tugged – and her mother kept up a constant litany of negatives, *Don't do that, don't touch that, don't go over there, come here, stop that, it's dangerous, it's dirty.* The poor child was practically immobilised, pale and energy-less. Her every action was under intense scrutiny, and was consistently stopped or interfered with every few moments. Her ability to flow with her own interests and intent, to make her own choices and follow her own needs and desires was severely blocked. Her capacity for enjoying her own bodily experience of the beach shrank rapidly. Eventually she sat down listlessly beside her mother, staring out to sea (whereupon her mother said, *Don't you want to run around?*).

I could only guess at what the little girl must have felt, and where her energy had gone. Up into her head perhaps? Into a vice-like grip on her feelings of rage and hatred? (or perhaps those were mine). That kind of treatment can't have started at this age, it must have been happening since she was tiny. It can lead to a heart and mind bent on escape, rebellion and revenge; or worse, perhaps, a withdrawal into passivity, compliance or depression. As an adult it can lead to a life lacking in authentic self-expression. And whatever else is happening, the child is not getting any feedback from her own discoveries of the real world.

Given enough of the right kind of support, we'll find interest and enjoyment in absorption in the choices we've made, excitement in exertion and wrestling with challenges, and satisfaction from achievement. Especially if it's been a tricky ride (back to apples being more satisfying to chomp through than porridge). And of course we'll store yet more feedback, more information for next time in our muscles and emotional archives. We're constantly updating from our real experiences in the real world, stretching ourselves with new challenges of doing things.

Separating things out, making choices and getting deeply involved and absorbed in a process is the next step in doing things.

But some of us find it hard to establish boundaries, to choose *this* and *not that,* or hard to believe that we have a right to make choices for ourselves, or focus on our own interests. You may find it difficult to make choices in one or more aspect of your life, even though you can be decisive in other ways. Alternatively, you could have reached a point where any choice has become difficult, and the need to make one leaves you anxious and tense. Being alone to focus on your own projects may leave you anxious and uncertain. Perhaps you feel uneasy if you allow yourself clear time and space to become immersed, even in something you know you want to do, so you find distractions. Skimming and dipping rather than getting deeply involved, you may find it hard to find satisfaction. You may experience tooth and gum problems; heart, bowel, and spinal difficulties (especially in the neck, shoulders and mid-back). You may have trouble growing your nails and hair, and find that sexual arousal fades rather than builds to a climax.

Difficulties like these may mean that you procrastinate at the CHOOSING and GETTING INVOLVED stage of the Action Spiral.

Stage 4
Completing

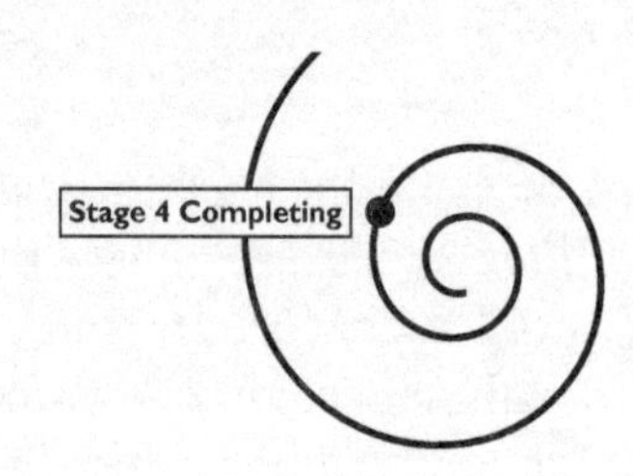

Being able to finish something and let it go is just as important as being able to get started. You can procrastinate about finishing something just as easily as you can put off beginning. Completing the task in hand means your energy will become available to you to invest in something else. So how do you know when something is done, or when enough is enough?

> Is the meal finished when you're full, when all the nice things are gone and there's only figs left (which you hate), or when you've forced yourself to eat them?
> Is it time to go home from the park when you're physically exhausted, you've had your fourteenth go on the swings, when it gets dark or when your big sister says it is?
> Is the sand castle decorated enough when the ice-cream comes, when all the available shells are used up, when the sand is covered, when it looks pretty to you, when it looks pretty to someone else – or when the tide comes in and you have to leave the beach?

If you're tiny, enough means when your body tells you that it's needs are satisfied *(no more milk thanks Mum)*. Instant feedback from our internal hunger monitors, regardless of the state or condition (or feelings) of the external source. That uncomfortable sensation has gone, and maybe even been replaced by a nice new one. So primarily, you know when you've finished when you physically feel that you have.

If you're well, well-fed and rested, your body's energy will naturally propel you into some kind of action, directed by curiosity and interest. Your energy flows towards something, gets deeply involved with it to the exclusion of all else, reaches a natural peak of intensity and then begins to recede, like a wave crashing on a beach. So, secondly, you let something go that you've been involved with because you're just not interested in it anymore.

The wave of your attention has receded, and moved on to something else that has become more attractive – *this old sucky thing was OK but that furry thing over there is moving; I like the bear you keep offering me but your earrings are much more tantalising.* You drop the spoon you've just been sucking, abandon your toes in favour of pulling someone's hair, let teddy fall out of the pushchair when your brother comes by on his bike. Quite callous in a way. But not intentionally. You're living in the immediate and following whims, infinitely distractible.

Once you start exploring and experimenting with things, getting involved, you notice that some processes have beginnings, middles and ends, and you start developing a broader sense of completion. You know when you've finished doing something or being involved, *because there's an outcome.* You've produced a difference, a change, something new – either in yourself as a new experience or in the thing itself. Sometimes it's a surprise, sometimes it's what you wanted as you learn that you can have intentions and find ways to fulfil them, sometimes it's disappointing, not what you had in mind. There's no more apple left to eat – *it's all gone.* All the petals have come off the flower – it looks different. You've slid down every slide in the park loads of times and you're happy, worn out and satisfied that you've conquered them all. The circle of shells goes all the way around the castle and meets on the other side. You've submerged every duck in the bath, and the baby-sitter says she feels damp enough. The story has ended, the lights are turned off and Dad says, *time for sleeping.* External events are now giving us a sense of completion as well as our internal feedback.

The end of a process has it's own satisfactions, in addition to our bodily fulfilment. And your internal feedback and the external circumstances don't have to exactly match for you to still get satisfaction. The big cardboard box is now in small shreds (That was great. *I've still got energy left, but that box has definitely had it*). You're upset that you have to leave the supermarket when you were just getting down to re-arranging the soup tins, but your big friend says come on, race you to the car *(Mmm, beating you by a mile is definitely more fun than crying, though that did buy me a bit of extra time with the tins.)* You'd like to carry on pulling

Dad's hair, but he seems to prefer it if you stroke him instead and it's great fun making him think you're going in for a good tug (*Ah look, I can be gentle; – but now can I bite your cheek?*) You're developing an aesthetic sense too, for example with the shells on the sand-castle, your own taste in what looks good *(Minimalism, schminimalism, give me Gaudi any day)*. Only you can say when it looks right to you.

We know we've got some power – we want to find ways of using it that make us feel good, physically and emotionally. We're developing new capacities – even starting to use words, in speaking and in thinking. We're finding out about relationships as we begin to notice the effects of our behaviour and activity on people and things and to care about the outcome. And building a sense of aesthetics, our very own taste of what is beautiful.

Other people's attitudes to finishing things are very important. If you are always told when something is finished, when you've got to stop, it may not match your sense or your timing, and you can't learn to discover what wanting to complete feels like *for you* from inside yourself. Nor can you work out when something has taken enough energy or time or when it just isn't right for you anymore. On the other hand, if people always wait for you, or let you wear them out, or let you hurt them or their precious things, or constantly interrupt their conversations or concentration, it can be hard to learn that your use of time and energy, and what you do with yourself, has an effect on other people as well.

And if your adults don't even notice how long you're involved with anything, it can be hard to learn when enough is enough in all kinds of ways, in doing, feeling, thinking, and in relationships to other people.

> As a child, Maria spent hours just staring in the mirror. She had no-one to play with, very few toys, and no books. Perhaps her adults thought she was fine because she was quiet. She wasn't. How could she learn how much time at the mirror was enough, in such a vacuum of neglect?

Learning to finish something in a reasonable amount of time is also related to there being *lots* of interesting and exciting things and people to be involved in – so completing *this* doesn't mean nothing else will follow. Observing our adults gives us information too. Copying them is a huge part of learning. Noticing when enough is enough for them, how they value their time, their energy, the things they've started and their relationships, tells us that completing can be ....

- satisfying (or not)
- important (or not)
- delayed and postponed from anxiety or, in the interests of perfection,
- resisted for fear of nothing to do afterwards
- never really accomplished properly leading to piles of half-finished things lying around
- lost amongst many things happening at the same time
- almost unnoticed or unmarked in the rush to get on with other, new, sparkly things

or

- savoured and marked in a relaxed way, leaving a sense which we will come to recognises as completion

Sometimes we'll learn to finish things to our own standards. Sometimes we'll learn that carrying on with someone else's encouragement brings a different result, maybe even better than we'd imagined (or not). And sometimes we'll stop sooner than we would have liked to. Which is fine, if you care about the person who is encouraging you to go on or telling you to stop, and if you don't learn that you only get smiles and warmth from them if you conform.

We need people who can really give us the message that what we do and what we produce is great, and how we do it is fine as well. Not wonderful and marvellous all the time, not always having to do or finish things perfectly. But because it's loveable old us doing what we're doing, then by definition it's well-intentioned, and we can be helped to learn when it's not good for other people. People who can show us that we are as loved and loveable and lovely if we don't produce something as if we do, and if the outcome is as we or they wanted, or if it isn't. People who can celebrate and share in our joys and achievements and help us struggle through our disappointments, independent of their own.

Knowing when you have had enough or done enough, physically, emotionally and mentally, and being able to let go of what you have been doing, are necessary abilities to navigate the completion stage of doing things.

But some of us may have problems in recognising how to complete. You may constantly put off completing, or put off completing *properly*, or never really quite *know how to know* when enough is enough. Difficulties here can lead to health problems like alcoholism, workaholism and other addictions, obesity, constant fatigue, hypertension, pelvic congestion, constipation, headaches, and weak orgasms that don't exactly make the earth move.

Difficulties like these may mean that you procrastinate at the COMPLETION stage of the Action Spiral.

Stage 5
Pausing and Reflecting

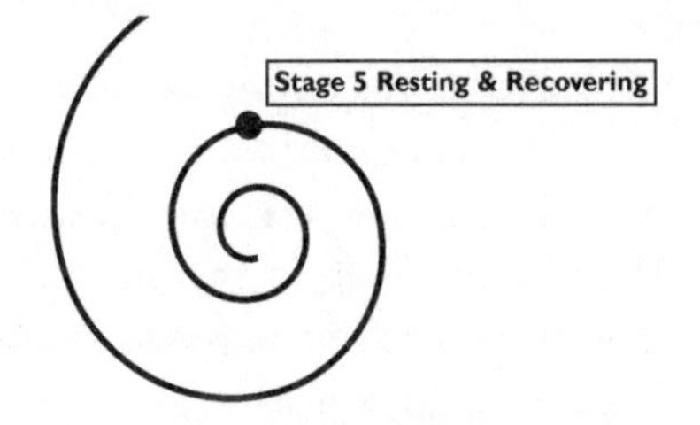

When you're very tiny, you tend to drop off to sleep in a rosy glow when you've finished drinking your milk. It's natural. Other body functions temporarily go into cruise mode whilst your digestion gets down to processing the food. Most of us probably feel like or could do with a brief pause after eating, to give our systems the same chance, but we often don't take one. *Pausing after finishing something, having a brief rest,* not instantly rushing onward to other activity, gives us a chance to complete the process at all levels (physical, emotional and mental) before starting out *afresh* on the next thing. And perhaps that's the key word – afresh. If you are someone who is always putting off pausing for rest and reflection *(I can't stop yet, I've just got to...)* – you may have lost touch with knowing what that freshness can be like

> I once heard a tale about a young English explorer in Arab lands in the early 1920's, who was taking a long caravan of camels, mules and men across the desert. On the first morning, he rose with the light to the sounds of men and animals preparing for the long day's march. As night fell, weary after the long day, the men pitched tents and built fires. On the second morning, the young man rose again to the sun and the smell of cooking, and the caravan setting off across the vast expanses of sand. It travelled until the evening and the second camp and a dinner of succulent roast lamb. On the third morning, the young man rose as usual, but realised immediately that everything around him was silent. He came out of his tent. The camels and mules were still tethered, quietly chewing. No-one else was up. He walked quickly to the tent of the leader of the camel drivers, opened the flap, and called the man out.

> *We need to get going,* he said
> *Where is everyone ?*
> The leader of the camel drivers looked at him sleepily, blinking in the bright sunshine.
> *They won't move today,* he said, smiling (no doubt) at the impatience of the ignorant. *They are waiting for their souls to catch up with them*

Now this story may have changed somewhat both in translation and in my telling of it. But the point remains. If we travel, we need to be able to recognise when we have arrived, for rest, replenishment and review. Charging on regardless may mean we go off to the next thing without enough energy, sensitivity or awareness, or indeed enough information learnt from our last experience. Which means that we never fully re-establish the state of relaxed "just being-ness" of the first stage of the **Action Spiral.** I like the pictures from the cartoon *Tom and Jerry* when one of them (usually Jerry the mouse) – tricks the other (Tom the cat) into running into a brick wall. Tom has been running so fast you can still see bits of him following on behind, so when he crashes into wall, he sticks there until all the after-images catch up. Then – when he is all of a piece – he flops to the floor, lies in a heap, and then miraculously recovers (until the next time). Photography shows we have after-images trailing behind us too; so perhaps on a quantum physics level, Tom has got it right. *We can't move on until we're all there.* Otherwise we leave bits of ourselves behind, forever trying to catch up. Moving on quickly may look as if we are flowing forward, but actually we're creating lots of sticky points of attachment to incomplete activities, projects, roles, dreams, places and relationships from the past.

So whether you call it waiting for your soul, or an after-image, or "merely" taking time to relax after effort, to review and reflect, come to terms with or celebrate what has happened, this is the point in the **Action Spiral** at which we need to *disengage from activity*. As little people, learning about Doing, we need to learn about Not Doing as well, about enjoying having quiet times and rests after lots of activity. We need to learn how to wind down.

We need to know we're going to be loved when we're quiet and drifty as well as when we're active and bouncy (and vice versa). And we need to learn that when we do take time out, we may feel droopy, and possibly even a bit sad, but that our energy and enthusiasm will return, no matter how long that takes. As does hope. It's a bit like going away for a break and for the first few days, finding you get more and more tired as all the weariness you've been pushing away catches up with you. You may feel depressed, moody or restless, and wonder what you're doing in this weird and rather peculiar part of the world. Then one morning, you wake up, refreshed, curious and excited, and you feel as if the holiday has just begun.

Different spirals of action require different lengths of pausing time, and different processes are at work. You may need more time now than you did when you were younger to rest and regenerate after a hard night on the town (or less, of course – who am I to say?) The energy invested in the action, and what value you attached to it clearly affect the pausing time needed too. Getting over losing your first love may bear no comparison to ending a three-week relationship at forty-five, or the loss of a long-term partner at seventy-five. The time you need to get used to a new car, settle into a new job or house, celebrate the first time you meet a sales target or have a baby, grieve for people, animals, capacities, opportunities, for the life lived and un-lived will depend on a vast array of variables. As will thinking an experience through to the point of understanding and new learning.

So our physical, emotional-relational, mental and indeed spiritual senses will let us know when we've had enough pausing, because we will begin to notice new things catching our interest, and find we have the energy to move towards them on the next wave. There will be the sense of freshness, even at times of moving on "older and wiser", having taken in all the good things from what has happened and what we have done, and, ideally, let go of the bad. We can never do this completely. It's not human nature to be able to process everything absolutely. What we hold onto, that we either don't want or can't let go of, becomes part of us. And that's natural too. It's a question of how far we can free ourselves to move forward effectively, and how much we allow past, incomplete, unprocessed action to hold us back.

Of course we don't ever completely stop all activity unless we're dead. (And even then some religious teachings suggest that you can't move on to the next life until there has been completion, either by your ghost or someone on your behalf, or unless you've been through a purging process to disengage your spirit from its former bodily life). But you can nearly always have a spell of hibernation, no matter how short. If you've been fully engaged in something requiring real physical or sensual exertion, mental concentration or emotional intensity, there is a natural sense of – *aahhh!* – when it's over, which, like the best orgasms, can lead to great sleep. But often completing something is more complicated, and the *aahh!* factor may be missing or hard to find. There may indeed be anti-climactic feelings such as sadness, regret, remorse, disappointment, frustration, or anxiety and fear, which can be hard to allow and make us want to rush onto the next thing. And if you often don't really complete things and you put off time for reflection and regeneration afterwards, then, inevitably, your *forward-going energy becomes depleted.* It means you have less energy available to be wholly committed to the next action, and it becomes hard to experience anything as a truly "fresh" start. This invariably leads to less of a sense of full completion at the end of the next activity, a sense of weariness and lack of hope. Back to the drag factors I described in Part 1.

As little people learning about the last stage of the **Action Spiral**, time out for winding down, we need lots of good role models who can show us how they handle endings. People who like to celebrate, reflect, take stock, look after themselves and each other when something is finished, and who respect their own need for regenerative time. We need experiences in which we can *know for ourselves* the natural desire to flop for a bit after total exertion (the first little girl on the beach will naturally acquire much more knowledge of this than the second). We need people who will respect our feelings when we are sad about losing something (not *It was just an old bear and you're too big for toys now anyway*). People who will take time to enjoy the paintings we've done.

Adults who can teach us how to learn from our experiences, by thinking through with us what we can build on, what we could do differently another time, and which bits are "just how it is". And letting us know what we're good at, our strengths and skills as we develop. We need support to take our time in this resting and processing, so that we are not constantly being rushed from activity to activity with literally no breathing space in between. We need idling time. This is very different to the kind of empty, isolating soul-destroying boredom of nothing but a mirror to stare at. It's a seed-in-the-earth-in-winter phase, rather than a barren suspension of life.

Pausing after doing something for rest, reflection and regeneration, is the last stage of doing things

But some of us find this process of letting go into what might feel like nothing very hard. You may fear that if you don't keep going, you'll just lie down and stay down forever. Or that if you stop you'll miss something, or be passed over for something important. Or you find yourself getting depressed or feeling worthless. You worry that you're being lazy if you don't have sixty-eight things on the go all the time, or if you stop to think or notice your feelings about what you've been doing. You may experience bad breath, poor appetite, digestion problems, constipation, headaches, ennui, difficulty sleeping, muscular cramps and blocked sinuses. You may use drugs and stimulants or cigarettes to keep yourself going, to find sexual arousal or to feel anything except a weary numbness. You may look for bigger and bigger thrills because nothing seems very exciting or interesting anymore. You may only find interest in new things, but increasingly can't seem to progress anything or get things finished properly. You may find yourself having inexplicable outbursts of completely-over-the-top anger, or bursting into tears. Or you may suddenly realise that you've been staring at the same piece of paper for over 15 minutes, and that nothing has gone in, or, to your horror, that you've just driven through a red light. You may develop serious,

even fatal illnesses, as you become incapable of recognising total exhaustion.

Procrastination should carry a government health warning. It can kill.

Difficulties like these may mean that you procrastinate at the PAUSING and REFLECTING stage of the Action Spiral.

~

Before looking at how procrastination develops at each stage of the Spiral, it's worth thinking about thinking for a moment.

Thinking and procrastination

A short tale of soup.

> There was a boy of 5 years old who never spoke a word. He could do everything else that the other boys of his age could, run, climb, understand what was said to him and pretend not to, ignore go-to-bed instructions, make things, ride a bike, chase the cat and so on. But he never said anything. One day the family were eating dinner, when to their surprise, little Gordon suddenly said -
> *This soup is cold.*
> The family threw up their spoons in amazement.
> *You can speak!* shrieked his mother, dripping. *How come you never said anything before ?*
> *Well,* said Gordon, letting the dog lick his face. *Everything's been fine until now.*

I don't suppose we all learn to speak in order to protest about the conditions, although it can certainly help if the people who are taking care of us are consistently missing our other signals. When we form words we are symbolising. The first words you understand and say tend to be about people, animals, things and basic actions or functions to do with what you want or like. *NO* comes in handy as well!! (and yes) You don't need much more than that to get about really (apart from *please, thank you and where's the station/airport/harbour* if you want to get home).

And as you learn to understand language, you can begin to think in words too. Thinking has been developing alongside our skills for doing things from Day One, and now, with the addition of words, our thinking can be summarised in sounds that mean things to us and to other people. Words develop relationships to each other inside us, as we begin to speak to ourselves about our own actions, and those of other people. The verbal life of the mind has started, and an exciting, rich, dull or terrifying experience it can be.

If we grow up being given permission by our adults to *follow our own logic* (within the boundaries of safety for us and respect for themselves that I have described), then the words that form our thinking will be grounded in our sensory and emotional experience of ourselves and the world. Our command of words develops through the desire to express our needs, feelings and interests and through the feedback we get from people and our environment as we explore and experiment. *If* we have physical grounding and permission to explore, *if* the full range of our feelings is accepted and validated, and *if* our ability to think for ourselves is encouraged and respected, our energy will be balanced between physical, emotional and mental worlds. Because thoughts carry energy too. Each thought is invested with a greater or lesser value and significance. So if our thinking is underpinned by our feelings, our feelings informed by our thoughts, and if our thinking and feeling connect in our body-experience, all within the holding created by our relationships with others, there will be a solid linkage and flow between our intention and action, feedback and feeling.

But some children get lots of permission to be physical, but very little permission to *think for themselves*. Their attempts to begin to work out and articulate their own logic meets little response or respect. So their thinking remains quite simplistic, or only develops slowly, no matter how many experiences they may have as they age (*just because you get older, doesn't mean you grow up*, as my friend Jane, wise psychotherapist, puts it succinctly). As adults, these ex-children may "parrot" things they were told years ago and have no idea they could question (or how to). They may act impulsively on feeling without much prior consideration of possible outcomes. They may think in very concrete terms, and find it hard to be imaginative or visionary. Their thinking is weak, stunted like a plant stranded in poor soil. It can't grow properly without good nutrients and a healthy flow of water and warmth. Such adults may well procrastinate about generating new ideas, planning and reflecting, as such challenges cause the anxiety of entering the unknown. They may get highly emotional and upset when circumstances force them to make choices they have no idea how to think through, or to express something in a logical, linear form.

At the other end of the spectrum, if there is too little permission for children to *express themselves physically,* then their impulses and enthusiasm and sheer energy have to go elsewhere. The mental arena becomes flooded with the re-directed energy and new forms of *substitute* action and expression are created. Some children are often rushed through the exploring and experimenting phase, given very little physical permission, support or encouragement. These children may develop highly elaborated patterns of mental activity, including rituals and obsessions (like the mutant forms a plant may grow into if it is given far too rich a dose of fertiliser or irradiated). But because their thinking structures are not sufficiently underpinned with physical experience and real world feedback, the thinking is based on inaccurate assessments of what is or is not physically possible or desirable. They may have strong imaginations and be capable of intellectual wizardry. But life gets tried out on the mental stage, rather than in reality. In the mind's eye all kinds of flights of fancy are possible; but not a lot can happen in the real world if you have no solid ground to push off from. These children may learn to procrastinate about life lived for real, and be highly anxious and unprepared for the physical world.

A third group of children may find only some segments of their emotional spectrum are acceptable to their adults. They are given little permission to *express their real feelings.* These children may be able to think quite logically, and maybe in good contact with their bodies at one level. But their logic is divorced from the warmth of authentic, bodily experienced feeling. They may compartmentalise, and hold contradictory beliefs at the same time. As adults they may act or make decisions without allowing their true feelings to inform their choices. They may have difficulty empathising with other people (or with themselves), or be selective or rather erratic and inconsistent in whom or what they support or condemn, with little basis in genuine warmth. They may panic and procrastinate when asked to take a moral position, or to commit with feeling. They genuinely have no idea how to direct their lives from a solid base of feeling-informed thinking.

Most of us have a hotchpotch of permissions and inhibitions across the three areas of thought, emotion, and the physical life of our bodies. If permissions are balanced, then healthy thinking, rooted in bodily experience, validated feelings and warm, contactful relationships, can develop, If not, then forms of mental activity emerge which are not what I call *real thinking*.

They include -

worrying obsessing intellectualising dramatising
hyper-criticism (self or others) re-gurgitating fantasising
detached, over-objective application of logic
and (of course) – procrastinating.

Procrastination is above all a mental activity, although it has physical, emotional and social effects. I believe that we develop it as a creative way to manage imbalance, blockages and disconnection between body, heart and mind, an attempt to adapt to the lack of crucial permissions from the world of our childhood. We don't consciously decide to start procrastinating – who would? – but we make the best possible choices we can when we are small, in the face of our circumstances. All choices have consequences. We can get trapped by the very habits that initially helped us to feel safer.

Procrastination may be the thief of time. As a habit it can become a killer. It gets a lot of bad press, and deservedly so. But it may have been the only way that any of us who have ever procrastinated could come up with to deal with unbearable tension. Learning how to go through any one of the stages of the **Action Spiral** may have been a real struggle, and it was the best we could do at the time. The next section of Part 2 will look in more detail at how blocking and being stuck comes about.

Each block around the spiral requires different resources and tactics to help you create new habits, to develop richer and more satisfying ways of following the logic of your own thoughts, in touch with your body, your feelings and other people.

Then you can allow your habit of procrastination
to retire with dignity, having served its purpose.
Enabling you to survive.

So How Does Procrastination Develop?

The reasons why people procrastinate are very idiosyncratic. We may be very clear about why we do it, or the answer may be just beyond our thinking. Some of the reasons may even be deeply unconscious. And there are probably different reasons for putting off different things, and these may change over time. But all is not lost. If you track your patterns over time, you'll get a better idea of what you're up to, and then you'll be in a much better position to start doing things differently.

I've divided the reasons we procrastinate into the five stages of the **Action Spiral**. As Part 3, ***Ways Forward***, which offers strategies to help you stop putting things off (and so get on with what you want to do) is often arranged in the same way, you'll be able to work out what is likely to help you with the Thing that might be looming around at the moment.

You may find that you can identify difficulties at more than one phase – maybe all of them. Don't worry! It probably just means you have a tendency to be over-inclusive. Which suggests your primary task might be to address the *Choosing*... (and thus excluding) *...and Getting Involved* phase, and practice *Involvement* tasks (especially physical ones).

Stage 1
Putting off Becoming Aware

This kind of procrastination probably means important things you need to notice and attend to just seem to disappear, or end up on the bottom of the pile on your desk or in your life. You may only wake up to their absence much later, even years later. This is the kind of procrastination where you say *Oh yes I must get around to doing that* – but almost immediately the thing goes out of your mind and you just don't do it, even if you meant it sincerely at the time. Some of us do this with domestic things, some life planning, some physical or relationship matters. We forget them, blank them out, no matter how attentive we can be to other issues. It's amazing how easily we can stick our heads – and any other sensitive part of our anatomy! – in the sand.

If you have difficulties at this stage –

....you might understand intellectually that smoking and being overweight are bad for you, and you vaguely think of changing your habits because your partner is worried about you, but you don't connect the information (or her concern) with your breathlessness when you climb a few stairs

....you might find your colleague is pointing out to you that the drains of your company's building are blocked. You vaguely remembering smelling something ages ago and thinking you should do something about it, but it quickly went out of your mind and you didn't check and you haven't noticed that practically everyone in the department has been complaining.

....you might learn from the garage that your car engine is beyond repair. You're very surprised, but your son tells you he's been telling you about the noises it's been making for ages.

....you might be amazed and aghast when your partner says he is leaving because he doesn't feel he ever gets your full attention and love. Although he's been saying this for ages, somehow you've put off making time to spend just with him because there was always work, or the kids, or the team, or your parents, and although he said he was unhappy, he seemed OK, he didn't mean he was really unhappy, did he .... ?

....you might not notice that the clock is ticking and you've left it too late to have a baby, to spend any time with your ageing parents, to strike out on your own, to appreciate your health .... and so on.

~

Procrastination at this phase is primarily connected to difficulties with *sensory and emotional awareness*. It means not being in the state of relaxed awareness I described in Part 2. Some people maintain a state of tension *all the time*, which may make them hyper-alert to some things, but numbed off to a wealth of other input. Alternatively, people can walk around in a kind of dozy trance-like state; awake and functioning, working, bringing up families, running companies etc. etc. – but not really firing on all cylinders in any area of their lives. As if part of their awareness of life itself was closed down. Difficulty with awareness means not attending to the sensations that your body experiences, either physical ones or the kind that tell us we are having an emotional response to something. You are probably very good at being alone, at being single-minded in some areas of life, and you are probably a faithful partner. If other people describe you as *living in a world of your own, above it all, head in the clouds*, or experience you as detached, forgetful, or inattentive, your habit of procrastinating may be rooted here.

People with problems of awareness are like the person who attends a party where there is a buffet, but doesn't notice he or she has more than one choice. Or worse. Doesn't even notice there's a buffet.

How we develop problems with awareness

People who have problems with awareness may well be surprised to be told they procrastinate. Because out of sight (or hearing, or smelling range and so on), out of mind. This is a tragic saying in some ways, but it may give a clue to where the habit started from in the first place. You know the old philosopher's question about whether the tree exists in the wood if there is no-one there to see it? People who have difficulties with awareness may genuinely believe they don't have certain feelings or experiences, or they believe, consciously or unconsciously, that the sensations they do experience in their bodies are either unimportant or unacceptable.

Physical sensations are the signals which tell us about our needs, wants, feelings, interests. So if you haven't got much permission to notice your body and its urges and feelings or to respond to them by giving them attention, you may have developed a strategy of not attending to them, or blocking them off. Or of pretending you didn't have them in the first place, to other people, and/or to yourself.

It takes energy and courage to keep pushing in the world for what you need in the face of resistance. It may just be simpler to anaesthetise the urge and carry on regardless. Except that we can't do that. Numbing is not a process we can control precisely, and it tends to spread. Use it or lose it, as they say. What may start as volitional shut-down can become atrophy (and is therefore painful to reverse, offering even less incentive to do so). It would be especially painful if you started to shut down awareness when you were very young, or if the reason you closed off to sensation was very traumatic. People who have shut down their awareness may not demand much from the world because they don't have much sense anymore of what they need physically or emotionally in a particular aspect of their lives, nor that it's OK to need or want it. They may be very angry about this, but the anger too may have been unacceptable, and therefore becomes ignored.

And if you neglect and numb yourself to your own sensations, urges and interests, then you probably don't notice other people's needs tremendously well either. It's hard to appreciate and prioritise someone else's body and their physical or emotional needs and feelings if you're not really in much contact with your own. You may not attach much significance to other people saying they feel tired, unwell, cold, hungry, in pain, frustrated or stressed, and you may put off doing anything about it even if it is your responsibility, or when you care about the person.

At a mundane level, you may not notice how you've left the bathroom. You may head for the Channel Tunnel even though your friend has said she is claustrophobic, or for the ferry even though you know he or she gets seasick. Equally you may not appreciate other people's feelings. You forget anniversaries and birthdays. If you experience sex as dangerous or threatening in some way and you've taught yourself to close down, you may find it hard to understand why your partner gets frustrated if you keep putting off love-making. You repeatedly put off making social engagements by prioritising work and don't understand why people get upset and the invitations stop coming. You put off writing a will, and are bewildered when your partner shouts at you that you clearly don't care. *It's not that you're being deliberately unkind*. It's just not allowing the information they give you about what is significant to them to register. Consequently, you can become neglectful.

You may find this puzzling, and you start thinking -

"If I care about this person (which I do), how come I keep putting off making him – or her – the priority?"

Yet you still do, without meaning to. The effects of numbing yourself to your physical and emotional sensations spread far beyond yourself. So why would anyone consider their body's messages to be unimportant or unacceptable?

No-one could tune in

In the last chapter I described the three things babies need from their care-givers in order to firmly establish a solid sense of well-being in their bodies. If, as a baby, you didn't have adults who could tune into and empathise with your helplessness and adapt themselves somewhat to accommodate and respect the range, intensity and timing of your needs, feelings and urges, you may well have had to do all the adapting and conforming yourself. They may have been perfectly well-intentioned, or they may not. They may have been emotionally present but physically detached or unavailable, or physically present but emotionally closed down themselves. They might have come from a background where their own body messages had been ignored or not tuned into by *their* adults, so they had no experience to draw on to tune into yours. They might have been struggling so much with their own lives and circumstances when you were tiny that they couldn't make space and time to attend closely enough to you even though they wanted to.

Whatever the circumstances, if there was a strong mismatch, you may have had too little experience of being able to influence your adults successfully; trying to let people know about your needs had little effect. You may have come to believe that your own cues of interest or distress were not important, because you had little experience of them being taken seriously. To continue to take them seriously would have put you into a serious conflict with how you were being treated, so closing down your own awareness of your body messages, or attaching less importance to them, became a mechanism for survival.

This can happen far more easily than you might think. Spend a day travelling by tube, if you are used to going by car. See how quickly you detach yourself from your physical symptoms of discomfort when you have little or no choice about making yourself more comfortable.

Feeling unacceptable

Babies who are not wanted take in the rejection in the first year of their life. These babies may have parents who find it hard or impossible to accept the baby they actually have, rather than the one they might have wanted. For example, they might have had a girl, when they passionately wanted a boy. They might have had a child with a disability which they found hard to cope with or a self-sufficient, placid child rather than a gregarious, interactive one. Or the child was born under the wrong conditions - wrong father, wrong timing. Any of these babies may internalise their parents' disappointment and other difficult feelings. The baby would experience the rejection and disappointment physically, via sensation, as he or she was handled. As time goes by, bodily reminders of being alive in *this* body become linked to rejection or disappointment. Solution? One way is to reduce connection to your body, reduce levels of discomfort, is to live in your head or in acting out your frustration and pain through difficult and therefore distracting behaviour. Seal yourself into a private, impenetrable world. Put off things that threaten to re-establish the connection.

Not everyone who was an unwanted baby, or whose parents were disappointed in the infant they had, grows up making these choices, consciously or unconsciously. But some do.

If you were "supposed" to be a boy, now you are a woman you may put off paying attention to anything which reminds you that you are female. If you were handled by adults who had real problems with bodies and bodily excretions, you may put off going to the doctor even though you know that there is frequently blood in your urine (*It's probably nothing, I don't want to make a fuss*). If your adults found to hard to cope with your upset or anger, you may no longer register these feelings very much, even when other people around you are livid on your behalf, and are exasperated about your lack of response to an unjust situation. They get angry for you, at one remove.

Of course this process can continue as we grow up and have all kinds of new feelings and sensations. Socially excluded people of all kinds may learn from very concrete experience that their needs are often not considered valid or acceptable by society. Where your very existence may be an issue, quietening needs by blanking them out of awareness, putting off prioritising them in the interests of not rocking the boat or sticking one's neck out, is an understandable tactic. If you are in a wheelchair, you may put off calling the council to raise the issue of ramps at the local library (yet again) in case you're seen as demanding. You're elderly, and you find you can't chew the meat meals-on-wheels provides. Your daughter keeps reminding you to say something, but somehow you always forget and end up giving it to the cat. You have mental health problems, living in your first independent accommodation, and you constantly put off telling your landlord that there is no hot water in case he complains about you. You're lesbian, and although your partner has told you clearly she values physical affection, you keep forgetting to hold her hand or give her a hug when you're out and about. You've become so used to suppressing your natural impulse to be demonstrative in public, because of all the negative and abusive reactions you've had from passers-by.

To remain aware of your physical and emotional impulses, to maintain that they are of importance, to prioritise them and not put off clearly asserting the right to equal treatment and respect, takes courage, energy and self-esteem.

Trauma closed the connection

Perhaps something happens which makes it impossible to remain aware, even if your adults gave you lots of respectful attention when you were tiny and growing up. In a period of sustained trauma, numb layers of dead emotional skin lie over wounds too painful to be healed. Putting off attending to the wound becomes habitual.

> A colleague of mine, Sarah, grew up and worked in the townships of Black South Africa. Her family and friends all experienced the violence and terrors of the decades leading up to the first democratic elections in the early '90s. She describes going to a funeral of a friend killed in the fighting, only to experience an attack on the funeral procession which left three more friends and relatives dead or seriously wounded. Grief compounded outrage which compounded grief. But no time to get over any of this before the arson attack on her cousin's home, and the mysterious small-hours disappearance of her best friend's son. You learn to put off allowing yourself to feel anything about it to another day, in the unspecified future.

The pictures of ethnic Albanians crammed into muddy fields in their escape from "ethnic cleansing" which filled our television screens and newspapers in the late spring of 1999 told a similar tale of the compound pain and grief that can numb the soul. Loss of children, partners, parents, friends, home, limbs and eyes, loss of language, livelihood, dignity, innocence, belief in humanity, hope – it is incredible how people survive at all. The refugees were given a profound message that their bodily needs, indeed their very existence, were unimportant to those destroying their homes. Adults in such circumstances are driven back to trying to tolerate the naked experience of raw, unmet need which infants must feel when they are left alone too long. To survive, adults, like the baby, may need to shut down sensitivity to needs and feelings. To pay attention to them is become aware of desperate hungers and traumatic memories too agonising to bear. The real effects of post-traumatic stress disorder are recognised now, whether through war, major accident or natural disaster, or something that happens to just one person. A numbing of physical and emotional sensation is one of the products.

This idea has been linked to how people and indeed children pass on physical, sexual and emotional abuse. Because they have become emotionally numbed themselves, they cannot empathise with the child or adult they are victimising. Witnesses to abuse may equally have become numbed by what they have experienced, and put off doing anything about it. A parent who puts off attending to her suspicions that someone is abusing her child, or puts off notifying authorities when she has proof, is doing likewise.

There are of course many people who have been profoundly abused who go the opposite way, i.e. becoming highly sensitised to other people, and develop deep empathy. But if you have learnt to experience violence as the norm, you can put off being aware of how much it hurts for fear of worse reprisal if you complain. People experiencing domestic abuse from their partner may have numbed off their sense of their own feelings to such an extent that the impatient comments of *Why don't you just leave him?(or her)*, which outraged friends and even professionals come out with, entirely miss the point. There may be so little awareness of yourself left, that being aware of the time of day is a miracle, let alone staying in touch with your ability to make your legs move towards the door. Let alone believing you have a right to a good life on the other side of it.

And it doesn't need to be extreme physical violence or abuse that numbs our sensitivity to our bodies. Some adults live asexually. Say you have grown up in a sexually repressive environment, where even sexual or erotic thoughts were considered sinful. As an adult you feel very anxious if you experience attraction or arousal. You might get so good at quickly closing down any thoughts that the process becomes automatic. So much so, in fact, that you hardly even notice the feeling/sensation that gave rise to the thought in the first place. You don't even notice that you put off meeting people who you might be attracted to, and you put off making yourself look nice in case you get attention. So you come to regard yourself as not much interested in "all that". Maybe true; maybe just well-trained in the art of self-censorship.

Cultural attitudes to needs and wants remain

In the UK, men born after 1942 were probably the first generation who did not have to go to war. Up until then, men were regularly dispatched to fight on land and at sea. Women traditionally stayed at home up until the late19th century (apart from camp followers who have always accompanied troops).

So for hundreds of years there has been an implicit culture of waiting, patiently or otherwise, and putting things off. Waiting for him to come home. Waiting until the war ends, until you can go home and put a normal life back together with her, if you can. Waiting until the country is back on its feet. Good things come to those who wait. Jam tomorrow, never jam today. If waiting has been a significant part of your psyche, bred into you for generations, then procrastination may simply be your way of carrying on the family or national tradition of putting off your dreams until the better time comes. The collective unconscious can function both faster and slower than the conscious mind. You may not have learnt that it is OK to up-date ways of doing things that were handed down to you, to create your own time-table and possibilities of action.

Not every culture has the same experience. The US is commonly seen as a *Go for it* or indeed *Just Do it* society, even by those who don't like what the outcome of the going and doing is.

Whereas, despite *Cool Britannia*, the UK is still viewed as far more phlegmatic and cautious (*Is that wise?*). There is still a strong tendency to knock success and being entrepreneurial. Amazingly, bowler-hatted gentlemen, county ladies trimming the roses, smog and Sherlock Holmes continue to prevail overseas as the central aspects of the stereotypical image of Britain, apathy the British disease, tooth-sucking and putting things off until you're sure, if it's allowed, part of the national character.

Religion may also inform your awareness of your body's messages, with rules and guidance to ordain what you may or may not prioritise or give attention to. The promise of a life after death may be based on how well you follow these rules. And even if you don't follow a religion yourself, you may be putting out of your present-day awareness things which your father's priest, rabbi or mullah told him *he* shouldn't dwell on, forty years ago. Class, income, housing, local culture of country or city, family rules, birth order, health care or lack of it – the list of variables which affect our capacity to pay attention to our body's messages is enormous, and often hereditary.

No permission to move into doing

In effect, all the previous points have been about lack of permission for just *being*. But there are others people who procrastinate at the awareness stage because they had *so much permission for being*, they didn't need, or perhaps were not allowed, *to do* anything for themselves at all. A kind of helplessness, a passivity, results. People who have had this experience may expect friends, partners and the world to continue to do for them what their adults did.

These people may look like adults, (although they often have very un-formed, childlike faces) but practically, emotionally and socially they remain infants made weak and truculent by excessive indulgence. If all our needs are met so perfectly even before we realise we have them, then why stretch our legs or our wings? Such people may be demanding, but they carry a lot of hidden shame. We all know we have to come out of the nest, one day. At some level, people who continue to bury their awareness that they could do things for themselves know that they are behaving like babies. They are likely to panic about the gap they'd have to bridge, getting wider by the day, in order to grow up and become the adult they could be.

Procrastination begins at the awareness stage of doing things. You may not even know that you do it. The key thing is that to begin to do things, we need to able to notice and become aware of the information gathered by our senses, either from the external world or internally. Then we need to be able to give ourselves permission to respond to these sensations by paying them some attention. If we have learnt to regard our impulses as either unimportant or unacceptable, we may see little point in doing so. Letting the thing we felt we wanted or needed to do slip out of our consciousness, it becomes hard to move to the next phase. To begin to prepare for action, by exploring and experimenting.

Stage 2
Putting off Exploring and Experimenting

Procrastination at this phase is connected to either -

Anxieties about exploring and experimenting

or

Getting bogged down in lots of experimentation
(including talking about what you're going to do)

If you have problems at this stage –

....you often don't know what you want; you put off finding out, or you frequently resort to saying – *I don't mind.*

....you know that you need to do something, but keep putting off doing anything about it, including thinking what the first step might be

....you might announce to family and friends that there is something you need or want, but you feel reluctant to do anything about it. Somewhere inside you lurks the feeling that someone else should be going something about it, but definitely not you.

....you might talk about the course you're going to take, the book you're going to write, the internet company you're going to start, how you're going to stop smoking, how well you're going to treat your partner, how much you want someone in your life. You think (and talk) about lots of possible routes but never take any action.

....you get lots of brochures from different dating agencies but you never call one to make an appointment. You read loads of papers but can't seem to start your essay. Your book-case is groaning with self-help de-cluttering books. You come up with lots of brilliant ideas for the new campaign, but you lose any sense of knowing which you want to go with. You look at far too many houses, kitchens, diet books, dress fabrics or investment opportunities, and have no idea how to start the selection process. You collect leaflets, but you always put off booking up the show, reserving the holiday cottage, or sending money to the charities you've chosen.

~

You're likely to know that you procrastinate at this stage. It might be a hidden knowledge, a secret that you guard rather shamefully, or it might be something everyone knows. If you were blocked from exploring in your early years, you may be a person who sticks pretty much to the familiar in other areas, places to go, people to see, paper to read, ways of thinking. You may have left school or college, taken the first job you could find or one just like your mother's and stayed there. You may have married your first-ever girlfriend or boyfriend. You probably haven't tried any new food or a new way of making love for years. You probably dislike change, moving and endings. You're probably really good at putting up with things that other people find infuriating or intolerable. When you are forced to change, however, once you've got over your anxiety you feel refreshed and wonder why you didn't move on years before. Other people take over when you keep putting off doing things (including identifying what you want or like), and when they do you feel a mixture of relief and shame.

On the other hand, you may know precisely what you need or want to do. But you tie yourself up in knots thinking of all the possible ways forward, all the eventualities and every possible outcome of each eventuality. You have a tremendous imagination. But it usually comes up with a negative evaluation of the future *(What if ... ?)*. This is so even at the end of a long chain of positives, like *how would I deal with the pressures of winning a million pounds on the lottery?* You probably have an excellent eye for detail, but you can't play chess.

You're probably a good conversationalist, maybe even a strong public speaker. You're famous for coming up with good ideas (for other people to implement) encouraging and enthusing friends or your team, and you're excited by new things. But you never seem to get stuck into anything, to follow up your innovative schemes. It infuriates you when you hear how someone else has made a fortune doing the same thing. You can come up with a huge range of convincing reasons why you had to put off what you said you'd do.

If you've got no problem with exploring but you're blocked about moving into committed action, then over-experimenting, flitting, getting hugely enthusiastic about lots of different things without much to show for it may be more the picture. You may even believe your own rhetoric, for years, even though somewhere you have a nagging suspicion it's all just excuses. It's the other people around you who get frustrated and infuriated, and saddened at the waste of so much potential.

For people who procrastinate about moving on from the experimenting and exploring stage, *All mouth and no trousers* is the standard epithet. It was been used to great effect in a Christian Aid campaign posters promoting the initiative to end Third World debt. Above the caption, a line-up of trouser-less G7 Finance Ministers wear underwear made of their national flags.

How we develop problems with exploring and experimenting

Lack or loss of internal permission

If you have permission to notice and give attention to things of need, interest and importance to you, you start finding out how to go about getting involved with them. When you're small you explore and experiment physically, without thought or calculation. As you get bigger, you have the additional facility of rehearsing possibilities on the internal stage of your mind, drawing both on your experience of the world, and on imagination and conjecture. Part of the experimenting may also be *to talk about what you're thinking of doing*, both to clarify thoughts by hearing yourself describe them, and to get feedback. You're mobilising your energy and getting ready to choose appropriate action, working out the best way to move forward with what you want to do.

But you may have been one of those children who experienced their interests as being (as best) ignored or side-lined, at worst deprecated, by your first adults. There was little or no negotiation of agenda; what interested you was incidental, and your experimentation was nipped in the bud. This may have been a repetition of what happened to your adults when they were children (being seen but not heard), or it may have been what they had to do in the genuine interest of survival because of your family circumstances. Now, as an adult, you put off pursuing things you are interested in or need, because if you start making them a priority, you feel uncomfortable, and anxious, and you get worried that other More Important Things or people will be or feel neglected.

On the other hand, your first adults may have given you lots of permission, but something happened in later life to undermine that confidence.

> Phil had a bad accident. His confidence in driving was severely shaken, and he put off returning to work for fear of a journey he'd done hundreds of times.

> Maggy received an obscene anonymous phone-call, and then had an abusive experience with a new date; she became highly apprehensive about meeting strangers, preferring to stay with immediate friends and family, and put off venturing further out into the world.

There may be social and cultural constraints on different kinds of experimentation. It wasn't really that long ago that women couldn't get mortgages, have our own bank accounts or get contraception if we weren't married - how much harder for that generation to explore being independent? (Or change their mothers' ways of doing things). Women receive permission to explore and experiment in, say, the areas of relationships and intimacy, but many, still, in 2002, doubt we can lead large organisations or manage finances assertively. We may have a huge range of highly marketable skills, but feel shy, apprehensive or even vaguely resentful about trying out ways to promote ourselves and what we can do. Conversely, many men have internalised permission to explore the world outside the front door on the broadest and greatest of stages, but even now have less permission to experiment with intimacy, show affection, or enjoy something for its own sake, rather than to master it and be the best. When boys try to express difficult feelings, they are often portrayed as needy or wussy; only indifference is cool.

Believing we musn't get our hands dirty

A necessary and healthy step on the way to being creative and productive is to fantasise and dream about the things you want or need to do. Our imagination and our powers of expressions can create play-grounds in which anything is possible. We need to muse, speculate, mentally rehearse, evaluate, and identify obvious pitfalls in our schemes, and hopefully we get better at this as we have lots of experiences and learn from them. Then we need to move into action. Unfortunately, however, you can get stuck. *Procrastinating through fantasising* becomes a substitute for action in the real world if physical involvement is under-valued or inhibited. In your first family there may have been a lot of permission and reward for discussion and ideas, but not much, or practically none, for real achievement through action.

If we were not given lots of opportunity and encouragement to explore and experiment physically when we are small, then we may start playing around too much of the time on the internal stage provided by mental activity. I don't think of this as real "thinking", (*see How Children Learn to Do Things*). This is precisely because it is not based on sound sensory and physical experience. But it can have its own strange little logic, and it can resemble thinking at times.

So for someone who has a very active mental life, procrastinating may have developed as a way of avoiding the discomfort of having to "get into" or "descend" into their bodies. Why should that be uncomfortable ? Ah, well, of course bodies smell, are clumsy, slow, messy, sweat, make noises, have feelings, and LIMITATIONS! In your imagination you can achieve things at the speed of sound, be the quickest, the sexiest, the most eloquent. In other words, perfect. In reality, we trip over, we get spots, we blush, we make mistakes. So we may think and talk about Doing Things to avoid getting our hands dirty, literally and metaphorically, when getting dirty is associated with difficult feelings and rejection.

There may not have been much permission in our first family for getting messy and mucky as we explored with all our senses. Being lusty, inquisitive and experimental may not have gone down too well. We may have been expected to be skilful far too early, rather than encouraged to value learning through playing, being curious and making mistakes as we went along and *having fun*. Some children are expected to get everything right first time. There wasn't permission for curiosity and the chaos of excitement in exploring all kinds of ways ahead before Getting Down To It. You had to get on with it and be good at it, or you were wasting time. Or money. Or using up people's rather limited capacity to be interested in you. And if you actually found out that you survived and even enjoyed the ups and downs of your experiments, you'd be contradicting all those *what happens if ...* gloomy fantasies that were supposed to help you anticipate the worst (but which actually squashed excitement and curiosity).

So now you put off finding out about things or starting anything new because you think you have to go direct to your goal, be immediately skilful, totally safe or absolutely confident of success. So as adults, gliding around on the heady (literally) breezes of the imagination and the daring flights of fancy involved in procrastination may feel preferable, and more enjoyable to *getting down to it*. Procrastinating may help us avoid the discomfort of having to go against the messages which we learnt from our first family which basically say DON'T!!!!! (be curious, sniff at things, dabble, make mistakes, get grubby, grazed, be loud, inquisitive, etc. etc.)

And actually, at the beginning of the millennium in the West, we are all encouraged to see ourselves as above *all that*, which really means our bodies, and nature. From a class perspective, the cool upwardly-mobile only sweat when they choose to, (when having perfect sex or winning at sports) and certainly not to earn a living. Use a voice-activated computer, you shouldn't need to touch a key-board. Pay your bills by e-mail, why should you have to share air with the clerk at the bank, or need to make relationships with real, imperfect people? Convert your garden in hours into a paved, controlled outdoor sitting room, rather than get out there in all weathers with your fingers in the dirt, meeting a few worms and thorns, finding out by trial and error what you can and can't grow, and revelling in the glorious feeling of the end of a hard day's labour rewarded with a cool beer. Time and space to muck about, try a bit of this, explore that. Touching and being touched by the world in her raw, ordinary state is valued less and less. (Bunjy jumping is an extreme – I'm talking about daily contact-ful aliveness, not death-defying thrill-seeking).

At the same time, reports indicate that more and more people in their 20's have disproportionate expectations of the life they believe they need to create for themselves by their mid-30's, ideal partner, amazing salary, lifestyle, home, perfect children, and so on, accompanied by a dread of failure. There seems to be massive pressure to be perfect, perhaps mirrored in the incidence of stress and depression, which, according to the World Health Organisation, is rising hugely. People crash into the reality that it just ain't like that, for most people, most of the time. Procrastination can be a way of avoiding this painful disillusionment.

~

Talking about *Doing Things*, especially Great Things, can equally become a substitute for action, especially if you can find an appreciative audience. Feedback from a responsive listener can be very gratifying. You might even be able to find different people who haven't heard it all before (counsellors, beware!) who express more admiration than your family and friends are willing to muster anymore. That might feel so good that it becomes worth the discomfort of carrying un-lived fantasies, dreams and plans around. Talking does release energy, so some of the tension built up by becoming aware of something you want to move towards can be dispersed. Writers are often advised not to talk too much about their work, in case expressing the ideas verbally takes away from the energy required to express them on paper. Of course the more you procrastinate about doing something, the more you may have to talk about doing it to relieve the internal pressure of knowing you haven't done what you said you'd do.

And talking about dreams can also seem as if we are preparing to do the thing itself. It might also be a way of getting attention where we don't feel we can ask for what we need, to help us take real action, in a straightforward way. If we haven't learnt the skills for being direct, this may feed us as we build the strength to do so. So our words can also create play-pens, which keep us little and limited. Thinking and talking become pale substitutes for the real thing.

Logically, it's inevitably less rewarding to live life simply by rehearsal, rather than to put on the play ...... but still we do it. We keep putting off action, we keep thinking and talking about what we're going to do rather than doing it, and we sustain our illusions.

Believing our fantasies are better than reality

Dreams and fantasies can be extremely enjoyable. A rich fantasy life can be a wonderful thing, maybe even better than trying to make the dreams come true. Procrastination can be a way of keeping the dreams intact, and deliciously energised. Your emotional, mental and physical muscles don't ache from effort, you don't find out you're not as good as you think, you don't realise that the things you thought you wanted won't magically make you blissfully happy forever. Some people have such a good daydream and fantasy life that they are reluctant to dip their toe in the waters of reality, in case they get cold. And the fact is, they might! In fact they might freeze! But they'll never find out what happens next ....

If you tell yourself doing the Thing is really difficult and that you need to put it off until you have more skill/strength/confidence/knowledge/wind from the right direction etc. - then you never get to test your theory. If you actually got down to doing it, you might find it easier than you thought. Then you'd be faced with several new possibilities:

- Theories you have about other things may be wrong.
- People from your past who taught you that doing things was difficult may have been wrong *(and therefore they could have been wrong about other things as well).*
- If doing the thing is so much easier than you thought, it might have been possible to do the thing – and other things – a long time ago.

Time may have been wasted. Opportunities may have been lost. These realisations can be hard to face. Too confusing or maybe even too sad *(for more on Grief see Part 3, Ways Forward)*

Having dreams is a way to make the reality of now bearable.......

A dream can keep you warm at night, can give you hope in agonising times, can help keep you going when reality fails to live up to expectations. We can never know how important someone else's dreams are to them, or how letting them go (even in the effort to try to make them become real, or to face the truth), may make the present just too difficult. We all let go of dreams at our own speed, and that pace deserves respect.

... and safer than finding out the truth

We procrastinate when we're frightened. If you're worried because you've found a lump or you're passing blood, you may believe you're going to die. You put off having to face the possible negative outcome of tests. Your procrastination maintains the fantasy that you're actually OK and that there is nothing to worry about. Finding a reason to be busy in the evenings may mean you never have time to confront your daughter when you suspect she's taking drugs. Imagining that the job of your dreams overseas would fall immediately into your lap if you didn't have family responsibilities, may be safer than going through the process of applying for the kind of blue-chip companies which take such issues into account, and finding you don't get an interview.

And ironically, fantasies can also prevent you from the difficulties of having to handle happiness. Say you are really attracted to your colleague. He or she might just say yes if you asked him or her out. He might just want to live with you, adore you forever and ask you to have his babies, or she might actually find you very attractive and interesting. Then you'd have to accept that you are loveable after all, and that life can be good, or even fantastic. Sounds great? Not for some people. It can raise tremendous anxiety or regret

> *"Now that I've found something good it's bound to be taken away"*
>
> *"I don't deserve this happiness and I better find a way to get out before I'm found out for who I really am"*
>
> *"More may be expected of me than I am capable of giving"*

For some people it's safer to stay with a tight, limited world view, and the fantasy that life could be better, than trust that reality could bear glorious fruit. Restricting, sad perhaps (in the real sense of the word), but a lot less risky.

Believing that someone might save you

When we procrastinate we create a delay. It may that you have the (unconscious) fantasy that the cavalry, Brad Pitt, Batman, your Dad/Mum or God will arrive in this period, who will take over and then either the thing will be done for you, or somehow you will magically be where you want to be without having to make the journey. This may have been your experience when you were small; maybe you did things at a speed which wasn't quick or good enough for your adults, and they always swooped down and did things for you. Perhaps you were indulged and babied, looked after a bit too much, and you didn't learn to find things out for yourself. It becomes harder to risk experimenting later in life, because things take time, you make mistakes and you have to wait. Things don't arrive in the refined form your adults were able to offer you. You might put things off because you have never learnt that your version was good enough. And you didn't learn or weren't allowed to struggle, carry on through a few scrapes, bumps and bruises until you found your own way.

You needed permission to initiate exploration of your own interests, from the adults who cared for you when you were tiny. Then you would have learnt to respect and to trust your ability to experiment and play around. But because you didn't learn that this phase could be exciting and rewarding in itself, now as an adult you try to activate the people around you to take over by discounting your own abilities. Pretending to be helpless can indeed bring rewards, especially if you are young, small, blond, have long eyelashes, a trembling lower lip or any of these in combination with great legs. Which is fine, if you can switch into being competent when you need to. But it can become habitual to procrastinate in the hope of reinforcement, and you may never learn to manage for yourself. When the going gets tough, the tough may have got going before you woke up.

It may not just be other people who intervene. Giving fate time to do things for us sometimes works as well ...

- People do win the lottery or huge prizes on TV
  So it was fine to put off asking for a salary increase
- Aches, pains and lumps do mysteriously go away
  You knew you didn't need to make that appointment to see the doctor
- Children do decide for themselves to stop smoking
  So you didn't need to confront them and risk their dislike
- Someone steals the car so it didn't matter you hadn't checked the tyres
  In fact it means the thief might have the blow-out! Ha!
- Your lover leaves you.
  Now you get to be the wounded party and you don't have to feel guilty for hurting someone else
- The prisoner is released
  Now you don't need to write letters of support
- Your boss leaves
  You don't have to be the one to stick your neck out to complain about his offensive personal comments
- Other people get impatient and hassle you into doing The Thing, or do it themselves
  (this one works really well for some teenagers, less well for people going through a delayed adolescence)

Procrastinating to create delay in which someone or something else may take over, is an indication that you haven't had much experience of the satisfaction of doing things yourself, or the relief of speaking or knowing the truth even if it is difficult. On the other hand, it might be because you have had that kind of satisfaction in buckets, and you are completely exhausted. In this case, procrastinating has become an alternative to asking directly for someone else to help you. Fantasising that people can or indeed should read our minds and know what we need (and then act on it) is a hangover from the babystage when we needed our adults to be able to do exactly that. We may revert to this when we're really worn out. As an adult, it's not an effective strategy, and it assumes that other people will respond negatively to a straight request.

Believing we are immortal

Life is short
No-one is young forever
We all die

Really knowing these truths with your whole being, rather than just as theories in your head, can be hard. You may have had to face up to the truth about death very young because someone you cared about died way too early. But knowing them can also be tremendously energising and motivating, enabling you to get going and have a go at realising your dreams, or confront difficult truths. Facing death can mean embracing life. Some people don't know that life is short until they are dying, and chances are they may be filled with regret.

When we procrastinate, we tend to forget these things, or compartmentalise our awareness by putting them to one side. Other ways of assessing and evaluating the importance of things tend to take precedence. We buy into the fantasy that there is endless time to go for what we want or to say the things we need to; that there will always be the same, or better, opportunities. We deny ourselves the chance to fully engage with the life we have by doing this, by denying the passing of time.

In a way, procrastination may be an attempt to avoid knowing these hard facts, to stay in a dream world, to not grow up and face adult responsibility for life. As if by living as if it's fine to constantly put things off, we could be the exception, the one who is given immortality and eternal youth. It doesn't work like that, even for people with great paintings in the attic.

Ultimately, procrastination involves a denial and fear of death. Not for nothing is procrastination known as the *Thief of Time*. It's interesting how many people who don't procrastinate very much have a strong sense that life is short. Constantly putting things off can be a way of bargaining with death. *I'll do it later* means we believe that we will still be around tomorrow, with just the same capacities and abilities, and that our important people will still be here too. But that isn't always true. Life moves on. Procrastination is like trying to put out a fire with an ice-cube. It won't work. But if we get the temporary sensation that it will, we may be able to trick our minds into thinking that we are in total control.

When someone really, deeply, truly understands that life is short and that time past can never be recovered – it can be amazing how productive, energetic and effective they become, sometimes almost overnight. It is not just something you can know in your head.

You know it in the way you know who you love.

Stage3
Putting off Choosing and Getting Involved

Procrastination at this stage is connected to

Anxieties about excluding

or

Anxieties about commitment and absorption

If you have difficulties at this stage -

....you often end up having flat weekends, dull or over-expensive holidays, because you put off making plans and clear arrangements in case something better comes along

....you are a "perpetual student", have a long line of short-lived relationships, a house full of stuff you've bought for interesting, practical or potentially money-making projects, which you start but never get stuck into; lots of different sports equipment but no muscles. You are easily put off if someone says, *don't get involved*

....you have a sneaking suspicion the best party/career/relationship/"real" action is going on somewhere else. You may have affairs

....you take your mobile 'phone into meetings or to dinner, and answer it even in the middle of discussion or conversation

....you read on the loo (and you sometimes get constipated)

....you have moved from job to job and ended up in one you never really wanted which is way below your capacity. You've studied half-heartedly, but never developed your skills far enough to set you onto a career path

....you make a decision, you know what the next clear and logical step is. Then you either change your mind immediately after making the decision, feeling overwhelmed, or just before the moment when action is necessary or imminent. You experience the process as stressful, maybe feeling very sick or having palpitations. This is only relieved by putting the moment off yet again *(It would be better to do it later – I'll definitely do it tomorrow/next week/when he comes back etc. etc.)* The tension is temporarily relieved, but each time you go through this incomplete loop of the spiral your anxiety, stress and sense of burden increase. You also have a sense of failure, disappointment or disgust with yourself

....you get especially stuck when trying to make major life decisions, when you see your entire world or happiness as depending on making the right choice, probably between two completely different courses of action. You experience high anxiety, and possibly panic attacks, and you begin to doubt your judgement on practically everything

....you try really hard to get down to things you know you need (or even want) to do, but even though you get started, when someone else needs you, you give up

....to be committed feels like suffocation, or like being abandoned

....you have teeth problems or dreams of losing your teeth. You may have problems with eating (too much or too little)

~

If you've done enough exploring and experimenting, thought and talked about what you want or need to do, you've built up a lot of energy. Your batteries are fully charged, your bags are packed, your tanks are full. Retreating from choosing and not getting stuck into action at this point means all that energy stays in your system. Adrenaline is meant to be used, not left un-spent to circle aimlessly round your body (where all it can do is create mayhem). Imagine a high-performance athlete on the blocks about to start a race, suddenly getting up and walking away just before the crack of the starting pistol. It would probably hurt a lot. Most people know what it's like to experience anti-climactic moments. The build-up of energy you felt, as anxiety or excitement, doesn't disperse easily. You're left with a fretful or leaden feeling of congestion, irritation, and heaviness. You may get on with the next thing, but these unpleasant feelings stay around for some time.

It's the same when you bring yourself to the point of doing something and then stop. In fact, *choosing not to choose* may be more uncomfortable than actually going through whatever barrier or objection you have come up against, and it may not really feel like a choice at all. Your day feels weighed down with the saddlebags of the unfinished business that you had prepared yourself to do. Your thoughts become unusually depressive, circular or obsessive; perhaps driven by the un-spent energy. Once you've recognised that talking about the Thing you need to do doesn't get it done, and forgetting isn't working, then you know the only thing left to do is to do it. Choose. Then follow through with action. If you don't, you're moving into different territory. A land of broken sleep, bad dreams, frightening fantasies, bad breath, a sense of staleness and at worst, life losing its lustre altogether. So people who procrastinate at this stage usually know they do, big time.

But strangely, your friends may not. People who procrastinate over choosing and getting involved in some things may be highly productive in other areas of their lives. The public persona may be very different from the private one. So you may have a job in which you are known to be decisive and effective, but have real problems choosing and taking actions in relationships. Or vice versa. Permission to decide and become committed varies according to the messages we have internalised from our families and society, and what we've done with those messages over time.

Uncomfortable is a mild description for the very real emotional, mental and physical torment some people experience when they are trying, without success, to force themselves to make an importance decision and then follow the logic of their own thinking into committed action. Hugh Grant, in the film *Four Weddings and a Funeral*, portrays this state extremely well. His character is in the church vestry, supposedly about to get married (to Duck-Face), and completely paralysed by agonies of indecision about whether he should or not. He clutches and squeezes his face, hyperventilates, pulls his hair and kneads his stomach, almost as if he is trying to wrench the decision out of himself physically.

If you have procrastinated for a long time about making and acting on a major decision, or getting on with a major project, you may feel entirely preoccupied by it, and experience frighteningly irrational and obsessive thoughts, possibly even delusions. You may have the sense that your world has hugely shrunk. Making even minor decisions feels practically impossible; you doubt everything from your ability to do your job properly to whether you love or are loved. You may feel guilty beyond forgiveness, deeply self-critical to the point of self-hatred, completely alone, or filled with dread and perhaps even suicidal. You often get cold for no apparent reason, almost as if your system is closing down (this is an indication of what you need, more of which in *Part 3, Ways Forward*). If you have never experienced this state, then you already have many of the skills necessary to transform your habit of procrastination, even if it's a large part of how you approach things. If you do know this experience, either in the past or if you're experiencing it now, or if you know someone else who is, take heart.

**There really are ways through,
and there is not only light at the other end of the tunnel,
but hope, laughter, and a renewed sense of being alive.**

How we develop problems with choosing

Choosing is a skill like any other. Some people procrastinate in order to avoid having to learn it. Ideally, we're given plenty of opportunities to practice choosing when we're small, chances not only to explore our tastes, preferences and values, but also to learn to take responsibility for and deal with the consequences of our choices. When you have teeth you can bite and chew through challenges and dilemmas. You can learn what is good for you, and you can learn to bite it off from what you don't want. You can learn that destruction, excluding, rejecting, is part of the process of creation. That you will still be loved when you exclude and reject. And that you can make choices which are respected and supported, whilst you and others remain safe.

No practice in or familiarity with choice-making

But some children are brought up with all their choices being made for them, like the second little girl on the beach in the previous section. It's as if no-one recognised that the child had cut her teeth and was still feeding her with semi-solids, keeping her as a baby. Procrastinating around choosing in adult life can happen simply because you have no experience or knowledge of how to make good choices. You draw a blank when others are "thinking things through".

> I was in the audience of a very effective, highly responsible speaker, who was discussing issues of personal development and finding life-paths. A young man asked how to go about deciding on a direction for his newly awakened awareness of his abilities and choices. The speaker advised him to think about what he wanted to do, prioritise and get started. The young man repeated his question, rather uncertainly, and once again, he was encouraged to think and act on his decisions. I think the speaker missed the point. The man asking the question didn't know how to think his choices through, and arrive at an outcome – he hadn't learnt. Many of us didn't. We may look like adults, even sound like adults, but inside the apparent swan there is a cygnet pedalling like billiyo to try to keep up, and most likely going in circles.

You may have had a lack of role-models who were content with themselves and their choices, and who could remain committed to their way of doing things, without making comparisons. There is more choice for nearly all of us than there was for previous generations. Many people have had to develop "choice-making muscles" incredibly quickly, in ways which their adults could not prepare them for. But where permission to trust oneself runs deep, past experience of good choices can inform the process in new situations.

When children are not allowed to make real-world choices, they emerge blinking into the light of their first-time-away-from-home with barely a clue how to respond to the demands of adult life, and with some very strange ideas about how life works. They are like plants which have grown in the dark, pale, sensitive and head-heavy. They don't have resilience and strength built through solid real-world experience. The only rehearsal for choice-making was on an internal fantasy stage. Such inexperience can bring with it confusion, shame, attempts to conceal lack of maturity with a veneer of a rather desperate sophistication, or in making wild, ungrounded and even dangerous choices that even other people of the same age find odd or misguided. Permission to mature in choice-making may be given in a limited way, over some aspects of life, for example studying and developing a career, or making a home, but no choice at all may have been offered over relationships, finance, balancing work and play, and so on, and it's these areas that throw up the difficulties later.

I think your teeth would probably fall out if you never used them; or at the very least your mouth would hurt a lot if you tried to bite something hard for the first time when you were an adult. If early on, you made a choice for yourself which brought unforeseen and very hurtful results, you may develop procrastination as a strategy for safety, especially if the decision had been very difficult for you. This is particularly true if your decision opposed "messages" you had received which told you that you couldn't make choices for yourself *(stay small, stay safe, stay home)*. Your sense of inadequacy can get reinforced. You may develop the belief that you make ineffectual, childish choices and a vague apprehension that is likely to lead to things going wrong *(because only your mother/father/God has the power to make the right decision)*. You put off making choices, and you don't get involved in anything of depth or substance. Your choice-making muscles atrophy or remain vestigial.

Not very logical, perhaps, since no new learning can happen

without contact in the world, nor moving ahead without trial and error. But then lack of real experience in choice-making doesn't help you learn to think properly, in a physically, mentally, and emotionally-connected way. It's a vicious circle. What grows up in place of clear feeling and reality-based thinking is doubt, which is an insidious and corrosive force *(for more on doubt, see the end of this section)*. To avoid relying on yourself in such circumstances, you may put off taking responsibility for choosing, and shelter behind apparently stronger forces.

Some people practically retire from life after making one bold stride out and being knocked back. Anita Brookner's novels are full of such people, and they do exist. This can lead to despair, when people recognise the cost of years of non-commitment and feel powerless to do things differently. But putting off choosing can also be a kind of loyalty to the people who brought you up not to make choices for yourself, in a demonstration that their way of doing things was the right way, no matter the cost to you. To challenge that way might be just too difficult. Children are fiercely loyal to their parents, even when, from an external perspective, there may be grounds to be more critical.

When the permission to choose is conditional

A second group of children receive very one-sided messages about choices; in other words -

> *"You can make choices, but our love and affection depends on you making the choices we approve of"*

If you were only supported if you made one set of choices, significant or otherwise, you were receiving a message to stay small and sweet by conforming and not to grow up into a decisive, incisive, independent individual. Teeth would decay if they were constantly bathed in sugary nothingness, with nothing clear and clean to bite into and chew on. Trying to make decisions as an adult may bring up all the old fears of rejection. This is a life lived by proxy. The cold atmospheres and disapproving looks are taken in by the small child, and as an adult they are re-experienced almost as soon as a "forbidden" choice becomes possible. Putting off making the choice is to try to avoid re-living the experience, expected now to re-occur in the present. Even when circumstances are different, and the original adults are no longer present, the "internal parent" may give the person a hard time with strong, perhaps unbearable feelings of guilt. In making choices that were permissible and approved of, of course, the person may look very decisive. But she or he constantly feels as if an invisible hand controls which paths may be taken, which are blocked.

Some children obey on the surface, but covertly rebel. Procrastination may be an adult form of such resistance. If somebody wants you to do something, or tells you you should be doing X, it may ring all the old bells of only receiving affection if you toe the line. Putting off choosing and getting absorbed can be a subtle form of revenge, even if it's being acted out on a present-day person whom you wouldn't consciously wish to hurt. Sometimes people turn their choices into duties this way, and then resentfully dither and duck involvement, almost as if they are still relating to the withholding parent.

Being allowed to avoid consequences

A third group of children are allowed to make decisions but are not given the chance to learn from the consequences of their choices by being repeatedly rescued and bailed out. So their choices don't have real-world implications, and they don't get to learn through their own experience. In effect, they are not taken seriously, so they don't learn to think ahead and evaluate their choice of action, or lack of it. As an adult, you may procrastinate about choosing because you assume, perhaps without even realising that you do, that putting things off won't really make any difference - someone else will clear up the mess. In a way, you're saying that your input doesn't count for much. External indifference mirrors internal anxiety that maybe you really don't matter. Procrastinating about choosing and getting involved can be a way of getting other people to demonstrate that your input does matter, by the strength of their frustration with you. Convoluted perhaps, but validating to a degree.

Using Drama as Deflection

Repeatedly revving yourself up for action and putting it off can stem from a kind of addiction – to drama. Procrastination is the stuff of drama, because it thrives on the highs and lows of adrenaline. Both your own, and other people's (the ones who are getting angry or frustrated).

> Mandy described how she prepared herself for writing an essay. She finds out the deadline, gets lots of books, reads, notes, puts off beginning to write, rereads, takes more notes, getting harried, tries to write, reads some more, puts off wrestling through the difficulties of thinking and writing, getting frustrated, searches for that one further book which would surely have the answers, struggles to produce words, feels pressured and panicked by the deadline, stays up all night, and presents her work the next day exhausted and convinced she could have done better. Her partner finds it very difficult to be around the tears, wails of despair, self-deprecating comments and heavy sighs.

Days and nights spoiled for both of them for three thousand words! Mandy is an intelligent, articulate person who enjoys discussing the subject she loves. But when it comes to committing words to paper – committing herself – you'd think she was facing a firing squad. She *squirms* on a grand scale, like a child who doesn't want to go to bed or to write thankyou letters. Sometimes people don't realise they can do things very straightforwardly. They haven't learn to channel the energy they build up and their thinking gets muddled by the quantities of unfocussed adrenaline buzzing around their system. It feels like something major is happening, when it really isn't.

Dramas are created for different reasons. This may have been the way your family behaved, or a significant person in it. There may have been permission for action, volume, being bouncy and on the go all the time, but little valuing of quiet concentration and deep absorption. Intense, emotionally-charged atmospheres and communication can mask a lack of genuine intimacy and relatedness. Heightened feelings predominate and clarity of thinking disappears. Maybe you didn't learn, or weren't allowed access to, other more productive ways of getting excited by real life. As an adult you haven't got internal permission to do the things that would really stimulate you, so you generate a substitute. You miss out on riches. Sexually you may be gorgeous, seriously flirtatious and the hottest thing on the dance floor; but in the middle of making love you may wonder what it's all about. It's as if you stay on the skin and surface of things, rather than getting into the heart and muscle.

Feeling that the choice is a matter of life and death

To choose to live fully you have to become aware of the life you cannot live as well as the one you can. In other words, that possibilities are limited and that each opening door will be accompanied by the sadness of having to close others. The drama which is created by procrastination may be a protest that you are not exempt from this universal truth. Putting off choosing and making a drama about it is a bit like protesting about being sent to bed as a child - if you do it long enough and loud enough it just might work. A kind of magical thinking, which of course will work sometimes, for some people.

And for other people, having to make an important choice and act on it can *genuinely feel like* having to choose between life and death (*see also the example of Becky in the next section, Putting off Completion*). We all contain a mishmash of messages and permissions, and sometimes the choices which torment people fundamentally differentiate between seemingly incompatible matters of permission and inhibition. For example, between being active or passive, between sex and love, mind and body, duty and pleasure, family and friends, home and abroad, principles or practicality. If you don't have an internal sense that you can find your own way to combine and integrate elements of these different and important aspects of your life, and survive taking a stand or having to let precious people, places and roles go, then you may feel that choosing will involve giving up a part of yourself.

Where different parents represented different strengths in any of these areas, it may feel like letting down one of your parents, or alternatively, becoming like the parent you didn't get on with. This is especially difficult if you were asked to take sides between your parents as a child, directly or otherwise, or if they divorced and you feared it was your fault. Old fears of betrayal and abandonment can be revived and experienced as if they are part of the present dilemma, no matter how old or mature you are now. No wonder you might put off choosing – no wonder you feel apprehensive. It's difficult to exclude if you sense that someone will feel fatally rejected or hurt – or abandon you. And your fears of hurting or being hurt get even bigger the longer you put off choosing what to do.

How we develop problems with getting involved

Not knowing if it's safe enough

Sometimes we know exactly what we need to do. We've thought it all out, weighed up the alternatives, excluded some possibilities, taken on others, devised the strategy, chosen the path. Now we '"just" have to take a deep breath and get on with following our logic and intuition, which is probably sound enough.

But somehow all the old excuses start coming up. We make little stabs at starting but then our energy and enthusiasm seem to tail away and we shelve the plans. We get a certain distance down the road, but then run back again. It's as though we keep putting off jumping in with both feet. We procrastinate in order to hold on. Even if you can see the possibilities of the way ahead, you put off taking the real step into commitment that will necessitate letting go your hold on the familiar, the step that means you can never go back.

To let go you need to feel reasonably safe. Some children do not have nearly enough experience of being released into absorbed play. Their adults needed to create a safe, supportive, non-demanding space for them to truly focus on the directions *their own curiosity* wanted to take them. Maybe the adults couldn't, or just didn't, protect the child's space, time and interest enough. *The child will have learnt to stand guard over herself.* This split divided her energy and attention. If part of you is always alert to the possibility of attack or disturbance, it's hard to dive into and fully concentrate on what you're doing. A bit like the bird in the field in the last section – you wouldn't get to pull up many worms if you were constantly having to look around for predators. So trying to be fully absorbed in something as an adult, with all your energy focused in one direction, can bring up all kinds of uneasiness and misgivings actually associated with a past sense of insecurity. Try leaving your mobile outside your next meeting.

To be absorbed in what you are doing, or in saying something valid and important, you have to be prepared to be alone. If you had a good-enough experience of a safe space being made around you by a loving adult, that separateness and isolation can be borne or even enjoyed. This is because you've taken in the quality of that person's care and have it with you even when you are actually on your own. To be separate without that "ring of confidence" can be a painful and cold experience, one which many people would like to put off. Some people develop a sense of the ring from their first family, but something happens to damage their confidence in it. Perhaps your trust was betrayed. Maybe someone violated your security physically, emotionally or mentally whilst you thought it was OK to be "getting on with things". You now have a vague sense that commitment to action will lead to something bad happening - so you put it off. If you have known the despairs of violated boundaries, it may be hard to be truly abandoned, in other words to truly let go into the absorption necessary for full engagement with whatever you want to do or accomplish. You may decide to -

> put off opportunities for absorption
> keep a foot on the riverbank
> keep a card up your sleeve
> build in an escape clause
> never commit yourself completely

.........and above all, stay in control.

Procrastinating to keep people happy

Alternatively, the child's parents or care-giver may have kept the child perfectly safe, but had little interest, enthusiasm or energy for what the child wanted to do. The adult wasn't able to put herself to one side, and she let it be known, overtly or covertly, that she wanted or needed attention herself. So the child had to split its attention between what he or she wanted to do, and keeping the adult happy. In adult life, putting off what you want or need to do may be an unconscious way to keep your early adults' approval, even if they are long dead. Such people, grown up, find it very hard to focus on themselves - you may judge your discomfort or guilty feelings as arising from being "self-centred" (still true for many women). So you keep one eye on how other people seem to be affected by what you want to do. You become distractible, and your energy is dissipated. You put your own interests off – it's far simpler than having to struggle with the old sense of guilt that everyone else should have been made happy first.

Members of minority cultures of all kinds may behave similarly in order to assimilate, not to rock the boat or attract a negative response. By minority, I am using the standard definition of an identifiable group in society, not necessarily a numerical minority, which is disempowered according to the features which determine membership. People who live with the daily reality of racism, homophobia, ageist remarks, the stigma of being homeless or having a disability may well procrastinate about involvement on the basis of a very valid anxiety. If you have learnt fear in the face of genuine danger and attack, how much harder to go it alone, to make yourself conspicuous by standing out, how much easier to keep others happy by marginalising and putting off your own interests, however aware of them you may be.

Fear of disintegration

When you do something new you change. It's impossible to stay the same. Nor can you exactly predict what the changes will be like, how you'll feel as change happens, or what life will be like afterwards. You may want to put off change, because you're afraid of uncertainty, of the letting go of the familiar way things are, even if you want the positive results you hope change will bring, and even if you don't like what is happening now. Procrastinating about moving out of a little pond into a bigger one, for example, means you stay smaller than you need to. In this way, we can become like plants which gardeners call "pot-bound". The plant is in a pot which is too small; the pot limits the development of the root-ball, and so the whole plant's growth is stunted. You have a business. It's doing OK, but it could do really well if you allowed expansion through external investment, or if you delegated some of what you do to new staff. If you are someone who gets anxious about needing to know everything, be in control, or if you think you're the only one who can do things properly, you may well dither about and procrastinate about expanding. And you may miss golden opportunities.

Or you may be working in a job which you could do standing on your head on a dark night in a bath full of strawberry jelly. You talk about leaving and becoming a consultant. You have business plan, finance, even potential premises, but you are always putting off the Great Leap because what you are doing is safe, it's familiar and Big Bad World out there looks cold and daunting by comparison. You feel claustrophobic, cramped, and stale a lot of the time, maybe uncomfortable and envious when you hear of other people making moves and taking risks. But at least you're warm and snug, and you know where you are. You won't have to worry about new ideas, new people in your environment, new demands on your time, or new feelings.

So we procrastinate if we have never learnt that not knowing, and not being in control can be OK. We may feel terrified that if we let ourselves go into the new experience we may never find solid ground again. We may never have learnt that every time you cross a shore-line you get turbulence, that each change undertaken requires an un-picking of the old to begin the new, and that this process can be, and often is, refreshing and enjoyable.

Fear of getting stuck – or never getting out

When you fully engage with something outside yourself, it can be like going down inside a tunnel. You may procrastinate about getting totally immersed, because somewhere in the past you got stuck, engulfed, overwhelmed, and had a bad experience getting out. The total involvement phase of the **Action Spiral** can feel claustrophobic, and painfully restrictive. When the necessary demands of The Thing take over, adults who had little permission as a child to affect relationships with important adults, who felt undefended or helpless in the face of unbearable conditions, can lose any sense of autonomy. Failing to get involved as an adult, in relationships, with our children's schools, our communities, even in responding to a call from a homeless person on the street, can equally arise from the apprehension that *once you get involved, you don't know what will happen.* You may fear being overwhelmed by no longer knowing exactly where things stop and start, or you may fear something coming into you or your environment that you can't control. You feel your boundaries under threat, if you are not confident of your ability to protect them. You might *be taken advantage of, ripped off, taken for a ride, made a fool of, over-stretched*, or even attacked. If we don't have a solid sense of our capacity to –

- look after our own needs (and thus respect those of others)
- negotiate and prioritise our well-being and autonomy
- know when and how to get out as well as how to get in

then we will resist involvement. These capacities form a crucial core of integrity. But if we did not have support in establishing this core, or if we lose our sense of our rights, it can be hard to take up the challenge of responsibility for our committments and involvements. And this apprehension is reinforced when the culture begins to define involvement as potentially suspect; when teachers cannot touch children to comfort them for fear of being accused of inappropriate behaviour, or a by-stander to an accident fears offering first aid in case she makes a mistake and is sued.

~

Of course the other side of all this is that you might be procrastinating about jumping into something wholeheartedly because part of you knows that if you did, you might like is so much that you would never want to come out again! You may be protecting your relationships, which would inevitably be challenged, if you were to get totally immersed outside your home. You may even be protecting yourself from having to deal with pleasure, or with the knowledge that the contrast between this pleasure and the rest of your life is too stark. You are allowed to have a great time with The Thing. But you may not believe this to be the case, especially if historically, pleasure has negative associations for you.

Believing that life should be pain free

With this belief comes the thought that if there is discomfort, or set-backs, then something is wrong, and whatever is causing the difficulties should be stopped. Procrastination achieves this, but reduces the opportunity of finding out what would happen next, and enables us to avoid learning how to overcome problems and to tolerate feelings we don't like. We sabotage ourselves by listening to our own worst fears, and *de-activate our potency* like a parent who backs down and gives in when a child objects to the undesirable, but sometimes necessary, pain or discomfort of an injection, or concentrating for exams. And because we sense the loss of our own inner strength and support at that moment, we protest and panic even more, and then we procrastinate.

I don't believe in no pain, no gain. Sometimes you can make gains in wonderful, exuberant, joyful ways, with no pain at all. However, becoming and staying involved can bring discomfort, distress or even danger. Overcoming mental, physical, emotional and indeed spiritual hurdles can be taxing. But there is a difference between the kind of discomfort which gradually wears off as progress is made, corners are turned, and mistakes are learnt from, and the kind that means there's something seriously wrong. You may prevent yourself from staying involved with the Thing because you get confused by the significance of the discomfort. Procrastination becomes a way of avoiding the hanging-on-in-there necessary to become clear and to carry on even when things aren't that much fun, or are downright awful.

Mis-reading difficulty

Why might you get confused? Surely it's possible to tell the difference and persevere when the problems are straightforward and easy to overcome. But you may not be able to distinguish. You may have had early messages that other people knew you better than you knew yourself. Those people may have been doing their very best to take care of you, but the message you got was that you should trust them more than you should trust yourself, and that your assessment of discomfort or difficulty was not accurate.

> Paula knows (or thinks she knows), she's not going to fall off the wall she's balancing on. Her grandfather, Ron, knows (or thinks he knows) Paula will fall. Ron tells Paula, to come down, because she might fall. Ron once fell off a wall and broke his elbow. He loves Paula. Ron's anxiety, based on his own experience of a bad fall (which hurt him a lot, and he got told off) may transmit itself to Paula, indirectly or directly. Paula loves her grandfather and listens to him. Paula may become nervous, less certain of her balance and fall. This confirms Ron's theory, and dents Paula's confidence in her own powers of assessment.
>
> Or Paula may get off the wall and believe that she would have fallen if she had continued. She has shifted the action to her internal stage and thus away from physical and sensory experience. Her memory of the event would be completed with an image of a likely stumble (which never happened) based on experience which was not her own. Her feelings about future walks on walls will draw on this memory. Paula might have fallen off anyway. Or she might not. Precisely because the relationship between them is strong, Ron's messages will have a powerful effect.

> *Of course Ron needs to warn Paula if Paula can't accurately assess safety for herself.* But Ron needs to make an assessment of Paula's own powers of assessment, and he's not always going to get this exactly right. It's all a question of how much Paula is more or less safely allowed to find out for herself, or not.

All of us accumulate inner knowledge by listening to ourselves and to other people, especially people who are important to us when we are very young. If other people's predictions for your experience or your feelings are frequently or radically different from your actual experience and feelings, you grow up with doubt and uncertainty. You many not be sure of your capacity to assess difficulty, or your capacity to survive and overcome discomfort. Here are some examples of messages that can undermine our ability to know ourselves.......

Physical messages:

You're not hungry, you've just eaten
You're not tired, you're just lazy
Don't make such a fuss, it doesn't hurt
You're clumsy, you're never gentle enough

Messages about abilities:

You can't dance, you haven't got a sense of rhythm
You can't climb that, you've got no sense of balance
You're not strong enough
You can't sing
You won't get a job anyway
It's too dangerous

Mental Messages:

You're not bright enough/Your sister is the bright one
You're no good at maths
You're not good at expressing yourself
It's too hard for you
What you say won't make a difference

Emotional Messages:

You'll be embarrassed
People won't love you if you get angry
Who do you think you are?
You mustn't upset them by crying
You're just oversensitive

Messages about relationships:

She's not good enough for you
Men can't communicate emotionally
We don't talk about that kind of thing
No-one will listen to you

Transferring old anxieties

If you repeatedly have to stop what you're doing before you have the opportunity to push through your anxiety and make your own discoveries, you don't learn that you can survive your initial nervousness and achieve new things. You're still hearing the old messages that disaster will follow if you carry on. You haven't been helped to contain, to tolerate the original feeling until it converts to excitement, or determination. Rather than a little anxiety being a little anxiety, like a signal which says *oh there's something new happening*, a little anxiety feels like it's just about to lead to A LOT, like a flood. Avoiding further involvement with things or people which make you anxious seems quite sensible, but it can equally set up more trouble.

> Fran was a quiet, softly-spoken woman who had a history of side-stepping difficulties with authority. Her father had been abusive and extremely domineering, and she had grown up sharing her mother's method of coping, by never making a fuss, always trying to avoid confrontation. She had a bad fall, which immobilised her for a protracted period, and in this time she had to rely on professional carers. One of them had a rather brusque manner, and Fran found it excrutiating to ask for help from her, preferring to stay in pain and trying to do things for herself. She

> transferred her fear of her father onto the carer, imagining that the woman's slight frown indicated a much greater anger waiting to explode. When the pain forced her speak, the carer did indeed became quite irritated, because Fran's delay made her condition worse. The irritation, naturally, re-inforced Fran's anxiety.

If you stopped every time there was a twinge in your muscles as you walked up a hill, you wouldn't get very far, or you'd get there but only very slowly. If you haven't learnt the difference between discomfort that merely means *this isn't very pleasant*, and pain that means you should stop, then as an adult yourself, you may procrastinate instead of carrying on when the going gets rough.

- You start having rows with your new partner.
  Does this mean the relationship should be called off?
- Your sales figures have dropped.
  Does this mean there is something wrong with the product?
- You're really not making headway in your studies
  Does that mean you should leave the course?
- The doctor sighs heavily and looks at her watch when you are talking
  Does this mean you should withdraw your complaint about the receptionist?

Or should you persist, and find out what you can do to improve the situation?

Wanting guarantees

Becoming and staying involved, in studying for exams, losing weight or giving up smoking, training for a sports competition, developing a career, building a monogamous relationship, supporting important causes, all require hope for a positive outcome, faith in your abilities and skills, tenacity and healthy self-esteem. Dedicating our resources, time, energy, love, and money in any one direction, is a risk. If you only have role-models for the avoidance of deep involvement in any of these aspects of life, you may put off jumping in yourself. There may also be active discouragement from others, as when children, especially boys, who want to study, are written off by their peers as "nerds". This is not a phenomenon limited to childhood; staff groups can generate their own culture of discrimination against colleagues who are seen to work harder than the norm, or not join in the distraction of office banter, especially where apathy has become institutionalised. Other peoples' fears and anxieties, lack of discipline or experiences of rejection and disappointment can compound your own, and it becomes easier to put off involvement than to take a risk.

Because you might indeed fail. You might pass all the exams and still not get a job, put your all into training and yet not win the tournament, leave a steady job to start your own company and end up losing your home, be left by the person you give your heart to, give up years to protect the woodland and still see it dug in for a motorway. You may indeed miss other important opportunities. Was it worth it? Only you would be able to judge. We put off making our best efforts because we want guarantees, and because there is so much pressure to be instantly successful, and to avoid being seen to fail (treatment of people who become bankrupt in the UK is much harsher than in the US, for example). We become distracted from our overall priorities by seeking answers to *what if ......? what if.....?*, looking for absolute certainty that our way forward will be successful. And the search becomes yet another to put off becoming immersed.

As children we needed to learn that just because we wanted something to happen, *it might not.* Life can be unfair. And that did not make us, or our wanting, bad, nor mean anyone was to blame. *It was just what happened.* We may not have been taught to value the process, only the "right" outcome. Without such early learning, adult experiences of failure can feel truly traumatic, and be needlessly avoided.

There are of course countless cases of individuals, in all fields, standing up for their vision and beliefs against all opposition. To separate yourself out, to say, whatever the Thing is, *This is worth it – this is worth my commitment* – can take unbelievable courage and tenacity. These qualities do not arrive overnight. They tend to grow "on the job", so to speak. But if you have little experience of allowing your courage and determination to grow, then you may put off getting involved because you don't believe you are that kind of person; as if the committed, the independent and the brave were a different species.

Doubt

When you procrastinate about making choices and getting involved, you strengthen your sense of self-doubt. You knock self-belief every time you say you're going to do something and then don't – a part of you starts saying, *really?* – and becomes cynical. And you may not have had too much self-belief to start with. If procrastinating at this point in the **Action Spiral** becomes habitual, then doubt can spread like an epidemic through your internal world, shaking even previously solid structures and beliefs. In states of extreme stress, you may develop all kinds of rituals to defend yourself; checking things, thinking magically, and driving your friends, colleagues and families up the wall by constantly asking for reassurance. You may even wonder if you're going mad – you're not, but it can feel like it. If you put off and put off becoming committed and involved, if you repeatedly promise yourself you'll do the Thing and then don't do it, you undermine your sense of trust in yourself and the world, and doubt and insecurity take its place.

Of course torturers have known the excruciating quality of profound doubt for centuries, and use it a weapon; depriving prisoners of certainty about anything from the time of the next meal, whether their relatives are still alive or whether they are going to be killed. For a person who has introduced profound doubt into their lives by procrastination, their experience can be very much like living in a prison, tragically of their own making. When people are lost in their procrastination at this stage, they often turn their frustration with themselves into attacks on their bodies (as described earlier in *Four Weddings*), hitting, tearing, squeezing their flesh. It's almost as if they are trying to extort action from themselves by force, trying to turn a truly terrified or paralysed *I can't!* into action. Mouths don't open to say the necessary words; feet won't move in the wished-for direction, thinking disappears. The mind is pure paralysed will set against a body which can't, by itself, produce the answers or take the step. Fear and doubt can become entrenched. It is a bully-victim state which must be broken for the person to be able to relax, think, keep going, and find the support he or she needs to move forward towards completion.

Images of change

Imagine the last time you went through a significant change Can you find a symbol, metaphor or image that can represent that experience?

Before....
How did you feel beforehand?
What were you saying to yourself beforehand?
What was happening to you physically? Emotionally?
Who was nearby? (actually present or in your awareness)
How were you taking care of yourself?

During...
How did you feel whilst the change was happening, or whilst you were making changes?
What were you saying to yourself about the process of change?
What was happening to you physically? Emotionally?
Was anyone else there?
How were you taking care of yourself?

After...
How did you feel once the new ways were established?
What did you say to yourself about the new situation?
How were you physically ? Emotionally?
How were you taking care of yourself?
Was there anyone there with you?

Through the process
Who did you look to for support in the process, if you did?
What other resources (from inside yourself or outside) did you have to help you make the change successfully?
What did you learn about yourself? About other people? About change?

Stage 4
Putting off Completion

Procrastinating about getting involved carried a strong sense of not *having enough* (love, support, knowledge, clarity, time, confidence in the future etc.) to really get absorbed in your task or project. Procrastinating over finishing is about feeling as though *you haven't done well enough – yet* – to be able to finish The Thing and let it go. It involves –

Anxieties about the future
Difficulties coping with loss
Perfectionism

If you have difficulties at this stage –

....you may suddenly lose interest or heart just before the end of a project. You put off finishing it properly or tidying up (some people's bathrooms have – *just those last few tiles* – left waiting for years). In other words, you finish your active involvement, but you put off finishing *completely*

....you use deadlines to their maximum, getting things done by the skin of your teeth, at well past the 11th hour. Without a deadline, you have little internal sense of how much (money, time, energy etc.) is appropriate to spend on something. You often put off making and acting on a decision until someone else, or circumstances, force your hand. You break deadlines repeatedly, because to act seems difficult to unbearable

....you are over-inclusive. You finish something, but then you start again, just to add that little bit extra – *just one more...*

- *comment at the end of an argument*
  - *tidy-up before we go*
    - *last thing I have to check*
      - *word to add to the sentence*
        - *thing to get from the shop*
          - *attempt to make this relationship work*

....you start out early, but you often arrive late. If you're a salesperson, you may be excellent at getting orders, but somehow they often don't get dispatched on time, or there is some problem with the delivery

....your office, study, house is a mess, likewise your drawers, kitchen, reports, computer desktop – you may never have heard of filing or spellcheck, or noticed where the local re-cycling bins are.

....when you're in a position of responsibility, you're great at making connections but prioritising can be hard. You lose perspective, can't stand back enough to see the wood from the trees and you get lost

....you tolerate uncomfortable conditions (low pay, stress, fatigue, difficult relationships etc.) far longer than anyone else you know. You find it very hard to be able to say you don't like something. You may be something of a martyr.

....you hoard

....you're often the last to leave the party, the pub, college, the "old firm". You have a huge Christmas list of people you neither remember much about nor feel anything for anymore. You think your school days/university days were the best time of your life, or that one of your early relationships or jobs was ideal

....you're a soft touch for a sob story. You can't stand the possibility of anyone being left out. You're nearly always the one who gets left in relationships.

....when faced with having to complete something extremely hard for which you are responsible, and which you know will have serious consequences, you have great difficulty being able to think clearly, or at all. You may feel sick, dizzy or unreal. You feel like a rabbit trapped in headlights, and behave like one. You have no sense of the future or the outside world other than the situation you must face; it can seem life-threatening, and all your instincts are focused on survival.

~

If you can't finish anything, you're never really in a position to start something new. You're system is furred up, like a calcified pipe or a blocked artery. Part of you is still engaged and tied up in the past, so there's less of you available to move ahead. The tiles you still haven't stuck on the walls irritate you every time you trip over them, but you still never get round to finishing. The bags of "unfinished business" you carry around with you, literally, from house to house, or emotionally, from relationship to relationship, leave you feeling congested, tired, and not particularly excited by a life which looks more and more predictable.

Your friends and family know only too well you have difficulties with completion. They know you're always late; if they are sensible, they no longer wait for you. They know you constantly take on too much and don't get through it all. They recognise the depression you fall into just before you try to finish something and they suffer alongside you. *They* get frustrated when they trip over the tiles, have to carry the bags from the attic in the old house to the new house, or have to hear the same old stories time after time. They wish you'd buy some new clothes. They wish you didn't spend so long in the bathroom. They wish you could have weekends together without your mother always coming along. If you have real difficulties knowing when to say *enough*, you may have it said to you. Sadly, the people who know you best may leave, for now or for good.

Paralysis

People who have the "rabbit-in-the-headlights" experience I described above may have a very serious problem with completion, repeatedly and habitually putting it off in certain circumstances. It's as if they have lost a sense of the continuity of life and have no sense that they will survive going through what they must do. The fear or even terror of the imagined consequences of their actions can be so great that they become paralysed, incapable of accessing that part of themselves that is usually competent, capable, decisive and so on. They seem to fall into a completely different state, or feel as if they are entering something like an emotional force-field. No-one else can see or feel it, but once inside they cannot find their usual thoughts, voice, integrity or even feel their own bodies as under their control. Caught between fight or flight, they oscillate between taking action and retreating in increasingly tight circles, hardly breathing. This exacerbates the tension and the anticipation of hurt. They feel helpless to have any say, or right to have a say, in their destiny. Taking a deep breath and doing whatever they must do feels like facing suffocation, drowning or being annihilated. To say – *just get on with it* – to such a person, is cruel.

Developing this kind of inability to complete can happen when the demands of the present circumstances have echoes of a painful or extremely anxiety-provoking event which the person experienced in the past. It could have been a one-off occurrence; for example being physically attacked for acting on your decision, for your beliefs, or for who you are. It could be that the terrible event, an accident, someone you loved getting hurt, or a great personal loss, occurred immediately after you did something, and the shock and trauma has become associated with being decisive and completing. Or you could have experienced a subtle but corrosive intimidation and negation of your reality over time. Torture, of course, is designed to have exactly this de-personalising and degrading effect on people. But the situation does not have to have been as extreme as organised violence to produce the same destructive result. Many children grow up without a strong trust in their right to follow through their own decisions, and still be safe and loved.

When people stay in physically, mentally or emotionally violent relationships, well-meaning outsiders often can't understand how otherwise bright, capable women and men find it so difficult to leave. What they cannot see is the disintegration of the person they know once that person gets home.

> Becky grew up in a strict family which had a strong need for everyone to conform, to "behave properly". She had negligible support for following her own thoughts, feelings and wishes with real action, and found it very difficult to stand up to her parents who refused to acknowledge the existence of anything they disagreed with. This had been repeated with her alcoholic, abusive husband. Becky was intelligent, well-educated and had a good job, met her responsibilities, and was responded to as a mature person in the adult world. But when she went home in the evenings, she felt like a bad and guilty child, who had no right to object to the way she was treated, even when her husband insulted her and hit her repeatedly. In their house she felt she was "going into glue", which gummed up her thinking processes. She lost all sense of herself as an independent person who deserved a peaceful, happy, loving relationship and home. Her inability to hang on to herself turned ordinary incidents into a nightmare of anticipating attack, that was literally unthinkable in her working day.
>
> In that situation, finding the words to say "I've had enough, I'm leaving", or even being able to think it, became impossible. However much Becky determined to leave when she was away from the house, her terror on walking towards her own front door and the mad-making situation within it destroyed her capacity to follow through her own decisions. It was as if she couldn't get the "forbidden "thought of leaving to stay in her mind when she was in her house; she had no support for its continued existence, no loving, stable, well-developed internal-parent to help her. And the more she put off telling her husband she was

> leaving, the more she became depressed about her inability to do so. So she exacerbated the demolition of her already diminished confidence. She literally could not imagine how she would go through the process of ending the relationship, and walking away. No pictures came into her head – all washed away in the swirling adrenaline cloud of fear. And for a long time, shame and fear prevented her from reaching out for support from anyone else.

Procrastination under such circumstances is understandable, within a dreadful logic. To live in this place for long can negatively affect everything a person believes about themselves, and bring their lives to a standstill. It fundamentally saps self-belief, self-esteem, undermines personality and, eventually, can even destroy the will to live. Putting off completing a major life task, such as ending a difficult or abusive relationship, can indicate that something is very wrong, and that real help from outside is needed.

How we develop problems with completion

Lack of role-models

Some children grow up in households where there are few models of completion. All around them are stacks of unsorted papers and bills, half-finished projects, dreams and schemes left in "pending", or an atmosphere of tension rarely cleared away by healthy argument and happy, loving making up. These children are likely to get into endless battles of will with their adults, which are unsatisfying for both sides. If you don't have adults who modelled how to bring about completion, how to clear the decks, break confrontational deadlocks, *and move on*, then you have a significant gap in your learning. You will have to find out about completion for yourself. Meanwhile, being immersed in The Thing, no matter how uncomfortable, has all the hallmarks of familiarity.

You might have learnt from one of your adults that putting off finishing dissuades other people from asking you to do something else. Expectations that more will always be demanded of you is a great reason for procrastination about completion. In your present-day life, there may actually be similar expectations from people whom you find it difficult to say no to directly, or you may be simply responding to old internal messages that said *finish this quickly and then I'll give you something else to do.* Putting off completing means you're still rebelling, even though the old pressure is off.

Fear of what will happen if we complete

We put off completing because we are afraid to enter the unknown, the unfamiliar, especially if we have limited role-models who survived going off the beaten track themselves. When you finish The Thing, whether it be a short task or pleasurable experience, a specific project, a long-term life-experience, like a career or a period of living in another country, a relationship, or a life stage, *you cannot know for sure what will happen next.* We enter – the *undiscover'd country (Hamlet, Act 3 Scene i,* by William Shakespeare), which is like a mini-death. We may have all kinds of fears and fantasies about what we'll discover. We procrastinate to avoid finding out.

Fear of failure and humiliation

Doing Things in the real world makes you visible. Procrastinating may be a way of avoiding the risk of being seen to fail when you complete The Thing you set out to do. Or not being as good, as fast, as skilful as either you or someone else thought you would be. Some people don't get the message that to have a go at something is valuable in itself, for the lessons to be learnt. That it's OK, and very human, to fall over and to fail sometimes. It happens. It needn't be the end of the world. But we fear humiliation if we have had experiences which have left us feeling de-valued and small when we failed, especially if we were expected to be wonderful and had no-one to help us puzzle through what we felt when we weren't. *You may wish to protect both yourself and other people from being disappointed.* We procrastinate to avoid these sad and heavy feelings.

So we put off completion in order to fend off criticism (imaginary or real), and the possibility of failure, by saying –

> *Oh yes, well of course I haven't put the finishing touches to it yet*
> *I'm still not quite ready for the exam*
> *I'll have succeeded when I've got just one more qualification/one further promotion/lost just that bit more weight....*

and so on and so on

On the other hand, your adults might have given you the impression that you were brilliant and perfect (and certainly superior to people who lived near you, or to the children who went to the same school). At home you may have felt bright, secure and confident. Outside the family, however, you were quite naturally rather less certain of your reception. So you may develop the habit of procrastinating about completing The Thing so as to avoid exposing the finished product, and therefore yourself as its creator, to having mistakes pointed out, or to being criticised. If you were never helped to learn to tolerate robust and straightforward criticism in a healthy way, a negative response can leave you feeling disproportionately devastated. Maybe you have the memory of feeling or being profoundly shamed in the past over a genuine mistake, and the awful feeling still lingers. How could someone like you have made a mistake in choosing who to marry? Which career to follow? Which course to study? So you put off leaving relationships, jobs or a life which no longer suits you, or makes you happy, or perhaps, and most sadly, never did. You smile till it hurts and feel nothing but empty inside.

Fear of having to deal with success

When they were very young, some people took in messages from their adults that they could get attention for *trying* hard. But if they succeeded, they would experience a confusingly cold response. We may believe that success will make us lonely, or that we will be envied and attacked, or that love we could previously rely on will be withdrawn. Some of these beliefs may remain realistic, but others will be out-of-date. So you keep trying, getting lost in more or and more complexity, which is a sophisticated way of procrastinating because it looks as if you're struggling to get the job done. It can also keep other people close, to give you help, which you may find hard to ask for directly.

If someone whose love you want is, or was, threatened by your success, you may be procrastinating about completing a project *in case you do well.* It can happen if success means that you achieve something that no-one in your family/company/area/class or race has ever managed before. You – or other people – may feel your success constitutes a betrayal, especially if it means you'll be able to move home, or job, or income bracket; if you have more freedom, mobility or fame, or even if you "simply'" become very happy and fulfil your dreams.

Fear of someone else's envy maybe the clammy hand pulling you back, and making you put off getting the job done as a way of attempting to keep your relationship with that person comfortable. And if that person is an important person from your childhood, you may still be listening to the old voices in your head which whisper – *don't leave me, don't outclass me, don't disgrace me by doing better than me.* Or they may be indirect – *don't use talents we haven't got, don't take opportunities we didn't have.* The person from whom you picked up the limiting messages may have been the same person who encouraged you most; this can lead to great ambivalence about completing.

> Barry was the first member of his family to go to college, the first to qualify in a professional field, and the only one to have moved to London and bought a flat. Although his parents encouraged his studies and seemed pleased about his achievements, they often made disparaging comments about "people who think they know it all", made much of learning through experience at the "University of Life", and generally gave Barry the impression that his success was not wholly welcome.

There can be major generational or cultural messages here, which are broader than our personal lives and take huge energy to identify and question. When we contemplate possible success, there may be a strangely guilty edge to it, as if we are hurting someone else by doing well. It's as if we don't have permission to believe we can be both successful, better at some things than other people, *and loved.* So we put off finishing and never get to the point of having to recognise the double messages we've been reacting to.

But who would you be leaving behind by risking success? Who is really asking you to stay small and wistful?

> "I can't go forward to do new and good things unless I take them both with me – I can't have good things unless the others do as well – unless I make sure that they are all right".
>
> Whilst Siobhan was putting off deciding whether to move abroad after retiring, she was protecting herself and her disabled sister from noticing the differences between them. She was also protecting her niece from being left alone with the responsibility. Siobhan may have consciously and genuinely wanted to take care of her sister, and felt torn; but putting off making the decision was a way of covering up for all of them the fact that there would be a cost to whichever choice she made.

If you don't have role models or experience of being valued in success, if you sense it's going to be cold out there (and it can be at the edge) then your concern about people you see yourself "leaving behind" may be partly for yourself. It might be true – they might really fear for themselves or be genuinely vulnerable if you do move on, and they may have mixed feelings about your success. But equally their vulnerability can be a fantasy on your part, a projection of your wish to be taken care of if you succeed.

In this we forget respect for other's capacity to take care of themselves, and our own ability to do likewise. We underestimate other people's generosity, and their ability to mitigate envious feelings with pleasure in and inspiration from the success of someone they love. Their capacities may actually be far greater than our own. Siobhan may never have asked her sister how she would feel if she went overseas; her sister might have been looking forward to having a larger bedroom, or she might have been planning to move out herself! By procrastinating about completing, we lose many possibilities of enriching our knowledge of each other, by not daring to walk into these new areas of our mutual experience. We try to hold back the rivers of messy and imperfect feelings which follow genuine ground-breaking by staying small and safe, putting off change, success and growth. We imagine that we can see the future, and we forget that our anxiety about change is distorting the view.

Fear of feeling empty

In the examples given above, other people's responses, both negative and positive, can affect whether we procrastinate. But we may also procrastinate about finishing because we feel there is no-one to notice whether we complete or not – that what we are doing is of no consequence, or holds no meaning for anyone else in the wider schemes of life. It can seem better to stay involved in what you're already doing, no matter how stale or boring it has become, than to finish it and feel a great gulf of loneliness and even less of a sense of valued identity.

If you don't have healthy, satisfying relationships and many different, exciting things happening in your life, this is an easy trap to fall into. If you don't have much faith in your innate resourcefulness for the future, it can be hard to be expansive and to open up enough to let go of The Thing and move on. So we endlessly put energy, time and resources into projects which should have been finished ages ago, for fear of the gaping hole which might open if we pulled free, closed the door, said *it's done*.

You may have learnt this pattern as a child, when your adults had little or no ability to say *enough*. If you lived in an atmosphere of tension which was never cleanly and healthily resolved, in emotional deadlocks which neither parent knew how to break, this will have become the norm for you, and the relief and freshness to be found once completion has occurred may well look like scary emptiness. Similarly if your adults had to endure difficult circumstances for protracted periods, and couldn't find a way to make improvements, you may have little internal permission to move on from unsatisfactory situations, which have the safety of familiarity, despite being uncomfortable or not particularly rewarding.

Clinging, and denigrating our capacity to survive the journey into the unknown, rigidifies our system. Procrastinating drains pleasure from your life; your vision gets smaller and smaller. What was simply one part of your life becomes all, and other important aspects are forgotten, or neglected.

> *"If I leave this relationship, will I lose my family and home as well?"*
> *"If I stop being a student, will I ever get a real job?"*
> *"If I sort out all the boxes in the attic, how will I fill my weekends?"*
> *"Will I be empty without The Thing? Who will I be when it is finished?"*

A great build-up occurs – we begin to feel we have to keep re-working, chipping away, perfecting, tweaking, adjusting, checking new angles – but we never seem to find the end – a kind of mental, physical and emotional constipation gathers. How many times have you obsessed about work and put off going out and having fun – *we'll go after I've marked all this homework - after the staff meeting – after the end of term – after the second year graduates?* Or continued to take in and chew over, like Mandy, when you should be finishing off? It's all about attachment as an insurance policy – needing something to weigh you down, in case you float off into thin air. If I let go, I'll have nothing, so I better keep taking in, put off producing until I've had enough. But somehow enough never comes.

Obsession with hanging on can reduce life to a single focus to which all else is sacrificed.

> Linda ended a relationship with Michael when he had an affair, and then became convinced that she had made a mistake. She was determined to find a way to re-unite them, and tried to identify what she had done wrong. Despite that fact that Michael was clearly no longer interested, she spent more and more of her waking hours trying to work it all out, thinking about him, reading and re-reading his letters and e-mails. Her appetite diminished and her sleep deteriorated. A free-lance interior designer, Linda increasingly found that her concentration was affected, and that so much of her energy went into trying to re-create events leading up to the split-up, that she could no longer focus on her work. Her hunt for her mistake became her way of staying attached, consuming and exhausting her in a desperate attempt to ward off the grief of missing the man she loved. She was constantly, restlessly, putting off the evil moment of recognition, and acceptance, of the end.

Revenge

Of course if you were expected to be good at something (or indeed everything) you could put off completing and achieving success – in work, relationships, in any area of life where you might imagine people would be pleased and proud for you when you do well – in order to rebel against those expectations. It's a kind of revenge. Unfortunately by depriving them (him/her) you don't get much satisfaction either.

> Stephen's father was a consultant psychiatrist who hoped his gifted son would follow in his footsteps. Although Stephen excelled in all the right academic subjects, got a place at medical school, and said he wanted to be a doctor, he regularly got extremely drunk and experimented with drugs. Just before his finals, he had a psychotic episode, and ended up on a psychiatric ward.

Wanting Perfection

If you have perfectionist tendencies you may well put off finishing The Thing because you have no concept of the expression *good enough*, coined by D. W. Winnicott, a paediatrician and psychoanalyst. Ironically, this can be true both if your adults were perfectionist themselves, or if you were reacting to their chaos. Procrastination becomes the way of preserving the illusion that you can and will reach perfection, and that life will then be fine. Letting go of the illusion that perfection exists can be extremely painful, because it means always falling somewhat short of your own standards. Tolerating disappointment, when the outer manifestation of our hopes and dreams doesn't exactly match up to the inner vision, is part of moving forward. If you can't cope with disillusionment and good-enough-ness, you may procrastinate to avoid these painful feelings.

The use of deadlines

Many people seem to thrive on deadlines.

> *Imagine yourself faced with one – what do you do?*
> *How far in advance of the deadline do you allow yourself to feel its reality? What does it do to you? Activate? Energise? Enable you to complete well before time?*
> *Or does it initially make you feel relaxed and nonchalant until being flooded with adrenaline (panic and anxiety) the night before when you realise how much you have to do?*

There's nothing wrong with using deadlines if they work for you. Having an end-point provides clarity, a boundary, something against which to push, a container for excitement. We all need limits. But if having a deadline becomes the rationale for stirring up yet another drama, then it may be counter-productive. It can be scary to trust yourself enough to say – *I'll do this until I know I've finished*, rather than – *I'll do this until the very last minute and then I'll be forced to finish* – in other words, abdicating responsibility again for what the finished product is like.

Because if you have left everything to the last minute, of course, there is no time left after completion to review, go over, un-pick, improve until you are satisfied by your own standards. So you may be left saying or thinking – *I could have done better (new fantasy) if I'd had more time.* You've just re-created your original fantasy of perfection. Your idealised project still exists, in your imagination. In other words you are still attached, you've held a little bit back, you've kept a little bit for yourself. Hanging onto the ideal is a part of the secret belief that what you were doing could have perfect, *if only.* Habitually using deadlines can actually be a way of putting off learning from experience how to exercise your own judgement, and of postponing letting go of an idealised view of ourselves. It's a way of avoiding taking responsibility and growing up.

Without the protection of *if I'd had more time*, we become open to imperfect life. Procrastinating until we come up against a deadline is a kind of control, masquerading as out-of-control-ness, a resistance, which ultimately robs us of the possibility of experiencing genuine renewal and freshness. Living by postponing action until the deadline can become a passive experience, even amidst all the adrenaline-charged hype.

Stage 5
Putting off PAUSING

Finally, you can procrastinate about taking a break, having a rest. Stopping. Chilling out. Doing nothing. Just being. It's as crucial a part of the **Action Spiral** as all the other stages; as essential as the seeming inactivity of plants in winter, as fundamental as the body-and-soul repair of sleep. But some people find apparent inactivity impossibly painful or uncomfortable. So they put off stopping for rest, refreshment and reflection until their bodies make it blindingly obvious that they have no other choice - through heart attack, stroke, or quite simply by dying.

I've called this stage pausing because nothing is ever truly completely still or stopped, even in death. It seems so obvious that we all need to take breaks, holidays, have quiet times. So why do we put off doing so ?

If you have difficulties at this stage –

....endings don't mean much to you because you're already involved in the next thing

....you find goodbyes extremely awkward, and try to avoid them if possible. When someone leaves you you find it hard to remember what they were like. If you're the one to go, you quickly forget what the past was like, and you don't really like to think about it

....you have often begun a new relationship by having an affair, or you start a new relationship within a very short time after finishing a previous one

...you find yourself making the same mistakes in circumstances which initially bore no resemblance to a previous situation (at work, in personal relationships, in choice of job, or house etc.)

....you find non-task-centred or unstructured time and relationships very difficult. The job is over, you go to the pub with the team, and suddenly you feel awkward and uncomfortable. You have no idea how to relate to them in an informal way

....although you are tired a lot of the time, maybe exhausted, you don't often take holidays. You have the sense of never being able to switch off.

....if you do have a holiday, you never really achieve the kind of relaxation you feel you need. You think about work or the things you "should" be doing at home. You don't sleep well, or you sleep very heavily, and you hardly ever dream.

....you get bored, agitated, depressed or restless unless you are very busy. You worry that your children are bored if their entire lives are not filled with activity. You worry that your lover/partner/friends are bored if you are not being entertaining. If there is nothing to worry about you worry about that. You can't stand queues.

....you rarely go for a walk just for the pleasure of it. You don't notice sunsets, the seasons changing, or the leaves coming out on the trees (or falling off). If you do then it reminds you of some job you have to do in the garden

....it's very rare that anything seems new or fresh anymore; your sense of smell is poor

....you hardly ever take deep breaths, or breathe out in a slow and sustained way

~

If you're someone who procrastinates about taking breaks, you're probably constantly tired. Either that, or you alternate between experiencing stronger bursts of energy than anyone else you know, and completely crashing out if you slow down even for a moment. You find yourself falling asleep on public transport, at your in-laws' after lunch, or (potentially) more dangerously, during a long, dull stretch of motorway. You may have completely forgotten what it feels like to actually *want* to get out of bed in the morning for the sheer pleasure of greeting the day. You often feel driven.

You're known for always being the one with an eye to the next thing, for getting things moving forward, for not sitting around crying over spilt milk – *for being able to carry on regardless.* Other people admire your ability to do this. But the same people who depend on this strength also complain that you don't like to cuddle after making love, don't see the point of discussing the finer interpersonal dynamics of the meeting or the relationship, and that you just don't notice the chaos – or indeed the spilt milk – left in the wake of your great strides into the future.

You have a huge sense of responsibility. You probably think that unless you keep going nothing will get done, or that if you stop you'll never get going again. In other words, *if I stop, something terrible will happen.* If you have to pause, because your plane or bus is delayed or because no-one is available to fill your one free evening, you may feel extremely agitated, restless, irritable to the point of mindless rage and aggression, frustrated, anxious or depressed. I believe road-rage, and probably other kinds of high-tension outbursts, are closely related to putting off taking breaks, and to the illusion that the only way forward is to keep going at the speed of thought.

People who constantly put off pausing at work, in or between relationships, or even in how they talk and think, have a strong need to be in control. They function from their will, driving themselves through life (or dragging themselves, as they inevitably get more tired). They often get pain in the mid-point of their backs, as if someone was constantly pushing them. Procrastinating about pausing often stems from a profound lack of trust. Each time you rush on to the next appointment, project, experience or person without pausing, you deny yourself the experience of the natural upsurge of your energy, creativity, genuine affection or feeling which would, if you let it, inevitably emerge to lift you onwards from the void in a new direction. No wonder everything begins to seem the same – life always follows the same old script.

If you put off pausing, you have foreclosed on the future, and you get hooked into repeating old and fixed patterns on the basis of what you've known before. Your future choices and vision are limited, if you miss the opportunity to integrate new learning which arises from *processing* experience, just as we do food, and waiting to see what impulses you develop next. In other words, each time you say *Well, I suppose I better get on now, no use crying over spilt milk, can't rest on our laurels*, rather than moving when you really want to get up and get going because your energy is rising in that direction – you further undermine your capacity to trust yourself or have confidence in the return of your natural urges and sensations.

Willing and wishing a new relationship to fit your concept of what you should have, rather than waiting to see what will develop, is similar. There is a sense that if you don't make something happen, then it never will. This is the opposite of the belief held by people who procrastinate at the *Choosing and Getting Involved* stage (which you have no problems with). In the absence of pre-determination, unexpected and exciting possibilities can emerge – relieving you of the burden of responsibility. But you might have rushed on too fast – or be too tired – to notice.

Procrastinating about taking breaks can be fatal. Serious workaholics who have reached the point in their condition where they are living and breathing work all the time risk their lives to maintain their habit no less than drug addicts or alcoholics.

> Rachel worked seven days a week, constantly initiating new tasks for herself and incapable of delegation. She worked literally from morning till night, prioritising business calls and meetings over all social events or relationships. She lied about how much time she spent working, and even secreted work papers amongst the novels she took on her much-postponed holiday, like an alcoholic hiding vodka bottles in brown paper bags. Her partner eventually left her after months of argument. Rachel had accused Christine of being possessive, demanding and manipulative. What Christine had done was simply ask to have some of the time which Rachel repeatedly promised they would spend together, "soon".

The best metaphor I have ever found for workaholism is that of deep-sea divers. There is a critical depth that a diver can go down to before certain chemical changes happen in the brain; deeper than this, you start becoming confused and disorientated, to the point where you start "thinking" you no longer need your oxygen mask to breathe. You may even try to take it off. Starting to take your clothes off on a freezing mountain is a similar early sign of hypothermia. If someone else tries to prevent you, you get aggressive. The terrible thing is that the person trying to rescue you must not swim down to the same depth - otherwise the same thing can happen to them. So unless they can somehow haul you up, all they can do is watch. Being close to someone who constantly puts off taking a break to rest, who is utterly lost inside their work, can be similarly heart-breaking. *You* can see that they are no longer capable of recognising when they are exhausted; you hear the reasons they give for continuing; further on, they don't even give you excuses anymore. They cannot be reached; they are immersed in their own flawed logic, which you can see will only end in breakdown as, increasingly ineffectually, they drive themselves harder.

A symptom of burn-out, the complete depletion of mental, emotional and physical resources, is the compulsion to maniacally initiate new projects whilst previous tasks are still lying around in a state of partial completion. To finish incomplete work properly is too hard, to face the space completion would create too painful. Rushing into the future seems the only way to find air, creating a false kind of breathing space in which the horizon looks uncluttered again. But inevitably the stranglehold of the incomplete and undigested past catches up, and the individual is left to move papers from one side of the desk to the other, to scan the computer screen without seeing, to stare blankly at the kitchen wall.

Emotionally, putting off pausing and reflecting after profound experiences can lead to an inability to feel, a kind of numbing.

> Jennifer's baby Sam died suddenly when he was 15 months old; she was told by the doctor that the best thing to do would be to "start trying for another". When she got home from the funeral, she discovered that her husband, Tom, had cleared out the nursery, and nothing of Sam remained. Tom wouldn't talk about the baby, or his death. Jennifer tried hard to do

> as the doctor had suggested, and to push Sam out of her mind. The couple did have another child; but Jennifer spent the next twenty years in and out of psychiatric hospital. A part of her was incapable of "carrying on regardless". Until she had allowed herself to fully acknowledge the horror and pain of losing her beloved baby, Jennifer remained attached to him, and simply went through the motions of carrying on with life, in a kind of haze.

Digestion, of food, events and experiences, thoughts and feelings, takes time. Assimilation takes time. Integration takes time. In our guts, too little time to digest, absorb, and assimilate nutrients can lead to stomach disorders and malnutrition, despite the quantities of food eaten. The only thing to do is to stop eating for a while, rest, and allow the processes of nature to take over. The process is the same when we allow ourselves time to reflect, which means giving up control of what will happen next. If we create the space, we allow all the banked-up, bottled-up feelings and thoughts which have been pushed aside, all the brown envelopes stuffed behind the vase on the mantelpiece, whatever-it-is in the woodshed, to come out into the light. Some of those feelings may be extremely hard to bear. The more there is unprocessed, the more people try to avoid the potential discomfort by pressing on, pressing on. Each ending gives us the possibility of experiencing the endings we have avoided in the past. If we refuse to do this, we become incapable of beginnings, either physically, mentally or emotionally. We become numb, disoriented, exhausted. Life loses meaning, sensation and pleasure, and we become incapable of excitement, spontaneity or even humour, all of which rely on being aware and appreciative of our inner sensations, not just our beliefs about how we want to force our lives to be.

By trying to avoid the pain of endings, the fear of the void, we may also skim over and never fully experience the joys and satisfactions. If we put off pausing and rush to the next thing, we miss out on the possibility of actually relishing what has happened or what we have achieved, appreciating and celebrating how far we've come. We miss out if we fail to acknowledge and enjoy feeling good about things that have turned out well. Rushing on devalues all the effort that has gone into what we have been engaged in; we may begin to believe that because we haven't experienced satisfaction, we should work harder next time, or aim higher *(then I'll be good enough)*. But of course there is less incentive, because there has been no reward.

Pressing on may become so habitual that the satisfactions of completion, the release of the final *aaagghhh!* when something's truly completed can be missed. Life becomes monotone.

> Dean is a sculptor, who looks at the work he finishes with the eyes of a negative critic, always under-valuing. He rushes onto his next piece to prevent himself from feeling too disappointed. He treats himself like a strict teacher, never satisfied, depriving himself of those moments of real pride and pleasure when he could say – 'Hey – I did that ! This is OK – maybe even good – good enough, for me, for now!'

And even if something has gone wrong, time to reflect can bring back the highlights of the event, the experience, the task or the relationship. When you can celebrate, toast, take pride in, feel good about what you have done and who you are, appreciate the good bits, grieve for and accept the bad bits, then you can relax and trust the flow of you and the things you bring to the world. Peacefulness, rest, excitement, interest, curiosity are yours, seeing the world with all its possibilities, without having to pre-determine exactly how they will develop.

How we develop problems with pausing

Can't stop now

Pausing often gets a bad name. From religion *(The devil makes work for idle hands)* to advertisements for youth-oriented drinks (*Fight your eyelids – Sleep when you're dead*) to business speak (*If you're not moving forward you're falling back*), pausing is associated with weakness. When life is achievement and speed-oriented, and status attached to having certain things and roles in your life (car, house, money, particular jobs, partner, active sex life), taking a breather, looking back over what's happened, can seem like wasting time. Your diary is full, often double-booked; even when you schedule in *take a rest*, having read in the Sunday papers that it's a good idea, it's the one thing you don't achieve because you feel guilty if you stop. Taking time to reflect can seem like risking criticism or failure. Deciding not to get involved in another relationship for a while after your divorce can look defensive. Choosing to take time to think about your next career move and to learn lessons from having been made redundant not only means you risk the accusation of falling behind in the skills market, but is actually penalised by the withdrawal of state benefit. The dehumanising effects of education systems which insist on achievement at all costs are borne out in the suicide rate amongst children, young people and teachers in countries where to pause, however briefly, even in the kindergarten, is to damage your career chances.

So there are many messages in the social milieu that can reinforce a tendency to postpone pausing. But it's likely that the pattern developed much earlier, either because -

- we had no effective role-models of healthy pausing, or
- something has happened which made pausing too anxiety-provoking, or
- action was encouraged and rewarded but "time out" was not

Lack of role-models

When we're tiny, we learn a great deal about pausing from our adults. One of my most precious memories is of my husband and I visiting our friends Ian and Louize in hospital, hours after the birth of their first daughter, Hannah. In the hospital room, the lights dimmed, our friends had created a peaceful, intimate, gentle place for all three of them to rest after the long journey through Hannah's delivery. It was wonderful to join them, to be part of that quiet and loving celebration. None of us spoke much, but there were many smiles, and little tender touches, and some tears. There may be many other times when Hannah's parents will not be able to afford the luxury of such a profound pause, but they know how to create it when they need to. They are establishing a template for Hannah by giving her and themselves time to pause, time to savour, to allow themselves to catch up with the huge experience they had all been through together.

Giving birth to a beautiful and healthy baby gives rise to celebration, and making space for it is condoned even in statute. When we finish something, we enter a period not unlike post-birth, and similar to bereavement, and we need the same simple things – peace and quiet, early nights, healthy, uncomplicated food, people who are willing to be friendly and contactable. But all this is based on sufficient resources to make it possible. Financial difficulties, and the social circumstances under which your adults lived, may have made pausing, or taking breaks and holidays hard, if not impossible. In this century there have been severe economic Depressions as well as two World Wars. Pausing, to rest, reflect, even to celebrate, can seem self-indulgent. Taking time to reflect on mistakes, difficulties, losses, disappointments, or failure is even more likely to have been put off (*you've just got to get on and make the best of it*).

It can be extremely hard to learn the advantages of pausing if you were never able or allowed to observe your adults doing exactly that. You needed to witness their survival of difficult feelings, their ability to tolerate a pause and to allow new feelings to gradually emerge and to lift them with new energy and purpose. Without this we may imitate our early adults' need or tendencies to keep rushing on, or to be workaholic. Children may never learn how to think through what has happened, nor how to learn from experiences, if such things are not discussed. If your adults kept putting off pausing because they felt they couldn't or dared not stop, then you – and they – missed the benefits of taking time out, and you also missed the opportunity to learn how to do it.

Whole generations of people have had to *get on with it* – pushing away tears, pain and rage in order to survive. When my colleague Sarah came to London from South Africa to train, she created a space in her life. For the first time, she began to experience nightmares and memories from the horrendous events which had happened years before. Had she dwelt on her feelings at the time, she would not have had the energy or will to continue the struggle to keep her family together and feed them. The psychoanalyst Alice Miller suggested that wide-spread cultural suppression of trauma will be played out within the psyches of the next generation; in other words, if you always put off pausing, it could be because your parents or even your grandparents experienced trauma too horrific to allow into consciousness. A family pattern of getting on with it, not talking about the past, not pausing to celebrate or to mourn, evolves. To pause, therefore, is to go against the family "script" of pressing on at all costs, which was "written" to ensure the family's survival in appalling circumstances. No wonder people sometimes feel something terrible may happen if they stop. It may be that it – the terrible thing – *has already happened.* Not necessarily to you yourself, but to someone in a previous generation.

Fear of not being held, and falling apart

When we finish something, we need to know that if we stop the world will carry on. As tiny people, we needed other people to hold us, literally and metaphorically when the known world had disappeared. Our adults' arms gave us that security. In time, ideally, the memory of that wonderful feeling of sinking into the safety and comfort of their bodies, smell, gentle sounds, their smiles and their ability to be solid and reassuring becomes an internal part of us. We can draw on the memory of it when we need to stop, confident that *something else* will continue to enable our survival. That security needs to be willingly given without us having to do much or anything about it at the beginning. Otherwise we will learn very early that the only way to survive is to divert our attention, from our need just to be and rest after action, toward either having to be active and do things (for example screaming for attention, trying to please people in order to keep them nearby), or just finding something, anything, to distract ourselves from the appalling knowledge *that there is no-one there.*

We need to be able to rest *in* something, and most naturally it will be with the people who care for us, or with their memory. We can use them as a kind of womb to retreat to. Without this, if that security was never established in the first place or if something severely traumatic has ruptured our confidence in it, we can feel very much on our own. In consequence we may unconsciously decide that to pause is just too terrifying or difficult. Because if we give up our activity, we may fear re-experiencing a ghastly emptiness that seems to have no end. If no-one holds us when we are tiny, as adults we can feel as if we are falling into nothingness when we stop, or into a space only filled with awful and ancient feeling.

> A couple at my local swimming pool were struggling to get their little girl into armbands. She was distressed, they were distressed, and to try to end her cries the father whipped her up in his arms and quickly ran down the steps into the water. He slipped, and they both went under; surfacing, her cries became screams. Rather than just hold her close and steady until she felt safe again, he tried to distract her by bobbing her up and down, pointing out passing swimmers, splashing her, laughing and holding her away from his body to try to float – all, unsurprisingly, to no avail. Her screams increased, until her parents gave up and took her out of the water. From the little girl's perspective, it was easy to see how life was getting more and more chaotic and frightening. She needed time to rest, protest and recover, rather than more and more complexity.

The gap created by pausing sets off an alarm in our psyches, and instinctive mechanisms swing into action to fill the space and protect us from finding out and experiencing the unimaginable and potentially threatening forces from the depths. We rush into action, and put off pausing to another day.

Lack of permission to pause

Finally, we may procrastinate about pausing because we were given the message that to be active and trying to get somewhere was acceptable, but to be satisfied and content was to be arrogant, to be sad or disappointed was being moody, to be quiet was being lazy. Adults have to accommodate a massive range of feelings in our children. If we have not learnt to give ourselves permission to experience the full spectrum, and to pause and withdraw where necessary. then we may feel an uncomfortable mix of anxiety, envy, guilt and frustration if our children take time out.

> When Guy came home with his school reports, his father always referred to the hard work he'd have to do for the next round of exams, even when they were a year away. When Guy got his first job in a City law firm, his father wanted to know how long it would be before he would be made a junior partner. Guy felt that his satisfaction and pride in his success were diminished by the instant reference to targets yet to come. He felt his balloon of natural excitement was deflated by his father detracting attention from his achievement by focusing on the future hurdles he'd have to leap. A bit like getting to the top of a steep hill, only to have the mountains pointed out.
>
> As a father himself, Guy noticed that he found it very hard to simply enjoy the fact that his daughter was very good at running. He found himself thinking of the next competition she could enter, the speeds she could achieve. One day she burst into tears after telling him about the race she'd won, shouting at him that he wasn't listening. He felt mystified and hurt, but she was right, he wasn't really listening. He was thinking about the next step, and wasn't sharing her glow of satisfaction in what she had just achieved. When he did eventually learn to do this, he noticed how sad he felt that his father had never been able to

> listen to him. Guy's father had experienced long periods of unemployment as a young man, with a wife and two small children to support; to "rest on his laurels" was inconceivable when he never knew how long he could rely on any income he found. A huge sense of responsibility and genuine anxiety led him to try to grip the future tightly, a habit he couldn't give up even when he had more financial security as an elderly man.

I am not suggesting that pausing, for celebration, for grieving or for rest, has no limits. We have to find a way of continuing even when there has been pain. To wait for all the difficult feelings to go away is to risk becoming entrenched in grief, regret, hurt and so on; it is inevitable that we will carry some of these feelings with us as we set out on new ventures. We have to learn what we can and resolve to use the learning next time. At some point too, we have to stop celebrating and get on with the more ordinary tasks of making the company live up to its pre-flotation promise, start the long haul of training for the next tournament, get on with the day-to-day challenge of loving our partners once we're home from the honeymoon. The more we are aware, the more we are likely to know the moment to move with most of our energy available to us, to learn the difference between moving on because we're running away, and moving on because we know it's about time.

Part 3 **Ways Foward**

Physical Ways Forward

Mental and Emotional Ways Forward

Giving Yourself Permission to Move Forward

Relationships

Other Creative Strategies

Grief and Loss

IT'S OKAY I'll FINISH
IT LATER

Ways Forward

If there was one obvious way to stop procrastinating, this would be a very short section. I imagine it would be entitled, *Just get on with it*, which you've probably said to yourself many times before. And if it were that easy, you would have got on with it, and sometimes you probably do; so if it helps, here it is again –

Just get on with it!

But if that doesn't help, and if what you've read so far has struck a chord (or if you've immediately turned to the "solutions" chapter!) you'll probably realise there are many other things you can do to help yourself accomplish what you want to do. Many ways of *allowing* yourself to be effective, rather than *forcing and straining* and getting nowhere fast. You can do a lot to nurture the conditions in which your natural ability to get going will flourish; concentrate on those, and your tendency to procrastinate will gently fade away. Here you'll find broad-brushstroke suggestions, as well as fine tuning for specific issues.

First of all, think about the Thing you keep putting off, and then think about... motivation

Question: Do you actually want to do The Thing?

(Pause for honest reflection)

Answer A: *No*

Aha.
Some things are simpler than they seem.
If procrastinating has been a temporary or habitual way of avoiding saying no directly, now's the time to recognise that and give up the dream, plan, or belief that you can make anyone, including yourself, happy with promises you don't really want to keep. If

you say *no*, you may find relief, whatever else you may lose as a result. Saying no can be creative. It can open up and refresh your system, and un-stick you from muddled situations. The energy you had to put into holding back that "no" will become available to you again, and you'll free the time you've been spending worrying, self-blaming and wishful thinking.
But if saying no is one of the things you often put off, read on.

Answer B: ***Yes, I do want to do the Thing, but ...***

> I want the outcome (*or product*) but...
> I don't want to go through the process to get there
>
> I don't want to be a school governor anymore (*outcome*), but... it's so hard to tell the committee without feeling I'm letting them down (*process*)
> or
> I want a tidy kitchen (*product*), but... I don't want to tidy it (*process*)
> or
> I want to know my teeth/eyes/cervix/prostrate are/is OK (*outcome*) but... I don't want to go to the dentist/optician/doctor (*process*)
> or
> I want to have written a book for the satisfaction it will give me (*outcome*) but... I can't stand the thought of spending a long time alone writing, editing and re-editing (*process*)
> or
> I want the outcome, and I know I'll probably enjoy the process, but... I just can't seem to get started, get down to it, or finish it off.

If you answered B, then Part 3 of this book can offer you a huge diversity of ways to make changes, physically, mentally, emotionally and socially. Some of the approaches have worked for me and some have worked for other people. If you have other strategies which aren't described here, please do contact me via the publisher - I'd love to hear from you.

This section makes suggestions. The important thing is to find what works for you. And to give yourself permission to explore and experiment, get some support and find ways to follow your logic and intuition that are effective, sustainable and enjoyable. And legal!

The suggestions are grouped with each stage of the Action Spiral in mind. Remember that you can procrastinate at different stages of the spiral over different things, so trust your own ability to choose what will help you right now. Any of the suggestions can help you re-establish the flow you need, of energy, feelings and thoughts, and they can free you to do the things that make you feel relaxed, strong, happy and good about how you spend your days.

Enjoy the process.
You deserve the time of your life.

Physical Ways Forward

It's time to move your body

If children are well, well-rested, adequately but not over-fed, and if they feel safe, they can't wait to follow their curiosity and get going. The natural direction of life is forward. As adults we often have to over-ride basic physical discomforts to "get the job done", but we still have the same basic needs. If you're over-tired, too hungry, unwell or feeling vulnerable, you're likely to regress to more immature ways of behaving, which may include procrastination. So at times of high distress, stress or fatigue (for example in bereavement) or if you've recently gone through any major change, including positive ones, noticing that you're procrastinating a lot may simply be a signal that you need to withdraw a bit from the world, and find rest and nourishment of all kinds. If you come out of your cocoon sometime later to find your perception has cleared and you're back to being active and effective, that's all you needed.

What works for you?

A walk around the block before bed-time, long relaxing baths, early nights, lots of drinking water (still not sparkling), adequate carbohydrate and protein, keeping warm, not taking on anything new, talking with close friends, good books - in other words, snugging up and adopting a temporary state of hibernation until you feel your batteries are re-charged. People worry that they will stay in this state too long - it's very unlikely. If you really give yourself what you need, once you're satisfied and rested, the next thing you'll become of aware of along the spiral will be a need for action.

But if you're experiencing a general inertia rather than exhaustion, a key strategy for changing energy levels and to induce a sense of well-being and vitality is to become physically active. Anyone who has every really loved playing sport, running, dancing, skiing, sailing, or horse-riding knows the fabulous pleasure of full engagement. Your entire body warmed, you can relish flow and fluidity, the experience of movement and sound and connectedness to yourself, the ball, the track, the rhythm, the wind - as good as, and sometimes even better than, sex. Complete absorption in the moment, all senses alive, total embodiment of concentrated energy in flow. Such moments are precious. You know you are deeply, thoroughly alive, body, mind and emotions in total accord. And afterwards? Pleasurable weariness and the natural pull towards the rich sleep of a body refreshed by exertion.

If you procrastinate, you miss this. Your energy is scattered, part going forward, part held back. You may get headaches, back ache, feel heavy and irritable. Your digestion isn't so good. You wake up after a night's sleep but you don't feel refreshed. Everything becomes an effort. Throughout the book I have been talking about the flow of energy through all our tubes which gets interrupted when we procrastinate. If you regularly build your cardio-vascular capacities, if you develop your strength and flexibility, chances are you will feel more alert, happier, more confident, sexier and more relaxed *whatever else you are doing with your life*. So even if you carried on procrastinating, at least you'd be healthier - you might even live longer and get more "tomorrows"!

Our physical, mental and emotional systems are not separable. So if you consciously and deliberately set out to increase the amount you move physically, quite simply, you won't procrastinate as much. You can watch your habit begin to disappear practically from Day One as you become more decisive, self-disciplined, relaxed and effective. Getting fitter and being more active will help, especially if you're someone who spends a lot of time in your mental world, either for work or because it's become a habit. It's also true if you are entangled in deep emotional struggles, or indeed if you're a person who didn't have much permission or encouragement to be physical when you were small. Humans love and respond to metaphors. Giving ourselves permission to move on the physical level sends strong messages to our minds and emotions about the benefits of flow.

**Being active can make you feel proud,
full of well-being and bounce.**

Procrastination can't. A moving body is less likely to develop digestive problems or constipation, which can also clog up thinking and create bogus depressive feelings and lack of confidence. A body which is glowing with good health and thrumming with energy has less and less place for the phlegmatism of procrastination. Imagine your body as the channel through which you can follow the river of your own ideas, dreams and desires into action. When you are physically alive and moving, as you build strength and flexibility, the channel becomes more boundaried, clear and firm. A natural rhythmic pulsation of action and rest follows. Thoughts and feelings don't puddle up in stagnant corners, nor is your system so over-stretched with action that it wears out. When you feel physically alive you notice a healthy, good-natured impatience with your own dithering and *what if's* and *yes buts*. Your increased strength and body confidence enables you to face issues that once seemed daunting. You become more robust.

Draw a quick doodle of your body as you see it when you are procrastinating. What kind of channel does it form? Open and free-flowing?
Or hunched up and twisted, constricting your lungs and digestive system?
Draw another doodle of how you'd like your body to look, or how your body does look when you're feeling happy and confident, and being effective.
What first step could you take in that direction?

from	*tired*	*to*	*refreshed*	*(a nap or a stroll?)*
from	*tense*	*to*	*relaxed*	*(a yawn or a stretch?)*
from	*worried*	*to*	*calm*	*(humming or exhaling?)*

When I talk about being physical, I'm not suggesting you should instantly initiate a three-times-a-week-in-the-gym habit (although you may do just that, which would be fine). It would be too dogmatic and prescriptive for many people, and if you give it up after the second week, you might start criticising yourself again, which is counter-productive. I'm suggesting you experiment to find out what you genuinely enjoy, whatever makes you feel good to be alive.

What does moving more mean to you?

It can be anything from - walking the children to school instead of driving, taking the stairs instead of the lift, choosing a current song in the charts and getting up and moving around every time you hear it on the radio, kicking leaves in the park, lifting your briefcase or laptop up and down, to doing lunges while you wait for the kettle to boil, going for a hike, making love or gardening. And of course it can also mean going to the gym, playing sports, dancing, yoga, swimming, running, rowing - you name it. Whatever you find you enjoy. Even now as you're reading this, you can consciously decide to flex your bum muscles, straighten your back and drop your chin, stretch your arms over your head three times (interesting if you're on the underground), do three sedentary breast strokes (ditto if you're on a plane!), roll your shoulders forwards, rotate your neck, squeeze your face muscles, make any of your everyday actions bigger ... the list is endless.

If you do any or all of these in quick succession, you'll probably notice that you start yawning - excellent. Your body is drawing in more oxygen - your tubes are just that little bit more refreshed. If you drew your body as a channel now, it would be that little bit straighter, a bit clearer, more smoothly flowing. It can be that simple - and the more you move, the more you'll want to move for the sheer pleasure of how it makes you feel.

Looking for opportunities to move consciously can quickly become a habit, once you begin to get a taste of how good you feel in your body when you do. Regular, formal exercise might already be or become a part of your increasing activity levels, but the important thing is noticing you have a body and allowing all of it to become energised each day.

There are particular ways of energising your body relevant to each stage of the **Action Spiral**. Love-making and walking fit into any category, and are best included often. Massage is also helpful, both relaxing and energising. The gentle pressure encourages better circulation. It causes a small build-up of fluid; when this is released, the fluids momentarily travel a little faster through the blood and lymph vessels. That helps wash through the waste-products and toxins which have accumulated around muscle fibres which haven't been moving much. The toxins cause the tightness, stiffness and aching which make you want to move even less. If you've ever had to be in bed for more than a few days, or if you've got out of the habit of taking exercise, you know what that feels like. A good massage also helps you know or remember where your body stops and starts, as you feel yourself being touched and moved. If you are procrastinating a lot, you have probably become rather disembodied and head-bound. Whatever you find that helps you re-establish contact with your body, its boundaries and weight, will enable you to be more clear, firm, confident and decisive. And being touched all over, firmly, gently and with respect, reminds your body - and you - that you are valuable and need cherishing. Nobody feels good about procrastinating - it can seriously dent your self-belief and confidence. Exercise and massage can enable you to re-assert feelings of healthy self-pride.

If years of holding back forward motion and being expansive have made you stiff and tense, find activities you can enjoy which will work to reverse the tension. Different activities emphasise the different aspects of ourselves which need to be strengthened. Here are some suggestions; *do get advice from a doctor or sports professional if you feel you need to check whether a particular exercise is suitable for you.*

Giving Yourself Permission to Move around the Action Spiral

Stage 1 – Difficulties with awareness

Emphasis on raising body and environmental awareness, gentle increase of overall circulation and flexibility

Being massaged with upward motion

Bending and stretching (and yawning)

Climbing stairs, exercising the dog, cleaning out the pond

Dancing, especially with a partner with a good sense of rhythm

Dusting

Having a shower

Indian head massage

Hiking, for the pleasure of smells and sounds and sights of the country

Pilates

Swimming, (for the experience of moving in the water, rather than counting lengths)

Stage 2 - Difficulties with exploring and experimenting
Co-ordination, balance and confidence. Further development of noticing and stretching. Experiencing our bodies in relation to the diverse and uncertain environment. Emphasis on building overall cardio-vascular capacity. Upper arm/upper body strength, leg strength.

Breast-stroke

Cycling, especially outdoors

Gardening

Gym exercises which involve: strengthening arms, especially reaching out and pulling towards your body, like rowing

Hanging up washing (arms raised)

Improvisational and contemporary dance

Jogging

Orienteering

Painting walls

Riding

Swimming, especially in the sea or a river

T'ai Chi

Table Tennis

Water-exercise classes

Window-cleaning

Stage 3 - Difficulties with choosing and getting involved
Emphasis on developing strength, endurance, tenacity, determination. Selection and rejection, pulling through, pushing off, kicking away. Develops strong legs and a standpoint. Putting weight behind something, committing and collaborating. Activity which requires counting and building on – core body strength, lengths, reps, weights, points, strokes, etc. possibly with a coach to encourage you

Athletics

Digging

Foot massage

Gym exercises which involve:
pushing away with arms and legs, and using weights

Hoovering

Kayaking

Kick-boxing

Martial arts

Partner dancing

Racquet sports (tennis, badminton, squash)

Running

Sailing

Skiing

Swimming, especially crawl, focusing
on improving distance and speed

Thai Massage (Vigorous and energising)

Trampolining

Stage 4 - Difficulties with completion

Emphasis on goals, activity with an end product. Develops need and capacity to deal with success and failure, comparisons. Develops awareness of completion within given time, and respect for seasons.

Archery

Competitive sports, singly or in teams

Diving

Exercise classes (especially with music)

Golf

Martial arts

Pruning, hedge clipping

Shot Putting

Sweeping

Tearing up cardboard boxes

Throwing out the rubbish, taking bottles to bottle banks etc.

Stage 5 - Difficulties with pausing
Emphasis on soothing, repetitive, low-key wind-down activity, and rest

Backstroke

Dawdling

Feeding ducks

Indian head massage

Ice-skating

Paddling

Swedish massage, relaxing, with downward strokes

Stroking animals or partners

Walking in parks

Yoga and stretching

~

Find what works for you. Use your imagination to create the right environment of challenge and diversity. Even if you're not entering the Olympics, there's no reason why you can't hear the crowds cheering in your head as you walk round the last bit of park or hang out the last sheet. You may never see yourself performing live at the Albert Hall or on Top Of The Pops, but you can still entertain the cat with the Carmina Burana whilst you paint the ceiling, and imagine music which really helps you kick into fifth gear when you swim. You can choose clothes that provide that extra incentive to get out there and get moving, rather than shapeless, old or faded things which pull your feelings down. Whatever helps you become and stay engaged with the life-long process of making the most of being inside every cell in your body, will help you lift the activity beyond the everyday, turn it into an exciting adventure and push procrastination to the margins of your experience.

A Caveat

Of course you may be using physical activity as a means of procrastinating.

> *e.g. I'll Do the Thing I'm avoiding after I've ...*
> *done the dusting/washed up/played another game of tennis/ another round of golf/had a swim/been to the gym(again) watered the garden*
> *...you fill in the gap!*

We've all done it! If this is what you do, then I imagine you experience less pleasure and less moments of complete absorption when you're being active than you'd like to. In fact you may even find that you chip the cups you're washing, plant bulbs up the wrong way or in the wrong part of the garden, lose form, your temper or your glasses. You probably end up feel irritated, agitated and a bit all over the place. It's because your motivation is split. Your energy and attention are not fully available for what you're trying to do. If you move around half-heartedly or guiltily, telling yourself off, your energies are scattered, and that scattering drains you. So you need to find a way to gather your energy back together.

If you realise that you're moving as a means of avoidance, the way to use this to your advantage is to admit that's what you're doing, and then get into that avoidance as much as possible - revel in it, be gleeful, celebrate your escape!

If you know you're running away, run, don't slink!
Push/wash/dig/swing/kick harder and faster!

Throw your heart and your energies into what you're doing. Enjoy the dusting, the game, the garden. That in itself will help create flow. Your perspective, sense of humour and ability to breath deeply will return. The more you commit to procrastinating, to making the experience as consciously physical and as much fun as possible, the more energy you'll create for doing the Thing you've been putting off. And you'll resent "having" to do it much less.

Environment

Sometimes it's easy to forget that a shift in the environment helps, and that you can break the procrastinatory pattern simply by moving away from it for a while. Holidays, a weekend away, even getting up earlier than usual and walking in a direction you don't know so well can awaken perception and stimulate action and freshness. Don't get stuck, even if you love living in the same place and with the same people for years. And simply noticing the qualities of the environment gives opportunities for movement - playing with leaves, sand, waves, snow, resisting the wind - it's all there waiting to greet you, for free.

Drink more water

Drinking lots of water has many advantages. If you have never experienced the benefits of drinking several glasses of water each day, it is definitely worth starting. Feeling thirsty is often a late indicator that your body needs water; you may have missed earlier cues like headaches or stomach ache. On the way to dehydration your mental processes begin to slow down, get confused, and you can flip back into that infantile state of feeling needy or agitated without knowing why - the perfect breeding ground in which the spore of procrastination will flourish. Drinking lots of water also aids digestion and gets rid of toxin build-up, both excellent metaphors for the flow you're trying to encourage. Drinking water need not be oppressive - just have a bottle on your desk or table, carry it in your bag or the car, and sip some now and again. Increasing daily water intake is good for the long-term shift away from procrastination, but drinking water to enable you to complete a specific task, be it physical, mental or emotional, can also be helpful, literally and symbolically. (If you drink too much in too short a time, you can cause serious problems for your kidneys, so gently increasing your intake of water, rather than swinging to an extreme, will help most).

Food

Action requires nourishment. Meals, as opposed to food consumed whilst trying to do something else (the sandwich-at-the-desk, snacks-on-the-run syndrome), help reduce procrastination. This is especially true for people who have difficulty choosing and getting involved, and completing; they are likely to experience a lot of mouth hunger (as opposed to real hunger) and feel that they need to keep putting things in their mouth. The action of reaching out for the food, touching and holding it, biting, chewing and swallowing becomes a substitute for the Thing they're finding hard to get down to.

> Mark found that when he tried to write a report to a deadline, his table became littered not only with more and more paperwork, but also with cups, plates, and chocolate wrappers. He leafed through notes and searched increasingly frantically through his computer files, accumulating information but at a loss to know how to integrate what he was only partially absorbing. He was taking in far more than the report required. Thinking clearly become more and more difficult: he deleted what he wrote almost as soon as he typed it, and kept interrupting himself to make more coffee, get another sandwich, or to use the loo as his stomach started to ache. He brought the food to his desk to eat whilst working, to "avoid wasting time", but still spent ages trying to get down to the actual writing. The whole process was torturous and agitated. Mark felt childish, despondent and physically dreadful. He was locked in the procrastinatory grip of never feeling anything he could take in or put out was enough.

When people behave like Mark, the food chosen is not usually very helpful, because it doesn't provide the kind of nutrition which will sustain committed activity. Procrastinatory behaviour and thinking can be sparked and certainly fed by sugary foods, caffeine, alcohol, snacky things which give you a quick fix and energy burst but which leaves you tired and lethargic in the aftermath. What we need for sustained activity is fruit, vegetables, carbohydrates, grains and proteins. Slow-release food like pasta and pulses provide a rich source of energy as well as feelings of well-being and of having "had a proper meal" - i.e. of having completed the first task of eating, and now becoming ready for new action. Putting off having a meal, away from the task-in-hand, is actually counter-productive (Unless you're using long-winded construction of complicated meals as a way of avoiding, in which case see above and revel in it!). Of course you can sabotage yourself by attempting a brain-task at 2.00pm just after a heavy lunch. Food requires digestion, the pausing-after-action phase of the Action Spiral, just like anything else, and in the working week a short after-sandwich-slump followed by a walk around the block is likely to be more productive of brain freshness and energy than trying to get down to work straightaway. Procrastination after lunch can simply be your body's way of protesting at the lack of digestion time, so let it be. Take a stroll, have a glass of water and start again.

People who try to lose weight by becoming extremely selective in what they eat probably procrastinate more than people who give themselves permission to eat a wide range of food they enjoy in genuinely satisfying quantities. This is because it's hard to be whole-hearted about food, to be fully committed to the pleasurable activity of eating, if your mind is always monitoring what you're consuming, or calculating it's ill-effects, like a strict and critical overseer. Of course we need to eat sensible things, but not allowing variety or indulgence makes the whole experience boring. If you're not satisfied, you won't approach the next task with as much gusto - once again, some of your energy has been diverted and is not available to you. So obsessive food-watching can contribute to procrastination, which is a painful irony for people who keep putting off losing weight. How to follow the logic of the need for weight-loss versus the need to enjoy food ?

Give yourself permission to eat food you love

Have slightly smaller but exquisitely delicious or just robustly wonderful meals, eaten with people you enjoy talking to. Find support and information as you re-educate yourself about healthy eating. Move more, and take vigorous, conscious exercise. Find creative things to do with your hands. Develop important, exciting relationships and interesting worthwhile things to do with your life, other than worrying about the scales or becoming size 0.

Eating has all the metaphors you could wish to parallel procrastination.

- Do you even notice what you're eating?
- Do you spend ages planning meals, can't decide what to have and grab the same old thing at the last minute?
- Do buffets leave you unsatisfied?
- Do you spend all day cooking for dinner parties, have no time for your guests, and still feel things didn't turn out all right?
- Do you have your mobile phone on during a meal?
- Do you wolf the food and wonder why you get indigestion?
- Do you feel you have to finish everything on your plate, or must you always leave something?

Here are some ways to experiment with how food and the different stages of the Action Spiral are linked for you.

Difficulties with awareness

Smell and look at your food before eating. Eat without doing anything else at the same time, and turn your mobile off. Put only one kind of food on your plate at once. Try new food with a friend. Talk about what you're eating, the taste, where it comes from, how it's grown. Eat with someone who loves food, and eats more slowly than you.

Difficulties with exploring and experimenting

Go to a new restaurant. Get up early and eat breakfast in a cafe or watch the sunrise with a picnic. Buy food from a new shop, or swap brands of the same food. Stop and buy food on the street, or during a festival. Ask a friend to cook you something you've never had before, recommend food you don't know or take you to their favourite restaurant. Eat the most expensive thing on the menu, or the cheapest, or a local speciality. Use chopsticks to eat pudding. Buy a vegetable you don't even recognise and look up how to cook it. Invent a new dish.

Difficulties with choosing and getting involved

Go on a wine-tasting course. Eat things that make you chew and chomp. Eat at buffets without overloading your plate. Learn to make spaghetti. Make your own bread. Follow a recipe from beginning to end. Only come back from the shops with what you went out to get. Only eat what you have ordered, not from anyone else's plate. Notice what is good about what you have chosen. Eat only at tables. Dress up to eat. Eat with someone who really enjoys eating out. Make a meal of it.

Difficulties with completion

Eat with a friend who can leave food on their plate when they've had enough. Stop eating when you're no longer hungry. Consult a friend on the quantities they cook for guests, and follow suit. Invite people to eat with you even when you can only give them beans-on-toast (or equivalent). Eat with a friend who eats faster than you. Send food back if you don't like it. Drink only still water.

> ***Difficulties with pausing***
> *Eat with a friend who likes to stop after eating. Pause between mouthfuls, and put down your cutlery. Take a book to the table and read for a while after eating. Play restful music while you're eating. Eat in beautiful locations and admire the view after your meal. Have a picnic whilst the sun goes down and toast the moon. Take a taxi home after eating out. Have breakfast or dinner in bed.*

Simple things to do, but each offers opportunity for fresh experience.

Caring for your body

When you procrastinate, your self-image suffers. If you've become really stuck, you see a dishevelled indistinct blob in the mirror, down-turned mouth, tired eyes, hair all over the place, who can't get on with things to save her (or his) life. It doesn't help. Attending to your appearance is a way of sharpening and enhancing body-boundaries, and giving yourself pleasurable feedback. Then each time you pass a mirror, you'll see a together, organised, cool, good-looking person, and that image will reinforce your belief that you can do whatever you need to do. Fitted, well-cut, clothes, maybe make-up, sharp hair, polished shoes etc. generally increase confidence, and help define your body like toned muscles. Their form holds you, just as strong arms could; visually, your body-as-a-channel is straightened. Power dressing is an art which you can define for yourself and turn to your advantage.

On the other hand, warm, snuggly, soft clothes may make you feel cocooned, reassured and safe, and able to face difficult encounters; they may be precisely what you need at the moment. Play with the difference in feeling between approaching a task you keep putting off in your old comfy clothes, or dressed to kill. How would you approach your tax return/essay/letter of resignation/that difficult conversation etc., for example, if you were wearing either -

a) *your sexiest, most elegant and dramatic dress, a suit or leather trousers, or*
b) *if you were in baggy sweat pants and tee shirt ?*

You need to dress as your idea of someone who isn't procrastinating

Even if you are putting off something serious, dress as if you're not. Dress as a valuable, decisive, much loved person, not as a worthless worm. Explore and experiment with what works for you, slick or comfy, and give yourself permission to wear whatever excites you and makes you feel good, however mundane the task. Borrow clothes from people you admire and who support you, and wear them as a talisman for effective action.

Procrastinating about self-care itself can be a covert message. Jo, who consistently put off looking after herself properly, coined the phrase *communication by neglect*. Imagine that you are trying to tell someone that you're hurting and wanting them to care for you, but they can't or won't hear you. Maybe you decide unconsciously that the only to let the person or the world know how bad you feel is to show them the effects of what you see as neglect. So you "forget" to eat properly and your skin suffers. Your hair gets straggly. You don't change your clothes as often as you should, or you put off finding colours or styles that suit you. You bite your nails. You communicate your feelings, and a covert request, or demand, that someone else should come and take care of you. But you also punish yourself by depriving yourself of nice things. And you punish others, even when they are no longer around, by depriving them of the opportunity to see you shine at your most beautiful and most healthy.

Of course self-neglect can be much more serious than simply allowing appearance to deteriorate. Having unsafe sex: procrastinating about giving up smoking, over-eating, over-drinking or doing drugs; never taking holidays: avoiding the doctor: driving too fast with worn-out tyres or brakes; not fixing smoke alarms - the list is long. It's often wrongly assumed that it is only people who do quite extreme things, like deliberately cutting themselves, who are trying to get rid of emotional distress. I believe we're all capable of neglecting ourselves - and others - at different points along the same continuum. If you've been displacing difficult feelings by procrastinating about caring for physical things such as health, safety and appearance, you may begin to experience these feelings again as you learn to take better care of yourself. Not all your feelings will be related to the present. You are allowing more flow now, so the river of your feelings is dealing with the backlog from upstream. You might want to write down what you are feeling, or find an ally to talk things through as you get used to having access to clearer, stronger, more spontaneous feelings. Like the ones you used to have when you were small.

**The more you can tolerate anger, anxiety, frustration and sadness without acting it out self-destructively,
the more you give yourself permission to experience joy, delight, satisfaction and happiness.**

Mental and Emotional Ways Forward

Building self-belief

Don't call yourself "a procrastinator"

Words are hugely powerful. The ones we use to talk about ourselves profoundly affect self-belief and confidence. Calling yourself a procrastinator can create an internal straight-jacket, defining you and your value by what you do (or don't do). And that really doesn't help. We all have the capacity for a mixture of creative and destructive thoughts, feelings and actions, and we have the responsibility for making choices about which bit of the mix we want to emphasise. We've got natural human tendencies towards being happy, creative and productive, and equally natural abilities to sabotage ourselves. Along with everyone else, including people who seem to be or actually are very effective, no-one's intrinsic value depends on being brilliantly productive. Nor does procrastinating make anyone an undeserving failure. So don't put yourself down as a procrastinator, or accept the label from someone else.

On the other hand, it is hard to feel bold, happy, confident and free if you constantly break your promises to yourself. We can all change, learn, be imaginative, adopt new strategies for managing life, and drop old ones, at any time. So the good news is you that can certainly learn to procrastinate less and emphasise creative, effective action more. You're already started by reading this book, so congratulate yourself! The slightly-less-good-news is that to make sustainable change we all need to –

- *Practice new strategies, in the real world, not just in our imaginations*
- *Make mistakes*
- *Practice some more*
- *Give up "trying", over-ambitious intentions, and yearning to be rescued*

- *Learn from our successes and disappointments how to do better next time,*

......and find plenty to laugh about on the way.

There ain't no other way. But it does work. Think in terms of expanding your repertoire of tactics for doing things, rather than trying to eliminate procrastination from your behaviour altogether. It isn't helpful to think this kind of thing –

"I never procrastinate"
"Even though I've procrastinated in the past, I'm never going to do it again"
"This time I know I won't procrastinate – I'll just do it even though I'm really scared"

You can almost feel the gritted teeth in these sentences! - which are not conducive to relaxation or the potential enjoyment of what you're trying to do. Gritted teeth tighten our facial and throat muscles, which in turn constrict the arteries bringing oxygenated blood to the brain - so from a purely physiological perspective, the conditions for rigidity and confusion are already setting in. Don't set yourself up for failure, or for reinforcing your self-definition as an irredeemable (and therefore useless and unworthy) procrastinator. Your system will rebel if you try to convince it that you're always going to be super-effective, from now on, or more likely, from tomorrow!, because you'll be trying for perfection. It's OK not to be perfect, none of us are! Rather than getting into wishful thinking, create the conditions in which your productive and effective behaviours are likely to flourish, rather than procrastination.

So for example, instead of saying to yourself,

"Whenever I have to arrange an audition/do my bills/write Christmas cards/ tell my boss the sales figures etc., I always procrastinate ... therefore I'm bound to do it again this time, which is dreadful, I'm dreading it, I'm an idiot ...."

and so on

– experiment with thoughts like these –

"Sometimes when I set about doing something, I procrastinate. Sometimes I get on with things with amazing vitality and energy, and I complete them in far less time than I'd imagined"

Which naturally leads on to –

"I wonder how it will be this time?"

This creates an attitude of *curiosity* rather than one of judgement, self-criticism and despondency. Your *preference* is to be productive, but now as you're less tensed up against the possibility of failure, you're more likely to approach the task with energy. And the shift of perspective doesn't have to be based on lots of experience of being effective. It doesn't even have to be particularly true! Even a brief memory of a tiny spark of energy, once, on a dull afternoon way back in the past, will be enough to give your system hope that it is not condemned forever as procrastinatory. It simply requires openness to possibility and encouragement, and reinforcement of the times when you did follow your logic and act clearly and decisively. If you can't think of a recent time when you had some energy because you're so run down by the present, then imagine yourself as spontaneously active when you were tiny – before you could think. Or imagine what your best friend would remember for you. Go for the positive possibility.

The creative technique is to experiment with presenting yourself with alternative images of reality. The more you tell yourself *I always put off doing my accounts*, the more your system will work hard to prove you right. The more you think or say *I'll never sort this Thing out*, the more you're building the walls of a prison around yourself, a miserable future stretching into the distance, an hypnotic trance which becomes increasingly hard to wake up from. If you convince yourself that you'll be the one person who can find nothing in this book to help you procrastinate less, you'll be right. And if being right is so important to you at the moment, then your strategy of procrastination is obviously something you must not try to part yourself from right now. Even so, please don't call yourself a *procrastinator*. Find something more playful and affirming.

The more you are open to new possibilities, the more you invite in freshness and movement, the more your system will support you with fresh results.

Drawing on Past Success

In Part 1 on page 7 I invited you to think of a time when you knew what you needed or wanted to do, and went ahead and did it.

> *How did you do that?*
> *What helped?*
> *What are the differences between that situation and the times when you procrastinate?*
> *What factors which helped you before could you replicate in the present situation, even in a different form?*

Physical factors – were you standing, sitting, still, relaxed, moving about, tense, indoors, outdoors, hungry, full, sleepy, wakeful – what were you wearing – what time of day or night was it?

Mental factors – what you were saying to yourself – what belief did you have about what you were doing – what enabled you to have confidence?

Emotional factors – how were you feeling – how had you allowed yourself to have that feeling – whose support were you drawing on – how had you obtained that support – what did you feel good about?

Thinking about experiences of being effective provides a huge amount of information for you – you can work out from those circumstances what is missing when you realise you are putting things off. You can identify patterns. Notice what you approach with excitement and energy, rather than a sense of duty and burden.

> *What enjoyable elements could you find in the situation you are avoiding?*
> *What are you depriving yourself of?*
> *What do you need more of?*
> *If you only spring out of bed at holiday times, what's missing from your everyday life?*
> *If you can say boo to a goose, your boss, or taxi drivers but not to your partner on this important issue, what's the difference?*
> *If you love writing to friends, but constantly put off reports, essays or your Will, what could make a difference?*

Building on your strengths reinforces your self-image as someone who procrastinates now and then, but for whom it's really not a big deal.

When do you feel most proud of yourself? You deserve to feel like this a lot. What kind of conditions, events or circumstances bring out the best in you? When in your life do you feel most effortlessly productive, most generous, most confident and happy, most glad to be alive? What could you do to replicate aspects of that time now? Often just a small change can make a huge difference. As you plan how to do The Thing you've been putting off, arrange your life so that the chances of feeling strong, calm and good about yourself are increased.

If you know you're more relaxed in spacious, airy places than in confined, indoor environments, take your partner for a walk and have that difficult conversation you've been avoiding on a quiet park bench. If you're gregarious by nature, and put off getting down to do paper-work on your own, have your favourite photo of friends or your family made into a mouse-mat.

Concentrating will be easier when you're reminded of the lively, loving relationships you have all around you, supporting you as you work. What you need to help you stop procrastinating may not always be obvious, nor is it necessarily an intangible like determination or courage.

> Rita is a teacher with a typically demanding workload. She had to make a difficult call to a parent who had refused to sign her child's detention form, and was known for being extremely short-tempered. Rita paced up and down, went to the loo, made other calls, avoided by every means. Time went by. For all her procrastination, Rita felt no more confident (we rarely do). Talking with a colleague, Rita tried to envisage what would help her, and came up with the idea of making the call seated on the lap of a huge and protective bear with thick fur she could hide in. They decided to "create the bear", by filling a chair in an empty room with cushions and a blanket. Rita wrapped herself up in it all and called the parent. The woman was as angry as Rita had expected, but Rita held onto the blanket and cushions and kept talking. The parent eventually agreed to come to the school to talk. The call had been made and contact, however tenuous, re-established between them. The warm comfort of the blankets around Rita had enabled her to 'hold' the parent in a way which helped them both move forward.

Procrastination requires both imagination and creativity – think what it takes to keep coming up with alternatives to the Thing you're avoiding! Use it in your own service, by envisaging what you need to get you going, more deeply involved, or to finish what you have to do.

In the same way, having understood that doing anything follows certain stages, you can identify *which part of the process you're particularly good at*. Perhaps you know that once you're underway, nothing can disturb your concentration, and you are clear about when enough is enough. So your focus would be on increasing awareness and giving yourself permission to experiment and prioritise the initiation of new projects important to you and others in your life. Or perhaps your awareness is high, and you're great at generating ideas and getting started. You only need now to focus on involvement and completion. If you break the whole process down into the stages of the **Action Spiral**, recognise where you already have strengths and skills, you may begin to realise that you're putting off a whole task for five minutes worth of difficulty.

Believing in yourself

Dealing with the internal critic or saboteur

We all have one of these, and they play a strong part in undermining our best efforts to be productive, creative and effective. As a crystallisation both of other people's negative messages to us, and our own tendency towards laziness and staying-safe-by-staying-small, the critical voice in our heads needs to be resisted if we are to minimise our procrastinatory tendencies. The form the criticism takes is often to disparage what you're trying to do, make, say and so on by suggesting that you're not self-disciplined, strong or smart enough, what you are trying to express is not worth saying, is unreasonable or not original. From one energetic perspective, nothing has ever been done before; I, Andrea, this combination of cells, molecules, electrons etc. have never before sat in front of this computer on this day to produce these thoughts in this order (it's a watery morning in May in London – the balcony is full of greenery shooting in all directions, and the laburnum opposite is a delicate white). We all have the right to make our own meanings and our own decisions about what is reasonable and valuable.

Reminding ourselves that each moment is unique and that what we have to say or do is valuable, is a good start.

But this is only part of the battle. To argue against the corrosive cynicism of the internal voice, to persuade him or her or them that what we want to do is worthwhile, or that our needs are important, can take a lot of energy. And the trouble is that the energy put into the internal fight detracts from the energy necessary for output. If we pay attention to the fight, it will inevitably grow.

So the trick is – don't engage in the fight.

Like this –

Saboteur:	*What you're writing is absolute rubbish*
Me:	*Maybe. I'm enjoying myself anyway*
Saboteur:	*No-one will want to read it*
Me:	*Martin, Jane and Petra do. But even if they didn't, I shall be pleased I've done it*
Saboteur:	*You'll never complete it*
Me:	*Yes well, even if I don't, I've done something which is more than nothing*
Saboteur:	*You're just saying that*
Me:	*(giving up the fight) Mm, well, I appreciate your concern (continuing to type)*
Saboteur:	*You know I'm right*
Me:	*Thank you for your advice (typing and humming)*
Saboteur:	*Hmmmph!*
Me:	*Taptaptaptaptap hum hum hum etc.*

Have enough of these kinds of conversation and the Saboteur becomes conspicuously quiet. Goes off to lurk and mutter in the lift outside your office, perhaps, or in the kitchen, waiting to pop out with some new and even gloomier theory as to why you shouldn't, you can't, you never will, you don't deserve to, you won't be good enough etc. And don't be fooled, even as you feel triumphant. The Saboteur is trying to protect you, in it's own way, and it won't give up easily. Have patience. Appreciate it's efforts. Each time you produce or say or express something despite its comments, your productive muscles are getting stronger, and your system is getting clearer.

It's especially important to ignore the Saboteur if you habitually change pleasure into duty, or if you know that you love doing what you keep postponing. Interrupt the stream of undermining comments with humming, singing, music, or dancing while you work; carry on, and notice how quiet it goes. It's also crucial not to give the Saboteur new ways of berating you. So if you think you won't keep a promise to yourself, don't make it.

It's much better to tell yourself –

"If I do The Thing today, that will be great –"

than to box yourself into a corner with a commitment that you really know you'll break. Don't give yourself huge deadlines until you've built your faith in your ability to keep to small ones. Trust mends slowly – if you've procrastinated a lot, you may need a lot of practice in learning to rely on yourself again. Treat yourself gently, as if you've had 'flu. Every day brings opportunities to build self-trust, little by little; each bit of building silences the Saboteur further.

Believing that other people believe in you

When we procrastinate, we have stopped believing in ourselves. If we lose sight of our best selves, we need to find reminders. And whilst it's healthiest to develop our own sense of self-worth, for being in the world and for continuing to learn from our successes and failures, other people who believe in us are great additional sources of support.

Who believes in you?

Write yourself a list of all the people who believe in you and your abilities; if you've had particularly positive comments, write them down as well. Keep pictures of your closest people nearby and imagine talking to them, listen to what they'd say to you. Phone a friend! E-mail your dad! Ask your best

> *buddy/mum/brother/partner/agent to meet you, take you out for lunch, walk round the park with you and keep saying "You can do it!"*

Sometimes if you're really stuck, and you just can't seem to stop procrastinating, you may get into a frame of mind where you can't remember anyone ever believing in you. Or you start to think, ... *Ah but if they really knew what I was like ... they'd know I wasn't any good.* You feel empty, miserable, defeatist.

The sabotaging part of yourself is devaluing these people. If someone else started to verbally attack your friends and the people you care about, you'd defend them. If someone belittled what your friend said, or rubbished her opinion, you'd be outraged, and rightly so. But here in your head, the Saboteur is busy making cutting comments like –

> *"no-one really believes in me or cares what I do"*
> *"if I asked her to go out with me, she'd be dismissive"*
> *"if I ask for what I want in bed, he'll feel inadequate"*
> *"he's no judge of my abilities, he's just been taken in by my accent"*
> *"they think I'm strong, but if they saw me getting so worked up about going to the doctor they'd know I was stupid"*
> *"if I present my ideas directly at work, they'll think I'm over-stepping the mark"*

Thinking these thoughts hardly helps! – yet somehow they sneak in. They carry no respect for the integrity, warmth or perception of the people who care about you. The same goes for strangers. If you're putting off applying for a new job because you're worried about interviews, chances are the Saboteur has been feeding you falsehoods about the kind of people who sit on panels. If you want to perform, but find yourself imagining that the audience will be derisive, why let the Saboteur influence you with such insulting and corrosive comments about people you have never met? Ignore it. Concentrate on what you value about people who value you, and assume that strangers will recognise your best qualities as well. Imagine how you'd like them to treat you, and superimpose images of this happening onto the cynical predictions. Notice how your energy grows.

***If you find such thoughts persisting, you might want to find someone to help you to challenge them. A close friend, counsellor or therapist can help you notice how and when you start doing it, and help you break the vicious cycle that denigrates both yourself and other people. They are only thoughts. But you don't need them; they create painful feelings and sap your energy.*

A more subtle kind of de-valuing other people happens when you tell yourself -

> *"they won't mind if I put off doing what I've promised to do"*
> *or*
> *"they won't notice if I don't turn up (on time, or at all)"*
> *or*
> *"when they say they do mind, they don't really mean it"*

It's amazing how silver-tongued and plausible the Saboteur can be. Not only does this mind-set undermine your self-esteem, but people do mind, and they do notice. You matter, and you make a contribution to whatever you're involved in. People mind and notice especially when they miss what you could give, see you unhappy or diminishing yourself, or if they get hurt as a consequence of your procrastination, directly or indirectly. It can be hard for any of us to let ourselves be aware of this, especially if we're struggling. But ultimately, loving implies caring about the effect we have on other people, and taking our share of responsibility.

Most people would like to be able to rely on someone effective and genuinely trustworthy in their lives. Most of us would like to be that person.

There's no point in bullying yourself into this role.

Encouraging yourself is much more likely to lead to change than any amount of forcing, straining, false-promising, over-generalising, regretting or wishful thinking. But shying away from the negative consequences of not doing The Thing will equally diminish your forward moving capacities. You need to find a balance between keeping the implications of lack of action in mind, and not frightening or de-moralising yourself by over-emphasising them. Access your own wisdom and clarity of thought.

How would the best parents you know guide and support their children if they started to procrastinate? How would they help a child who was feeling deadlocked? Think of the of things they would do and say to help those children get on with difficult things; calmly, firmly, gently and with humour. Imagine a good friend is just beside you, encouraging you – what would you hear? Say the words to yourself, or write them on a card to look at again. Which part of your body might he or she touch? (Your arm, your hand, your shoulder?) Stroke that area yourself, whilst you repeat their words of encouragement. Take a deep breath, through your nose. Stand straight with soft knees; feel your feet firmly on the ground. Imagine energy flowing down from your head and flowing up from your legs, combining in your belly and heart, to enable you to move ahead, with tenacity and clarity. Breathe out slowly, with a sigh.

The process of dealing with The Thing you've been avoiding may be much more peaceful and less dramatic than you had imagined. It may even feel more elegant. And it will be infinitely more satisfying.

Finding the thought

When I was in the relentless and obsessive grip of a procrastinatory knot some years ago, a chiropractor I was seeing suggested I should resign myself to living as I was, rather than struggling to move on. That one tiny phrase gave me ground to kick off from, and to face the real difficulties involved in making the changes I needed. To have resigned myself would have felt like being buried alive; even thinking the words made me feel intensely claustrophobic. His suggestion revealed my desire to fight for improvement, and the energy to do so which had been hidden under despair.

Most people object when their lives are not as they would like them to be. This objection must be based on the belief that they deserve better. Find the thought that can inspire your need to kick away the clammy hands of your procrastinatory habit, and keep kicking until you are clear. It could be from a song, a poem, something someone said, even a homily from an old calendar. It's well-known that people give up smoking when they find the reason that works for them, which may be different to everyone else's and not necessarily linked to the most obvious logic. It's the same with procrastination. There is a phrase linked to your deepest value system, that will galvanise you into action. When you find it, use it. My current favourite is,

What have you done today, to make you feel proud?

Affirmations, positive statements which name and strengthen important qualities for you, can be helpful so long as you don't set yourself up for failure, as I described earlier. Find phrases that have meaning to you. Write them on cards to carry, stick them on mirrors, put them up on your office wall, repeat them at difficult times or whenever you remember. Affirmations which help you stay simple are usually best – for example,

- *I am willing to take time to become aware*
- *I really enjoy my capacity to be effective*
- *I appreciate my ability to learn from mistakes*
- *I am safe and can allow myself to be fully absorbed and excited by my tasks and interests*
- *I can let go with love*
- *I relish both action and rest*

The time it takes

How long do things take? How do you calculate this? How often do you set time limits on the tasks you have to do? How long will it take you to send six e-mail job-applications? Telephone Aunt Susan? Sort out the attic? Lose a stone? Write a cheque and send it to your favourite charity? The general consensus seem to be that projects, habits to be changed, forms to be filled, desks to be cleared, anything we allow to become The Thing can very easily expand to fill any time available, and then some more. Procrastinatory dramas are responsible for large chunks of the time spent, consuming emotional energy, everyone's patience, and often money as well. The actual time spent doing The Thing can be stretched out endlessly, by agitating around the edges, getting distracted, talking about how hard it is, etc. etc. It's amazing how many things we avoid which, when we eventually really get down to doing them and concentrate, take much less time than we had imagined. It is as if we don't even stop to calculate how much time will be needed to accomplish The Thing once we've slapped on the label *to be avoided and postponed*. This puts us into a baby-like state of not having a sense of time, or of the ghastly present seeming to last forever. *(This is very closely linked to knowing when enough is enough, see below)*

Working out how long something is likely to take you can switch your focus from –
how hard it's going to be
to
what can I do once it's done?
(far more interesting)

Knowing more or less how much time the Thing will take reminds you, as an adult, that life, in the majority of cases, goes on, however hard the task or rocky the journey.

How long will The Thing you are avoiding take to complete? An hour? Two hours? A week? Six months?
How long are you prepared to give it? How much time is it worth?
How long would the people whose capacity for effective action you respect give it? What will you do afterwards?
Remind yourself that you have survived that length of time before, watch your watch or the calendar whilst it happens. Noticing time grounds you in the reality of the present, because without it, you may get the feeling that you will be stuck inside the awfulness of The Thing you are avoiding, forever.
You won't be. It will soon be behind you. Time passes.

And what reward will you give yourself once The Thing is finished?

Deadlines

Deadlines help to put a boundary around a long or difficult task, so that you can envisage the end and life *after* that end. You need to know whether you function best if you give yourself a deadline, or if you have one imposed by someone else. It may depend on who that someone is. Notice how you regard different deadline setters – *aim to set deadlines with people you respect, and whose good opinion you care about*. Some people will do anything to sabotage other people's deadlines, so be wary of inviting other people into a drama. Tie your deadline into a reward. What would be good for you? (see below). If you associate deadlines in your mind with suffering, sweat and struggle, experiment with minor issues and see if you can re-associate to something more pleasurable – elegance, excitement, serenity, relish, satisfaction perhaps? Then get an image in your mind of reaching the deadline and feeling that way.

Is any time a good time?

Telling yourself – *Now is not the right time* – is a favourite procrastinatory line. If you're talking about a health issue, like going to the doctor because there's blood in your urine, or you've got severe pains in your chest or left arm, go now. Don't wait, even if there's a public holiday.

But when you're putting off a difficult conversation, for example, some times genuinely are kinder, more appropriate, more likely to have better results, than others. Generally speaking, it's a good idea to do what you've been avoiding *well before or sometime after* major events like birthdays, Christmas, weddings, or the night before your partner's big interview. If you try and take the plunge at those times, the strong emotion which is already in the air is likely to affect the result, and other people, quite justifiably, may be more upset or angry than they would have been on a more neutral, less loaded date. Future anniversaries may carry and possibly be spoilt by the memory, for both of you. And you will have an association of deepening distress to add to your memory of *this is what happens when I try to do what I've been avoiding*. Everything is heightened by the drama of Big Day, which would detract from your involvement in what you need to discuss, and from completion. It's the stuff of soap opera, not real life. So don't sabotage yourself.

But if you notice that you keep putting things off because of events you consider significant, (*oh but after Easter it's his mother's birthday – and then the children have got their exams, so I wouldn't want to rock the boat then – and then we're going on holiday and I don't want to spoil that, so I'll have to wait till September and then it's nearly Christmas*) – then you're probably just listening to the voice of anxiety in your head which can make the anniversary of the first landing on the moon a good reason not to get out of bed, let alone discuss your finances or relationship problems. Don't forget that you can't predict the future. You may think that doing the Thing you're avoiding will be easier *when.........* but you don't know what unexpected thing will crop up, to make that time actually *harder than now* (illness, accidents, major changes in circumstances, new demands on your resources).

There are occasions when you're struggling to get The Thing off your chest with the relevant person, and every time you start trying to speak something else seems to crop up, a distraction occurs, or you have the sensation that to keep talking will mean you'll have to make huge efforts to get the words out, almost as though you're swimming through porridge or trying to push against a force-field. If this is happening, it's likely that the other person involved has some sense of what you're about to say, and doesn't want to hear it. In such an uphill battle, your own reluctance, guilt, anxiety or embarrassment on this subject is being compounded by theirs. So be heartened – you're doing this work for both of you, and you'll probably reach genuine new ground if you persist. Imagine how you would like to be told about The Thing, and have a go.

For some things, and with some people, no time is ever going to be the right time. That's just how it is. And the sooner it is behind you, the sooner you can start re-building your strength and resources, and starting afresh. And so can the other people involved.

Giving Yourself Permission to move forward

Once you identify at which stage in the Action Spiral tends to be hard for you to navigate, then you can practice *giving yourself permission* to change that struggle into confidence. You can invent opportunities to do things differently, experiences which will reinforce the permissions you need to see the stage as a molehill, not a mountain.

Permission to become aware

To raise your general levels of awareness, you can experiment with paying attention to information coming in from your senses at any time. Becoming more generally attuned to yourself and your environment will increase the likelihood of you becoming more sensitive to the parts of your life you keep putting off, neglecting or forgetting.

Relaxing into awareness,
rather than straining,
remains the key.

Environment

Sit in a park, a garden, even at a bus-stop in a busy street or in a room near a window. Allow yourself to breathe out gently. Notice sounds. Make a little list in your mind of everything you can hear – leaves rustling, footsteps, laughter, a bird, the swish and vroom of traffic, your stomach gurgling. Pay each sound a little attention, and notice your internal world softening and slowing down. Another time, notice what is moving. Branches, people, a crane, a cat, a plane, litter, clouds; pay each sight a little attention, noticing shapes the movement makes. Notice patterns and colours. Notice your internal world warming and becoming richer. Yet another time, notice smells, and what you can taste. Look around your environment and imagine what the people you care about would like. Take a deep breath. Stretch your arms. Notice how you feel, what you want to do, and what happens.

Becoming aware of feelings and thoughts

Learn the difference between feelings and thoughts.

Feelings *are simple and felt in your body. They can generally be grouped into anxiety and fear, joy and excitement, anger, sadness, surprise and disgust.*

Thoughts *come in words rather than sensations, and are located in your head.*

If you have a feeling, where do you feel it in your body? Is it familiar?

Learn to trust even faint feeling, breath when you experience it, and you will gradually experience more.

Notice different thoughts as they occur to you, as they float by; notice the thoughts you have about thoughts. Experiment with controlling them, scrambling them, melting them into

images and sounds, allowing them to be central or peripheral to your attention.
Play with tuning into your body, feelings and thoughts in turn, and notice the quiet aspects of yourself which are both part of and beyond all three.

Sensations, thoughts and feelings come and go, and they do not define us.

Becoming aware of people

Slow down for a moment, put what you want to say to one side, and really listen to your partner, child, colleague or friend.
Watch how his or her face changes, lights up or closes down, the tiny muscles working around eyes and mouth. Notice his or her voice-quality, the words being used, and the feelings expressed through them. Repeat back what this person has said, and ask him or her whether you heard correctly.
Notice when other people mention their feelings, especially if you find yourself disregarding or dismissing their experience. You can do this with real people or even with characters in films or in books.
Have you ever had that feeling? What was it like? Imagine yourself in that person's shoes. What else would you feel? What would you be telling yourself? What do you imagine you'd need or hope for? Could that be true of someone you care about today? Have you asked?

You may of course have great awareness and sensitivity in some areas of your life, but total blocks and blanks in others. You may be a highly effective "people-person" with antennae a mile long, but you continue to stuff un-opened bills in drawers. You may be punctual and meticulous with the company accounts, but you completely miss the fact that the bathroom is filthy. You may be the best teacher, social worker, therapist, politician, vicar or doctor, but you never manage to join your family for a spontaneous picnic.

Which family member blanked awareness on the same kind of Thing that you procrastinate over? How would you have liked them to handle it? Which family member stayed most aware? How did they do that? Has there been a time in your life when you were more alive to and aware of this Thing? How did you maintain that awareness? How could you draw on that experience today?

Awareness can vary over time, especially with major life changes.

> I went through a period of not using a diary, and missing engagements. Then I started writing appointments down, but continued to miss meetings by "forgetting" to look at my diary. I had a busy, enjoyable life, but dates were falling outside my awareness. I found this disturbing, especially as I had lived a diary-driven life for many years previously, but the more so because it meant I let friends down.

If you are finding it hard to stay aware of what you know you want to prioritise, you need to interrupt your day-to-day life with reminders.

So – use your senses to call your attention to The Thing you keep forgetting to do. Wrap a note to yourself around your bus-pass. Phone your answering machine, mobile or voice-mail and leave yourself messages. Arrange an early morning alarm call and place the phone some way from your bed-room. Stick a note on the front of your filo-fax or put a large piece of paper with the details in your shoes. Obscure your mirror with a notice. Put a big sign beside your front door. Write the date of that crucial appointment or deadline everywhere you can think of. Build your awareness into a regular schedule (it's Wednesday, I can go to the gym, it's Sunday evening, the night I call my sister) Use a picture of

the people you care about as a marker in your diary and practice thinking of their needs as you plan your day.

~

Permission to explore and experiment

Allowing yourself to be curious, to play around, to see what happens can be tremendously liberating and/or scary. When you're trying to move into effective action, it's easy to assume you must get everything right first time. You need to give yourself permission to explore and try things out long before you go for the solution. The key in whatever you do is to experiment in reality, not in your mind. There is great sense in going slow and starting small - there is no need to be embarrassed if you are out of the habit of trying new things. If you're recently ended a relationship or been widowed, for example, and you're putting off going anywhere new alone, you can feel pleased if you go to an exhibition by yourself, or a park; don't try a full-blown holiday or even party until you're ready. If you have put off learning to drive, start with an instructor who is happy if you spend the first lesson simply getting used to sitting in the driver's seat, playing with the mirrors, pedals and gear stick. *You* experiment with and dictate the speed at which you feel safe enough to progress, until you're ready to risk letting someone else take control of the pace.

So – notice or remember the role or exploring and experimenting in your first family. Develop the most helpful patterns further in your own life.

Put time aside for unstructured experimental time, with the explicit aim of going out into the world and finding out what happens, not for being good at or achieving anything particular.

Join an evening class in a new subject, and keep reminding yourself that you are an absolute beginner for at least the first dozen sessions and don't have to get anything right first

time (if you do that's interesting, but it's a bonus).
Read a different paper every day for a week. Watch documentaries for a week if you always watch soaps, and vice versa. Go to a paint-your-own-pottery shop and play around. Find lots of different ways home. Open books at random and find something of interest you wouldn't normally read. Tear images and phrases you like from magazines and make collages. Make sandcastles or snow mountains, and then kick them down. Listen to music you think you won't be able to stand.
Try to find a grain of sense even in opinions with which you habitually disagree. Cultivate a response that says – that's interesting, and teach yourself to wonder how that person arrived at that conclusion.
Find people you enjoy who can help you brainstorm ideas or alternative solutions to dilemmas, especially if they are used to a bigger world than you are. You don't have to follow their ideas, but your own ideas will be expanded by their sense of the possible.
When you're feeling bold, ask someone you trust to plan a surprise afternoon for you, and agree to go along with everything they come up with (within the bounds of safety and legality!)

If experimenting is hard or unfamiliar, you may close down new ideas or thoughts automatically, or you may find possible negative outcomes of the idea flash into your brain at the speed of light. These are purely mental habits. Try saying – *yes, and* ... to other peoples' suggestions, instead of *yes, but* ... for a whole day, and finding something of value in each comment. Notice how that makes you feel – you may move from a position of rather gloomy certainty to one of slightly apprehensive uncertainty, but this is only to be expected for a while. When you start something new, or return to something you haven't tried for ages, practice suspending judgement about whether –

> it's good, bad, worthwhile, or worthless,

or > you are good at it, hopeless, never going to get the hang of it, too old for all that

.........and just let yourself experience what is happening for a little longer than you might normally do. This way you allow yourself to be informed at a deeper level than the automatic thoughts would otherwise permit. You may not like what you have undertaken – but at least you will be responding to it from a position of actual real-world experience, not just from a thought about what it might be like.

~

Permission to choose and get involved

Choosing

If you procrastinate about choosing which way forward is best, the world is your practice-oyster. These days it's hard to even get a coffee without having to make a whole list of choices (latte, cappuccino, espresso, filter, mocha, sugar, no sugar, sweetener, which blend of coffee bean, caffeinated, decaffeinated, small, regular, large, take away, drink in etc. etc.) let alone if you want a peaceful night in a hotel! Noticing how you make choices tells you a lot about what you like, value and believe in, all of which can inform you when it comes to The Thing you are putting off.

Do you regularly say "I don't mind" and then find yourself less than happy with what happens?
Are there some areas of your life in which you "know your own mind" and others in which you hardly know which way is up?
Are you worried that you may exclude something important, or give offence by rejecting an alternative view or option?
Do you give the same amount of time to small decisions as you do to big ones? Do you know how to differentiate?

You need to give yourself permission to make your own choices, knowing that you can learn from whatever outcome results. If you don't have much permission already, or you've lost confidence, you can develop your ability over the simplest issue, including coffee. Even really tiny choices – which kind of water to buy – is an opportunity to identify and express your own taste. Don't pass by the little choices thinking that you only need flex your decision-making muscles over big issues. You need to keep them supple. Of course some choices will have far bigger impact on your life than others. Choosing a drink dwindles into insignificance when it comes to whether or not to have the operation; have IVF or try to adopt; whether to move in with your partner, or get married; talk to your family about your sexuality; take the children out of school to go for that job overseas; make a whole team redundant; or confront your daughter about her drinking.

The more confidence you build in making small decisions, following through with action and surviving the consequences, the more you can learn to trust yourself to know how to make the big ones.

Decision-making – following our own logic and intuition into action

It is possible to become paralysed by the need to make a decision, and to put it off in the hope that the answer will appear overnight or over time. Sometimes "back-burn-ering" an idea can have precisely this effect – we wake up after a refreshing night's sleep with a new thought or some resolution.

But two other things may happen instead. Either

(i) the decision goes on hold and out of our minds altogether, in which case we are no further forward when we try to think about it again,

or

(ii) we can't stop thinking about it, continue to fret and agitate at the problem with no new information, and just get more tired and more stressed.

Neither route is likely to bring considered resolution – putting The Thing off has not resulted in thinking through.

Many people have never been taught how to think a problem through, and have little trust in their ability or even right to do so. Strong feelings, especially anger, fear, anxiety and panic, can wash away clear thinking, even when you know you can be competent at other times. Ideas and feelings swirl around like a jar of shaken-up pond-water, but nothing seems to emerge or settle in a coherent, solid pattern that can be built on. A single thought can get stuck in the mind like chewing gum on the carpet, and the whole world shrinks to this seemingly irresolvable issue. For others, decisive in sorting out things for themselves, separating out conflicting options can seem insuperable when other peoples' feelings get involved.

> *"Nothing is happening in my head,"*
> said Raj, who kept putting off a major life decision,
> *"– except panic.*
> *Every thought I have, I undo.*
> *Every decision I make I instantly reverse, and then I reverse it again.*
> *If I make a decision, I immediately think the choice I didn't go for was the right one.*
> *If you ask me to make the decision in 6 hours time I know I will be no clearer."*

This is a hell-like state, a sense of disintegration, of drowning in darkness. Your world can start to crumble, as you unpick and rubbish past decisions. Other decisions begin to loom disproportionately, and simple choices look overwhelming and will be put off. You become very difficult to live with. Anna, a woman in precisely this position, once turned to me with genuine anguish on her face and asked,

> *"Do you know how many kinds of butter they sell in Sainsbury's?"*

The major decision which was tormenting her had rendered her brain acutely raw and over-sensitised to having to make choices of any kind. This kind of paralysis can be undone, but it takes time.

If you are this stressed, be very gentle with yourself. *Your whole system of channels and tubes are so congested and twisted up nothing can flow; you cannot force real thought. Get rest, fresh air and go walking. Notice what minimum requirements you have for survival. Build short points of relaxation into your day. Breathe slowly, and concentrate on breathing, or even gently blowing, out. Notice the sun on your face, and the quiet that can surround you even standing at a bus-stop. Feel the air patting your cheeks.*

Sit down on a park bench; watch the ducks and listen to the sounds of the trees. Remember the ducks and the trees will be here tomorrow and build them into part of your daily routine. Look at your address book and remind yourself of all the people you can call on if all else fails. Call them, now, or go and see them. Keep yourself safe. Don't drive when you are very upset, and don't get drunk. Be with people around whom you feel good about yourself. Write down simple ideas or comments that are helpful, and distil them down to one line which you can remember or keep on a card to look at. Recognise that this is a really hard time for you, and that life will not always be like this. Keep warm.

Thinking through requires understanding the issues and options involved, the ability to draw on feelings, priorities, beliefs and values, to arrive, within an appropriate time-scale, at the best decision at the time. Not the perfect solution, but the clearest way ahead for now. One which recognises, but is not stopped by, uncomfortable obstacles. One which considers other people, but is not constrained by their expectations, real or imagined. To make such a decision, you need knowledge of your own values, needs and preferences, and the belief that you have the right and ability to make decisions as well as to survive whatever outcome and response results from your decision.

Making Your Decision

Working out what you need to do, and what you need to help you, can be broken down into a simple series of problem-solving steps:

1. Describe and define The Thing, task, problem, etc. you keep putting off, in one short sentence (call it A)

2. Describe and define the outcome you really want (again in no more than one short sentence) (call it B)

3. Describe how you will know when the outcome (B) has been achieved

(try and be as specific as possible – not just "I'll feel better", for example, but "My stomach muscles will feel more relaxed, I will feel able to take a break without feeling guilty, I'll have more confidence in my ability to stick with a decision" and so on)

4. Brainstorm possible ways forward from A to B; write down the alternatives

5. Identify what you will need to get from A to B in each alternative. (support, information, resources of time, energy, money etc.)

6. Decide what you are willing to give up in order to achieve what you want, and how you'll manage this (ninety-nine times out of a hundred there will be something)

7. List positives and negatives for alternative ways forward.

8. Choose the best possible way forward (as you see it at this time)

9. Break the best way forward down into steps

10. Take the first step (and then the next, and the next, and .... until you can celebrate completion).

What would help you go through this process?
You could – meditate before you start to get into a clearer state of mind: make sure you feel safe, secure and rested: find objects which represent how you'll feel when you've

tackled The Thing, and keep them nearby for inspiration: involve an ally in helping you through the process (see later): do the whole thing standing up or walking: sing or write a poem about it. Go to a favourite spot in the country with a view to getting a wider perspective of the issues.

Draw a picture of now, and another of how you'd like things to be. Notice what is different, and see if you can bring about any of the minor changes now, even if you can't see how to solve the whole dilemma just yet.

Make a list of past decisions you made which turned out well. Work out how you made them and use the same values, beliefs or sources of support this time.

Write your thinking down in a letter to a friend which you may or may not send; include completely daft alternatives that you know you'll never do in your brainstorming, to get your mind moving, make the process more enjoyable, and less of a chore.

Complete sentences which start

- *"what I'd really like to do is ...,"*
- *"If I had a magic wand I'd ....."*
- *"The main thing I need is ...."*

– and see how your spontaneous answers help identify your way forward.

If you are at a point where you can't sustain the knowledge and belief of your own values, needs and preferences, you probably need support to explore them with someone else. Find someone whom you can trust, whom you recognise is good at thinking with feeling, and someone who has a healthy respect for the life of the body, (someone who is fit or exercises). You also need practice to strengthen both your ability to make and stand by minor decisions before you go on to make big ones. You need practice to build confidence in your right and ability to choose and make healthy decisions.

And you need to keep breathing

Many people who procrastinate a lot have a problem with "*post-decision decision-making*", that is, beginning to question a decision as soon as it's made. If you keep doing this over small things, then you're probably rather short of pleasure or purpose at the moment, because undoing decisions is a great time-waster/filler. Or you may be doing it instead of tackling the really big Thing you know you're avoiding. If you're doing it whilst you are with someone else, you may be attempting to displace frustration and irritation, perhaps even about an entirely different issue, because that is certainly how your friend will end up feeling. Try suggesting they go off for a coffee whilst you sort out your decisions alone; and see if you can get to grips with what you're up to.

Frequently unpicking or reversing decisions will undermine your confidence in reaching decisions in the first place. It is as if you ignore or disparage all your previous reasoning. The hard truth is that many choices involve sacrificing the benefits of the alternatives. *Not feeling particularly good about the choice you've made is not necessarily an indication that your decision is wrong*. Acknowledging and honouring the difficulty of this is more helpful than going backwards over old choice-making ground again and again, trying to resist the inevitable. Talk to someone about how sad you feel about what you will have to give up, or how scared you feel at carrying out your decision; keep reminding yourself of the advantages you will be gaining. Don't lose or sabotage the benefits by comparing life as it turns out to the alternatives you've given up. You will never know what would have happened. The more care and attention you pay to what you have and do, the less those given-up options will glow with tantalising meaning. And arriving at a sense of peace about a major, life-changing decision may be instantly relieving, or it may take time. Sometimes the fact of making the decision, and living through what happens next, is as valuable as the choice itself.

> Recognising that a dream he had had to live by the sea was not working for him or his partner, Jack decided to move back to Salisbury. The couple put their

house on the market, and started the process of finding a new home. But even whilst he was applying for a mortgage and going round with estate agents, Jack couldn't stop thinking about how to stay at the coast, and secretly wanted to stop potential buyers viewing his home. He kept trying to convince himself that living by the sea was not the right thing right now, but part of him protested loudly. Jack had promised his partner that he would move, and he knew it had to be the priority for both their sakes, but he felt torn apart. Walking on the beach one day, the wild (im)practicalities and financial implications of trying to keep both properties, or contemplating driving to work each day from the coast, was making him feel half crazy. He suddenly stopped, exhausted and looked out to sea. A new thought entered his mind. *I'm sad*, said the thought. *I'm really, really sad*. Jack let the tears run down his cheeks whilst he stood there with the gulls circling overhead. He realised that all the mental activity had been a way of trying to avoid that simple feeling. When he allowed herself to cry, Jack noticed that his mind felt freer and clearer; he felt stronger and somehow more dignified about the decisions he'd made. He felt ready to face the move. Jack was able to honour his choice and keep his commitment to his partner, value what he was giving up, and look forward to the future, at the same time.

~

Notice or remember how your first family members make choices. Develop the best strategies and borrow others from people you admire. Remember a good choice you made in the past. How did you arrive at your decision? What values was it based on? Could this process be adapted to the present situation? What will you be giving up by going with your present choice ? What does that mean to

you? What will you not miss? What are the advantages of the choice you have made?

Getting involved and staying involved

Concentration is an art which can be practised and will develop in depth and satisfaction over time. Interrupting yourself, with distractions, intrusion of other demands, or by provoking arguments with your partner, children or the electricity company are great ways to rupture the bubble of absorption you need to get into and stay inside when you want to move forward. If you were someone who didn't have much permission to get absorbed in your own interests or tasks as a child, then you may disrupt yourself now to carry on the tradition. Or you may unconsciously nominate someone else or something else in your immediate surroundings to do it for you. You need to hold onto the knowledge that your time and priorities are important, and to remind yourself of the consequences of losing opportunities to be absorbed.

Notice if you are the one who always initiates conversations at work when you're involved in something difficult, and practice delaying making a comment. Notice if you are so attuned to other people's discussions or needs that your own tasks or interests extend endlessly, or get marginalised. Practice estimating the time you need and sticking to your own deadlines.

Remember times you have felt totally absorbed and involved – what were you doing? How did you achieve that state? Could elements from that situation be found now? Involvement thrives on regularity, so time-table periods of absorption, with beginnings and ends, and stick to them (including the end-point). Let the periods get longer. Remind yourself of how far you've come already. Notice or remember how your first family members regarded concentration and involvement; re-establish and develop the best habits in your own patterns.

Choosing and getting involved can mean giving up on other projects, tasks, interests or people, temporarily or forever, and you may find sad, lonely or even guilty feelings associated with this isolation or separation. Cater for these feelings in advance, by planning social time as a reward for a stretch of solitude. If you live alone, and work at home, find other people who can meet up in the day and activities that give you a lot of social contact in the evenings or at weekends. To make the desert of your involvement flower, you must find regular nourishment and replenishment, otherwise you run on empty and wonder why you keep putting off getting down to what you need to do. You'll notice you've really given yourself permission to get fully involved once you start resenting intrusion and interruption, rather than welcoming it! If you feel you've neglected other people by allowing yourself to be absorbed, offer them time and attention afterwards.

Sticking with things that are difficult may mean you have to negotiate for more time, money, support etc. than you are used to asking for. It may feel easier to give up than to ask, but staying with it brings satisfaction.

> Priscilla got anxious every time she had to do even a simple calculation. In her first family, Priscilla was the pretty one, and she got a lot of approval for being sweet and clean but not very bright. When she was asked to do anything numerical, Priscilla got flushed and felt panicky and made beautiful eyes at other people. This usually worked; someone else, usually someone with lots of permission to be a numbers thinker, would step in and do the calculation for her. But Priscilla became determined to do her own figures. By saying she needed time, by handling the discomfort of feeling self-conscious by looking at her desk and her calculator rather than at other people, Priscilla started to work out simple calculations for herself. This felt like a huge achievement. So was learning to tolerate discomfort and finding out that actually she had a good head for figures, and that she

could even enjoy the challenge. Anxiety turned into interest and curiosity.

During a long task or extremely difficult process it's almost inevitable that you can find yourself thinking *I can't do this*. Especially if it's a project or a cause which involves working and re-working, re-visiting, repetition, opposition, set-backs, other people's objections, hurt or anger, etc. Usually what we mean by *I can't is* –

"*I want the outcome but I don't want the process*" or
"*I'm having an awful time*" or
"*I'm scared I won't succeed or maybe even survive.*"

If you're saying or thinking, *I can't*, you're probably feeling quite young and tired and lacking in self-belief. If this is the point in a process at which you normally stop, remind yourself that what is happening is similar to physical training when you've come to the end of your "first wind" in warming up. This is the crucial time to carry on, even if you build in a short planned break. Then you'll find the mental equivalent of the "second wind" kicking in, and you'll notice that you can carry on much further, like a long-distance runner. Determination and tenacity both develop with practice.

If the thought that usually disrupts you is *I can't*, think this thought as well:

Old voice: "*I can't do it*"
New voice: "*I can do it, but I don't like it, and right now I need a ....to make it easier*"
Meanwhile – just keep going!
or "*I can't do it, but look at that ! I'm doing it any way (I must be amazing)*"
Meanwhile – just keep going!
or "*I'm not doing it – I'm not going to do it – I absolutely refuse to do it !*"
Meanwhile – just keep going!

This is just playing with words to help you stay involved - and you can find others. The point is, the new thoughts interrupt the old. Try them, invent what works for you. Procrastination is a habit, and the voice in the head is a habit. Create new habits by thinking new kinds of thoughts. New thoughts can keep you going through those times when you feel like giving up, and they can help you find a surge of motivation that might even tip you unexpectedly into a creative burst that will mean you miss all the television you'd planned to watch and don't remember to eat until 2am all because you're on a roll and look at that! The Thing is practically finished! And time has flown.

Or you will find yourself speaking the difficult truth, directly, rather than squirming around and hinting at what you want to say, only to run away again, ashamed and despondent. Your face gets flushed, you feel hot and maybe even shaky, but you don't disintegrate as you talk to the person you fear. You're crying, but rather than run for cover, you notice that it really isn't so bad to keep talking whilst the tears run down your face. You suddenly arrive at the other side of your dread and notice that your thoughts are coming back, you are fluent and angry yourself, and then the air starts clearing and there is energy exchanged between you again, and you feel you have come through an immense passage to emerge into daylight and now you are walking with firm steps on unexpectedly new and exciting ground. You feel bigger, stronger, proud of yourself, close to the person you were speaking to and no longer afraid. You could almost imagine doing it again tomorrow! (almost).

Survival

Sometimes we procrastinate because we have no clear sense that we will survive what we know we have to do. Other people may see our situation very differently, and wonder what all the fuss is about. Sometimes their robust encouragement and challenge of our over-dramatised view of the world can help us to step forward into The Thing, even if we tremble a bit. But when fear is overwhelming, the kindest words evaporate. Knowing that *putting The Thing off to tomorrow* will only make it worse may exacerbate rather than help our nervousness, or even tip us into dread. If you really have to do The Thing alone, and you are feeling paralysed, you need to find simple strategies that help you hold your own hand, as a good parent would when we were small.

Survival Techniques for moving through the Action Spiral

Let's say you have been putting off going to the dentist, but you've eventually made an appointment, and **you're on your way there:**

1. *Breathe slowly, focusing mostly on gently breathing out.*
   Listen to your environment, and make a little mental list of all the things you can hear; feel the air on your face, and the ground beneath your feet
   Drink some water
   Breathe out slowly, gently, again, and focus on yourself.
   Flex your wrists as if shaking water off your hands, gently rotate your neck and straighten your spine.
   Picture yourself handling the situation beautifully. Notice what helps you do that.
   Picture yourself after the Thing is over, walking away.
   Imagine what you'll say to yourself afterwards
   and what you'll do as a reward.
   Imagine how you'll feel about yourself

2. *In your head, keep repeating a supportive phrase a friend has said, or your basic aim in what you are doing, or a relevant lyric from a song. Keep it very simple and repetitive. Picture your friend's face; imagine he or she is close by.*
   Think about the pleasant things you can do afterwards, *especially involving people you care about*
   Hum

3. *Keep breathing slowly.*
Keep warm
Say yes to the protests in your head – for example,
yes this is really hard and I don't like it or want it,
yes I may well feel sick or cry
yes I may not be able to think quickly
and then add
but it will be over soon, and then I'll...

You arrive

4. *Keep breathing slowly*
Push down with your feet on the floor.
Tuck your chin down and relax your shoulders
(so relaxing your neck).
Use one thumb to slowly and gently stroke the other
from wrist downward.
If you are sitting, feel the support of the chair behind
your back.
Remember that if you feel sick, it is an indication that
you are now facing the difficult situation, and therefore it
is closer to being over. You are moving through.
Give yourself time to think before you speak, if you need
to.
Tell yourself,
I'm moving through it. I'm doing it.
It's happening.
It will be over soon, and then I'll...
Notice your watch. Notice the time moving on.
Notice your surroundings, the colours, the shapes, the
patterns; make a little list of the sounds you can hear.
Keep your feet on the floor. You are moving through.
Remember your phrase or lyric, and your friend's face.
Hum

5. *Don't feel you have to look everyone in the eye if it doesn't help you.*

6. *Have something solid, like a small pebble from your favourite garden, in your pocket and hold it from time to time, or throughout.*

7. *Remember to keep breathing out, slowly.*

8. *Remember where the door is, and your right to leave. Imagine yourself leaving, who you will see and* ***what you are going to do next.***

It's over

9. *Keep breathing slowly, focusing mostly on breathing out*
   Listen to your environment again, notice what you can hear; feel the air on your face, and the ground beneath your feet. Drink some water
   Congratulate yourself – I did it and I'm fine – remember how you got through
   Take a short break; go for a walk, and find something really lovely to look at, touch, taste or smell

10. ***Do what you promised yourself you'd do afterwards***

Giving up and starting again

If you do give up, the important thing is not to beat yourself up about it. You do need to register and appreciate disappointment and frustration at having done less than you hoped, because it is partly that which will help stimulate you to have a go again. Those uncomfortable feelings are useful and informative. But beating yourself up (*I'm useless, a failure, no good, hopeless case etc.*) rarely works as an incentive.

> Some people treat themselves like donkeys. They think the only way to keep a donkey going is to beat it, and they are afraid that if they stop beating, the donkey will lie down and never get up again. What they have forgotten or never learnt is the True Nature of Donkeys. If a donkey is well rested and well treated, why on earth would it want to lie around all day? It would want to go for a trot, or an explore, or a chomp of some good grass, or a nuzzle of its best-friend donkey. We are no different. So please be gentle with yourself.

Set a boundary around what you're trying to do, or how long you're going to do it for. If I get really stuck during a day's writing, I get more water, set an alarm for one further hour, and then stop. Take notes rather than write the full speech. Aim for a passable speech rather than a brilliant one.

Break the task down into manageable sections and learn as much as possible about how to continue.

> Julia hated making "cold calls" to potential customers, but had decided she needed to do this as part of marketing her skills as a consultant. She felt that she didn't represent herself well enough on the telephone, and was afraid that she'd come across as unconfident and incompetent. She found all kinds of things to do to avoid picking up the phone; the task

loomed larger and larger, and she became really anxious. She felt like giving up.

Julia had assumed that she would only succeed if the call immediately resulted in work. Once she realised this belief was blocking her, she broke her goal of getting work down into stages. She set herself a very small first target of making three calls before her next break, regardless of the outcome, and was pleased when she achieved this. Once she became familiar with the words she wanted to use, which she learnt with practice, she made getting something from the call the next goal; an address, a piece of information about the company, a contact. She learnt that often the people she called were surprisingly pleased to hear from her and to help. When she finally did secure a contract, it seemed almost effortless, but Julia realised how far she had come from her first call, how unrealistic her first expectations of herself had been, and how much she'd learnt in the process.

~

Permission to know that enough is enough, and to complete

If you feel your sense of *enough* is underdeveloped, then you could try noticing how other people determine when something can be finished. We all have the capacity to be perfectionist or dilettante. Find people who seem to balance both qualities and get things done. Ask people you trust to tell you how long things take them, and how they notice when something is enough. Experiment with setting similar time limits if you have observed that you have a problem with endings.

When Martin and I were creating a logo for our company, I was horrified that he seemed quickly satisfied with one of the first designs we came up with. Left to

> my own devices, I would have mulled over what we had created, come back to it again in a week's time, talked to the designer, thought of some new angle and eventually sent off something I thought was really "it". He, on the other hand, pointed out that our first sketches drew on the principles we agreed underpinned the company, had good strong colours, and that whilst something else might well be perfect, these were good enough and had already taken two or three hours of our time to sketch out. I enjoy savouring and crafting, and in other circumstances that would be fine. But here we might have become diverted into trying to become excellent designers, rather than making headway with all the tasks necessary to create the company. We sent off the originals, the logo was created and we like it; we had paid it enough care, time and attention.

To evaluate *enough-ness*, practice balancing how much time, energy, money etc. you are willing to allocate to the task in hand, by recognising how much it actually contributes to the overall strategy of moving ahead with whatever you want to do.

Practice knowing when you've had enough by pausing for a moment and checking.

Notice the difference between feeling a bit full, satisfied or stuffed, a bit tired, pleasantly weary or exhausted. Notice when you're keen to read the papers on a Sunday, watch TV or read a book, and notice when your interest wanes.

Notice when you are warm enough, cool enough, rested enough, exercised enough, when you have enough food in the house, when you've had enough time with people or enough time alone.

Experiment with saying and acting on "enough" long before or long after you would do so naturally, and notice the difference.

When you buy something new, throw away something old Notice your internal response to "enough" if you're spending money, not finishing your task because you keep having ideas for new "improvements", doing research, hunting for something lost, arguing or being involved in a confrontation, or worrying about something uncontrollable.

If you've thought the same thought a hundred times, (or even ten times) interrupt the thoughts, tell yourself you're bored and want to think about the issue a new way. Notice what you consider to be good enough or not good enough behaviour, in your opinion, even over small matters. If you are feeling bad, ask yourself whether you have suffered enough, for long enough; find ways to forgive yourself, to change or move away from the circumstances in which you are feeling bad.

Notice or remember how your first family did or didn't set limits, and see whether you still agree with them. Notice whose "enough" you are still listening to, and check that it is your own. Build on the patterns you see as most helpful.

If you're the kind of person who gets bogged down in detail, practice sitting back and asking – how relevant are these details to the completed task? Are you putting off completion by over-valuing the minute? If you're a heart surgeon you must make sure you've retrieved every bit of your equipment before you stitch up. But if you work in retail, you know that your stock count is never going to precisely match what you have on the shop floor, and there is no point in counting the same shoes, books, or coffee packets yet another time. When you travel, you know you have to set off for the airport even if you haven't checked the door-locks for the fourth time. Even if you're a Presidential candidate, there will come a time to say enough, even if the votes haven't all been counted for the umpteenth time. And if you're committed to being honest, you know the truth needs to come out, no matter how much courage it takes. We have to bear the overall purpose and priority in mind. Of course some decisions need a great deal of thought, some tasks require enormous commitment of every resource you have to hand. Learning to discriminate and prioritise frees you from unnecessary expenditure of all kinds.

Completely clear everything on your desk or your bed-side table or on top of the kitchen cupboard into a box. Keep the surface clear for at least 48 hours, only taking out what you need from the box as and when, and then replacing it. When you wash up, dry up as well, and put everything back in the cupboard. After washing your clothes, fold them up and put everything away. Notice how you feel when you look at the clear surfaces. Notice how you feel when you look at other surfaces.

Once you've said *enough*, you can complete. Completion needs to be marked in some way. That means taking time to celebrate the triumphs, mourn the losses. Then you will be able to carry on, after a pause, with *regard*, rather than regardless. Marking your completion means not rushing into the next plan, project or relationship before you've properly finished the first. If you don't have a clear sense of an end, it will be much harder next time to convince yourself that difficulties or struggles do eventually finish.

Walking away from something, literally, puts the memory of the end into our leg muscles.

If you envisaged what you'd do after something was over, do it, as part of your completion. Follow through with rewards. This strengthens the capacity to visualise next time, and continues to build self-trust – that you can confidently expect the nice things in life, as well as the tough! It also means you get a change of pace, fresh air, and the opportunity to relax after effort. Honour yourself in completion as much as in starting out. Which could mean celebrating, in whatever way makes you feel all the effort was worth it. Can you allow yourself to feel good about completing? Could you take a break? Have fun? Congratulate yourself on effort expended and difficulties surmounted? Ring up everyone who helped you on your way and tell them that the dreaded Thing is finished? What would be appropriate and enriching?

Little completions are important – you don't have to wait till something major. On the other hand, as you become increasingly effective, you'll gallop through tasks that used to take you forever, so the completion and reward pattern will shift. Don't forget to notice a completion just because the Thing has become easy.

Who was able to handle endings and completions well in your original family? Who noticed the little things? Who experienced satisfaction? Who could invite other people to share endings, large and small? Who knew how to really celebrate? Who was able to handle difficult endings well in your first family? Who was able to tolerate and share painful feelings? Who built on lessons they had learned from previous distress, or from failure? Notice the patterns, and develop the best for yourself.

~

Giving yourself permission to pause

When you pause after completion, you allow yourself to experience the effects of what you have just done. You may feel elated, full of pride, delight, joy and satisfaction, and full of yourself in the most generous and life-enhancing way. On the other hand, completion may bring difficult feelings – sadness, disappointment, regret, panic, heavy weariness rather than pleasurable tiredness – even hopelessness. These feelings are real, and also need to be honoured, even as you acknowledge that you will, in time, be able to learn something from the situation. This is not about prematurely bouncing yourself into the forced cheerfulness of *well, it's all part of life's rich tapestry*. Trying to instantly cheer up may completely miss the mark, and simply leave you feeling low for longer. But you do still need to go for a walk, have fresh air, drink plenty of water, because all these things help to keep your whole system alive and open.

Where failure or pain has been hidden as something shameful in your first family, you may not have much idea how to learn or even benefit from failure or disappointment now. You need new role-models (*see below*). And of course many endings will bring a combination of both feelings. Leaving a house you hated at long last may be a massive relief, but you may not have realised how much you valued the neighbours who helped sustain you through the worst times. Only when you have settled into your new place do you realise you miss them. Leaving a difficult relationship may bring you face to face with all the best in your partner which drew you to him or her in the first place. Winning the long fight to prevent a shopping mall being built in your local park can mean you miss the camaraderie and sense of purpose. And getting the excellent promotion you always wanted may mean your joy is tinged with sadness or anxiety at no longer being "one of the gang".

Life Lived and Unlived

When The Thing is over....... ask yourself these questions:

Experience	Feelings: *Glad*	Feelings: *Bad*
Happened	*What happened that you were pleased about?*	*What happened that you're still sad or angry about?*
Didn't happen	*What didn't happen, and you're glad it didn't?*	*What didn't happen, which you're still sad or angry about?*

Example – Tom is leaving his job

Experience		Feelings: *Glad*	Feelings: *Bad*
	Happened	*I learnt a lot and met some great people*	*My mother died before I got the promotion – she would have been so proud*
	Didn't happen	*The team wasn't broken up in the re-organisation – thank God!*	*Our team should have been re-located – everyone was prepared to move, and all that planning time was wasted*

~

Rest

Being willing to pause means going into a not-knowing-what's-going-to-happen-next place, in which you experience many different feelings, and find new ways of thinking about what you've done and what has happened. It's a lying-low, even a temporary hibernation, a digestion of the past in preparation for the turn toward the future. It means not being *on-the-go* all the time, but trusting that sleep, rest, quiet and dis-engagement from the same kind of activity or from new relationships, will bring refreshment, new energies and enthusiasm.

If you exercise, you know that you need to have breaks, and to sleep enough – it's then that the muscles knit back in response to exertion. Without rest, you're simply burning tissue, and you won't build strength. Similarly, if you don't get enough sleep, your mental processes start to get ragged at the edges; everything looks harder and you're likely to procrastinate more. When you sleep deeply enough to allow dream-sleep, your system is charging its batteries, and you're more likely to feel like facing the world.

If you regularly miss lunch, work over the weekend, cut short holidays or don't book them at all, you need to consider what you would say to an employee or friend who behaved that way. You'd recognise in an instant that this person was heading for burn-out. Sometimes people don't even notice that they are continuing to work – their minds are so fixed in the same groove that whilst they *look* as if they're on holiday, they are actually still wrestling with the problems they left in the office. Strong feelings take time to recover from as much as hard work does, so you might need a break after a big emotional upheaval as much as you do after several late nights finishing a report. Even if you don't consciously register the need for a break, you can act as if you do, and make a space for yourself. Sometimes feelings take time to surface; if you constantly rush on you won't know what you're burying until something surfaces unexpectedly. Putting off taking breaks means your system may surprise you by insisting you take one – like the workaholic who fell off his motorbike and broke his leg. Don't push your system into clocking off altogether.

Who was able to stop, rest and recover in your first family? Who was able to breathe? Who was able to appreciate their surroundings in an unhurried way? Who could be quiet and peaceful?
How did they recover their sense of freshness and enthusiasm for life? How did they regenerate their energies? Who remained curious? Notice the patterns you feel were most effective, develop them further for yourself.

If resting is really hard for you, then imagine bulbs under the soil in winter. Console yourself that although nothing seems to be going on after all that breathtaking flowering and leafing, there is actually a huge amount of cellular activity taking place. If you need convincing, keep a bulb through winter in a cupboard and watch what has happened by spring. Challenge the Saboteur in your head which says that resting = doing nothing = being lazy/getting behind/being a hopeless case, and take a break. Sometimes a brain, especially a tired and over-stressed one, comes up with the ludicrous notion that nothing we do or experience is of value unless it is involved and in control. It is only the arrogance of thoughts like these that prevents us from allowing nature to take over as she should. When our brains relax, they resume their rightful, co-operative role with our bodies and spirit. Seasons provide the metaphor and image for how we need to treat ourselves – it really is impossible to be in the flowering phase all the time. Think of crops being rotated from field to field.

Allow yourself to savour the phrase, "to lie fallow".

What would help you lie fallow for a while? When do you find you rest most? What do you need to do, have or let go of which will help you unwind, slow down, and breathe deeply? Do you need to be alone or with people you love? Do you need to snug up at home or do you need to be out in the fresh air? What helps your brain to let go of all that noisy, buzzing preoccupation, and start idling?

Often before we can achieve replenishing, enjoyable rest, we have to go through a phase of discomfort; feeling guilty, perhaps, or restless, or not knowing what to do with ourselves. It's tempting to pick up a task or rush onto the next thing to get rid of these feelings, like people who go on holiday but come back exhausted, needing another! But if you hang on, stay simple, concentrate on doing physical things, allow the verbal froth in your mind to settle, you'll find you move into a place of deeper sleep, more energy, and that you have much more enjoyment and appreciation of being in the present. And you're more ready for whatever comes next.

Relationships

Our strategies for coping with life evolve in relation to other people. Our own creative and destructive tendencies get reinforced and expanded by things we learn from and with them. As an adult you can take responsibility to use or discard what you've learnt, and you can find the right kind of people who will help you to fulfil your purposes and follow your own logic and intuition. Other people's love, support and affection can represent the kind of muscular holding which we initially had from the womb, and subsequently from strong, kind arms. These people co-create a kind of supportive tube around us, even when they are not present, and whether it feels too constricting, too draughty or just right depends on how we nurture, negotiate or neglect relationships. As we replace procrastination with effective action, our important people can stand-in for the parts of ourselves which still need strengthening. And we can fulfil a similar role for them. Such people become allies.

Allies

Allies remind us of permissions we've had but forgotten, and help us give ourselves new permission where there is a lack. Choosing the right allies is a good test of whether you're really ready to do things differently. If you turn to a new-found friend for help with something you've procrastinated over for ages, for example, you could be using the discussion to put off making genuine changes, perhaps hoping that this new person will somehow enable you to avoid the inevitable. On the other hand, if you find exploring and experimenting difficult, a fresh view can sometimes give the spur you need. It 's useful to find someone who doesn't procrastinate at the same stage as you; but having said that, most of us are better at helping other people than overcoming our own limitations, so someone who knows the signs from the inside could be your best possible asset ! At the end of the day, the choice is highly individual, and the only proof of a good ally is that with their help, you get the job done, and you move on.

Procrastination often isolates, especially when people feel ashamed of their habit. Agitation and futile consumption of time, energy and emotion create distance from other people. To have someone come alongside you, even briefly, can be very helpful. A friend who wants to get going with his business plan at the weekend would like to know that he can have dinner with you on Sunday evening as a reward. Your sister, who's been putting off getting the results of her tests, wants you to go to the hospital with her. A colleague who's been procrastinating about asking for promotion wants to go through what she could say to her boss with you. Each is asking for support to get their show on the road, to move into action. If they can ask for support, so can you. It might be for rehearsal or company. It might be for modelling (*tell me what you do, show me how you do it*). It might be for rewards for each stage of a process completed. You need to work out what you need and then find the right person to ask. Different people may be more appropriate as you go forward. The same person who can help you come up with ideas for example, may not be the right person to help you complete, or vice versa.

Awareness

Someone who points out to you an aspect of life that you haven't noticed is not only an ally but a godsend. Whether it be your boss who says your clothes smell, your partner who says that she feels neglected because you keep forgetting to prioritise time together, the doctor who tells you that your liver is suffering because of your level of alcohol intake, or the technician who tells you your computer is over-heating because of all the paper work stuffed round the back, these people open your eyes and all your other senses to the fact that you are a real person in the real world of people, feelings and consequences. You are fortunate if you have people in your life who have the courage to honestly let you know the impact you and your behaviour are having. It may not be comfortable; sometimes it might be shocking. And it will take effort to stay aware long enough to make changes. But becoming more widely aware can enrich and deepen your experience of life. Your allies can serve to provide feedback if you can ask them to point out if you go into "oblivious" mode again. You don't need to blame yourself, or be attacked. You do need to listen.

Exploring and Experimenting

People who are good at trying new ways of doing things or looking at life are refreshing to be around. Brainstorming alternative solutions to dilemmas with someone else gives you access to totally different ways of thinking. Remember that to develop your capacity to explore and experiment, you need an ally who doesn't always need to get things right, or to stay totally safe and/or approved of, but who is genuinely interested in whatever emerges. Someone who is pro curiosity and creativity. Someone like my friend Bruce, artist, therapist and brilliant salsa dancer, who is totally supportive of his friends' efforts *to have a go* at whatever inspires them. He has a profound sense that life is too short to stay timid and small. Find an ally with a sense of adventure and experiment together, or report back to him or her with discoveries you make and experience on your own. You don't have to wait until you can bungee-jump in New Zealand – you may never wish to. Simply get up two hours early, drive home an unfamiliar way, or arrange to meet in a different place; even such tiny changes introduce the new and strengthen your internal confidence that new doesn't always mean overwhelmingly scary. Allies help calculate the risk, and don't invite you into danger. Nor do they undermine you with their own doubts. They validate and share your experience, revel in possibilities, and ask what's next.

Choosing and Getting involved

Having people you can run through options with is useful. Someone who will give you an opinion when you ask is great. It isn't so helpful if that person can only see what you're doing in light of what they'd do themselves, or say things like *it's obvious, or you should* ... and then get stroppy or impatient if you don't immediately follow their logic. An ally can help at this stage by listening to you going through pros and cons, adding information, noticing if you are de-valuing yourself or if you are making assumptions etc. They can also point out when you are running through your options (again) as a ruse for more procrastination; in other words by speculating about outcomes and "just" needing a bit more information. Constantly generating new alternatives does not create forward motion. People who are experienced at procrastinating have got wonderful imaginations, so this is a real danger. Good allies will notice when they're being led down the garden path and round the bend! The point of looking at options with them is to find a way ahead, the more-or-less best option as far as you can see at the moment, and then for you to go forward down that path *through real action*. An ally will help you identify the first step, and wave you on your way.

What support would help if you have difficulty coming out of fantasy and getting into real life and action? If it is still safer and more comfortable to avoid and ignore reality, to talk and dream, than to act? Most importantly, people who will love and believe in you whether you don't do the Thing you're avoiding, or if you do. You need people who will be honest with you and give you straight answers, and not attempt to persuade you that your concerns about pain, hardship or the effort needed for the task are invalid. On the other hand, these same people won't lose sight of their own understanding or experience when you are panicking, and if they think you're making assumptions or unhelpful generalisations or winding yourself up with fears, they'll say so. This kind of ally can wince with understanding and say, *yes, that sounds difficult*: but he or she will be sure you'll survive and succeed, and maybe even offer you help. He or she can also, and quite rightly, eventually get tough with you if you keep saying – *I'll do it tomorrow*. They will confront you with the empty quality of words without action. They will not hide their disappointment and hurt if you let them down, and they will protect themselves from the worst effects of your avoidance.

> In Daughters of Copper Women (Women's Press 1990), Anne Cameron describes a custom of the Nootka women on Vancouver Island in Canada. Each woman is allowed to bring her troubles to the women's discussion circle three times. The other women will listen, three times. They will offer suggestions from their own experience, hold and comfort the woman who is describing her difficulties, three times. If the woman brings the same problem a fourth time, having done nothing with the support and advice she was given previously, the other women do not listen. Neither do they criticise. But they get

> up en masse and go elsewhere to form their circle. The woman is left behind. The group has symbolically demonstrated to the woman that she is choosing to stay with her difficulties. They respect themselves sufficiently not to expend their energy on something she is not willing to address for herself. She can rejoin them and not refer to the problem. Or she can do something about it, and then talk again.

I like this very much, although it can seem tough. Good allies will offer us the same kind of self-respecting support, and we can give it to ourselves. A good therapist will probably listen to you more than three times! But will also help you to understand what benefits there are for you in staying stuck, and to decide whether you want to keep them. If you don't, he or she can help you identify the first small step necessary to move forward, and be alongside as you take it.

Allies can be asked to be nearby whilst you get stuck into something, without intruding. If you live alone, you might find it helpful to have a friend in your home, not necessarily talking but nearby, in order to free you into concentration and commitment. Alternatively your ally can clear space and time for you to do what you need to by making the dinner/looking after the kids/doing the shopping/taking the dog for a walk etc. and being well away from you when you are working. You can offer them the same space in return on another occasion. Remember the absorbed play-space a child can enjoy when it is well and safe. This is what you're trying to re-create, however serious the task; children's play is serious too. You need to negotiate for its creation, and to find out what components are most constructive.

Good allies can look after themselves whilst you're doing what you need to do for you

And if you are frightened of what you have to do, it is totally reasonable to ask someone to be with you. I'm sure this sounds simplistic, but it never ceases to amaze me how easily people deny themselves the simple, reassuring solidarity of someone else's presence, either alongside, waiting in the waiting room or in a nearby cafe or park, or on the other end of the phone for a pre-arranged call after a difficult meeting, discussion or interview. People generally like to be asked to be supportive. Being wanted and viewed as a source of strength is a compliment. If you haven't had much experience of asking for or receiving support, either in your first family or recently, you may feel you are being weak, or making a fuss about nothing. Maybe – maybe not. The priority is to move forward, so practice asking for and accepting help. As you increasingly develop your capacity to get and stay involved, you and your allies will be able to tell the difference between a procrastinatory drama, and genuine anxiety or terror, and act accordingly.

On the other hand, you may have experienced "help" as controlling and smothering, or given in a way that left you feeling diminished, helpless, or inept. To avoid those feelings now, you do things alone, but you procrastinate over anything that leaves you feeling vulnerable and exposed. You keep your life little by not daring to go into those areas which were once controlled for you. In this case, it's important to be able to identify allies whom you can trust to really listen to you, respect your need for going slow and support you in ways you identify as right for you. Gradually, as you gain confidence in their capacity to do this, you can give up your need for complete control and become more robust, and you'll be able to accept the odd buffeting which comes from a helpful friend blundering around trying to be useful. People recovering from sexual or emotional abuse, who have decided to stop putting off being intimate, need this kind of sensitive support.

Allies keep bringing the cups of tea, 'phoning or e-mailing just to say hello even when you are in the slough of despond, even when you're behaving, feeling and looking your worst. They tell you *to get on with it, you can do it*, with love and exasperation. They hang onto the knowledge that life won't always be this bad, and they keep a tight grip on hope and purpose for you when you're too tired to hold on yourself.

Completion

To support completion allies need to hold onto priorities, and to have a good sense of enough being enough. It helps tremendously if they are good at completion themselves, and won't get caught up in your 'end-games' of *just one more, I have to be perfect, I'm useless, I can't, force me* and so on. These allies value their own time and energy, and yours. They help you keep a time perspective, by making plans with you for the future, or by clocking off themselves. They may set self-protective deadlines and limits, and whilst you may hate it, help you by sticking to them. They'll shout encouragement from the sidelines whilst you're going for the last big push, convince you you're nearly there, and when you've finished, that you're amazing for how much you've done. Then they probably need a stiff drink and a good rest themselves.

Pausing

Once you've finished what you need to do, allies can help you celebrate! They plan surprise parties! They queue up to have a drink with you, watch a movie, hang out and go on holiday with you! Allies know the importance of completion, and esteem it as highly as the start of the journey. They are there as part of your reward for completion, and are the first to cheer your success even if it takes you away from them.

Allies suggest rest as much as they propose action. They won't rush you on when it's obvious that you need some time out. And if you have failed, or if finishing leaves you sad, disappointed and depleted, and the pausing makes that apparent, they can help you learn from it, and be there whilst you gather strength for the next hurdle. Post-completion you will have more space and time, and your allies will be pleased to see more of you without the old Thing looming over all your heads.

~

Much as it may sound like it, allies do not have to be angels, although it would probably help! The more these people stay themselves, imperfect, impatient, loving, as liable to make mistakes as you, you can draw on them for support.

The key to any relationship is mutuality – you will be offering your strength in return

And the stronger you become, the more you have on offer.

Role Models

If you procrastinate, you can draw support from people you admire. Choose someone whom you think of as effective, efficient, productive and who enjoys doing what they do. I say *think of as* .... because for all you know that person might well procrastinate over things you don't even know about. It's amazing how the people you least expect to dither over anything will suddenly reveal that they do. But it's their ability and courage to overcome their tendency to put things off, carry on to succeed and accomplish what they want to do, that can be of assistance.

There are 4 kinds of role models:

- People you know or have known
- People you may never meet but you know something about them, e.g. people in politics, the media, history etc. They might be alive or dead
- Fantasy figures from stories, myths, and legends, including creatures and animated objects
- A different aspect of yourself, or self that you aspire to be *(e.g. the part of you that is highly creative and productive that you located in Part1)*

Think of someone now (Nelson Mandela, Martin Luther King, Mother Theresa, Matthew Pinsent, Miss Murray the chemistry teacher, Michaelangelo, your mother, Inspector Morse, Van Morrison etc.)

Imagine the person in as much detail as possible
Find something nearby that reminds you of that person. (If it's an artist doodle one of their paintings. If it's a relative, find a photo, or a part of your body which is like theirs. If

it's a politician or sportsperson, write a sentence on their finest achievement)

Imagine this person doing the thing that you are procrastinating about.
How would he/she go about it?
How would he/she move? Would he/she be standing, sitting, walking?
Would he/she be alone or with other people? Silent or talking?
What would he be feeling ? What would she be thinking ?
What aspect of the person helps them to accomplish the thing you find so hard?
If they had the same difficulties as you, how would they overcome them ?
What advice does this person have for you ?

To "hear" the advice, all you have to do is watch the person in your imagination, or seat them across you at a table, ask them the question in your mind and listen for the answer. If you hear – *I just get on with it* – "ask" them to be a bit more specific about how they do that, what they are telling themselves, or how they overcome difficulties. In your imagination, by the way, all these people are willing to help; there's no point in conjuring up people who refuse to give you an answer because they're too busy being productive! Imagine this person as your personal trainer or coach. If your role-model is a real person you know, you can talk to them in person, or watch them in action. People are generally surprised and pleased to be asked.

Write the core advice you get on a card and carry it with you.

Find something that will remind you of your role-model and have it in the place where you procrastinate most. Look at the card or repeat the advice as you go to make that difficult phone call, arrange the dreaded meeting, wait to see the specialist, get changed to go to the gym. Repeat the process with several people you admire and make a collage of their advice or images of them. Picture it, when you feel like smoking but know you don't want to; when you start the conversation with your boss which you've been avoiding for so long; as you allow yourself to finish the letter of resignation and put it in the post-box rather than opening it to correct it yet again. Draw on the strengths of the people you admire as you retrieve and build your own.

Because, of course, you have the same strengths, which you can identify more easily in other people. Sometimes we lose sight of our own capacities, and our abilities to be productive and joyful. It's like not being able to see the sun behind the clouds. But the sun is always there. We just have to find the way home - having role-models can create a short-cut. You may find you have different role models over time. Noticing who you admire and how this changes is an indication of how you are changing - finding more and more sophisticated ways of dealing with procrastination.

Respect and Responsibility

Procrastination often feels like a lonely-making habit, which puts you into a time-warp, but it doesn't occur in a vacuum. Putting things off frequently has a negative effect on someone else. It's natural to feel hurt and bewildered when the person you respect or love and have trusted proves untrustworthy, doesn't follow through, or spends long periods belittling their abilities, looking like a wreck and getting more and more miserably self-absorbed (especially if they don't explain what it is they are putting off, or why). Energy taken up by procrastination may also have been withdrawn from the development and maintenance of our relationships, so it's not surprising if our families, friends and colleagues protest. If you are someone who's had a real problem with procrastination, reading the next section (*If someone you know procrastinates...*) may be very uncomfortable. If it is, then you are already moving in the right direction, because your discomfort is a recognition of your effect on other people. As you start to procrastinate less, you'll notice the (at best) irritating and (at worst) damaging effect putting things off can have, not only on yourself, but also on the people you love. It's tragically true that we often most neglect the very people we care about most, as if they were an extension of ourselves.

Noticing this, however sad that may make you feel, will help to strengthen your determination to do things differently. Allow the sadness, but don't allow it to undermine you as you make changes. The trap would be to fall into a deep and murky puddle of self-recrimination, and need for reassurance. Regret can feed the Saboteur who can use it as a stick to beat us ever more accurately –

> *You've broken so many promises, no-one will believe in you again*

> *You've let so many people down, you don't deserve to be happy*

Regret becomes an energy drain in this way – and who does it serve? Certainly not the people you care about. If you feel regret for how you have behaved, and how that has affected others, so be it. Such feelings can be the great energiser that enable us to think about how to do things differently, and to follow our own logic in behaving in new and more constructive ways.

So apologise already, as they say,
and get on with doing things differently.

If there was someone you had neglected, who would it be ? Notice the first person who comes into your mind. Notice their expression, and imagine what simple thing they might need right now. A 'phone call, a hug, a glass of wine? What would it take for you to get up and give it? See what happens if you let yourself do that, next time you see them, without further thought. Nothing complicated. Just simple. Whatever you can do as a start.

Overcoming procrastination is ultimately about learning to love more fully. Where there is respect for ourselves and for other people, it's very hard for a habit like procrastination to survive, because every aspect of ourselves, who we are and what we do, the people we care about, our communities and our environment become precious. Time, energy, effort and emotion will no longer be squandered, because we recognise all too well how important these resources are, in making all our lives richer.

If you have children in your life, your own or other peoples', you probably want them to have the best possible example of someone who faces things squarely, who is aware and fully, joyfully alive, can initiate, get involved, learn from mistakes, complete, celebrate, mourn and rest. Someone who doesn't deny the difficulty of things, but faces responsibility, bites the bullet, takes a deep breath and moves forward. This can be you. You don't have to become that person overnight, nor do you have to be perfect. All our children need examples of people who can tolerate their humanity. People who can laugh at themselves and at life, whole-heartedly.

Other Creative Strategies

Humour

One of the key ways in which you can break out of the habit of procrastination is to develop your sense of humour; hence the cartoons in this book. By draining our days of colour, light, life, value, meaning and energy, procrastination can also rob of us of a basic human need and pleasure – to have a really good laugh. Laughter makes you take in more oxygen, and relaxes muscles all over the body, so it's great for snapping you out of the kind of doleful trance you can find yourself in if you keep putting The Thing off.

So if you do nothing else having read this book, increase the possibility for finding laughter in your days – it's good for your health, for your relationships, and it might just help to shift your perspective on why you keep putting things off. Life may be short, but it doesn't have to be humourless. You are going to have energy left over now that you're not losing it in the old agitated procrastinatory dramas, so enjoy it !

Take out comedy videos, ask everyone you meet to tell you a joke, write them in a note-book and them pass them onto your friends; laugh with a small child. Lie on the floor or on a bed with someone's head on your stomach: say HA HA HA loudly and with each HA try to make their head bounce with your stomach muscles. Then put your head on their stomach, and let them try the same (even if it doesn't trip you into spontaneous giggles, you'll still have had some exercise scrambling round on the floor) Make faces at yourself in the mirror; find 10 different ways of crossing the living room apart from walking. Pretend you're an orang-utan at the dentist. Remember the last time you really laughed and enjoy a smile at the memory.

Lists

List-making and ticking things off lists help some people so long as

- *list-making doesn't become a new way of procrastinating*
- *the list can be found amongst all the other things you keep meaning to get round to*

and

- *you do the important things on the list rather than add trivia and do that.*

I know these things! I've done them all. Use different coloured pens, sticky stars, reward systems, pin the list in the most accessible place and sing each time you tick something off – if this works for you, enjoy it, and glow with virtue.

Sometimes people who make lists notice that each time they make a new one, key items from the old ones keep returning. If this happens several times, you either don't want to do these items or you need to find new strategies for addressing them. If you had to simplify your day, your week, your foreseeable future to one priority, what would it be? Make that your focus. Do the important things first. The other thing that list-makers have in common is that they often forget how much they have done in addition to what's on the list, and tend to focus on what wasn't done. If this is you, notice how this can undermine your belief in your effectiveness. Write a list of everything you have done, and compare it with the one you set out to do. You may be surprised.

Learn to recognise and hate waste

Procrastination steals the time of our lives, and gives us very little in return. As you procrastinate less and less, you will notice how precious your saved time is, how much richer, more enjoyable and less tense your life is becoming. More of you is available to experience life more fully – it's as simple as that. You need never go back to that place of life-on-hold and marking time so long as you recognise your own form of procrastination and the waste it generates. If you notice yourself beginning to go down the road to *I'll*

do it tomorrow again, WALK AWAY – yes, really, get up, put one foot in front of the other and walk away – from the place in which you're standing or sitting, having the thoughts. Look back at where you were, notice how capable you are of being effective and taking action, and begin again. The more the muscles in your legs get used to doing this, the more you'll find yourself naturally moving away from stuck places and moving on.

Throwing things out

Sometimes sorting out a cupboard or desk or room full of things is exactly what you're avoiding. You can start by taking one thing, one small piece of paper or one spoon or one whatever from the pile or out of the drawer and dealing with it. Then you can have a rest and a bar of chocolate.

> "*What!?!*" I hear you explode,
> "*that won't get the job done!*"
> Hmm. Got a better idea?
> Two things?
> Six? Eight?
> Set yourself a tiny target *and then stop*.
> or,
> Use the momentum and energy you build up to keep going till you're done, and then you'll experience that wonderful, fresh feeling of freedom from *stuff*.

When you're throwing things away, find ways of putting physical effort into the process (music may help) and having fun. If you feel listless to start with, be listless in an even more languid and droopy way (think melodramatic silent movie characters). Dance or sing. Tell your papers, old clothes, your general junk what you're doing, invite them to fight back. Revel in discarding it all, and celebrate as you see fresh space emerge.

You can use throwing things away simply to generate fresh energy, or to solve the deeper, more difficult issues you've been putting off. The more you attend to the little piles of clutter, the more the important questions and challenges, and their resolution, will become clear. When you throw something away, you complete your physical relationship with it. You may still have emotional and mental connections to it, like old photographs or love letters which you liked and will always remember. But physically, the thing has gone, and it leaves space. Which we badly need to help feel fresh and open to life again. The point is that if you are feeling bogged down, any completion will help.

> Naomi was trying to write a long report and kept putting off getting totally involved and completing. She had started several sections, partially completed others, got herself lost in a myriad ideas but she couldn't hold the thread of her argument. She felt agitated and frustrated and had a strong sense of wanting to give up. One afternoon, she completely abandoned her work, and set about clearing the attic instead, feeling both guilty and sulky. At first she only threw the odd thing into a black plastic sack, but as time passed she found herself making more and more radical decisions and chucking out things she'd had for ages. After dinner, feeling full of energy, Naomi went back to her report, and amazed herself by finishing it painlessly – in fact she even enjoyed it. When she read it on the train to work in the morning, she was delighted with the fresh, simple and clear quality of the writing.

Visualisation

Imagining how you will feel once you've completed The Thing, and what you needed to help you get through it to a satisfactory conclusion, is very helpful. If you have a strong imagination, (and as someone who procrastinates it's likely that you have), then you can probably *pre-create* the good feelings you're likely to experience if you concentrate. You've probably conjured up a strong sense of the unpleasant feelings that may occur, so use the same powers to envisage a taste of a positive outcome. Of course no-one can predict exactly how you'll feel afterwards; although, when you are procrastinating, you probably imagine that you can. So you may as well imagine that at some point after you've done what you need to do, you will feel positive. Or maybe even during the process. The more you practice this, the further back in the process you can locate pleasant or at least relaxed feelings.

Another way to use visualisation is to project yourself forward to the last days or last minutes of your life (you don't need decide how far in advance that will be). From that position, looking back in time to now, how would you like to see yourself act? What would you like yourself to do – how, and when? Allow that older, wiser you to guide your thinking, decision-making and action.

Play with posture

Sit slumped in a chair, shoulders down, corners of your mouth pulled down, and your arms crossed tight round your waist. Then lean forward and mumble,

"I'm going to do The Thing."

Now stand up straight, feet a little apart, shake your wrists, open your arms and fingers wide, palms forward, look straight ahead, and say, firmly and clearly,

"I'm going to do The Thing."

Any difference?

Once you can feel the difference, you can envisage yourself standing and saying the line, whilst spreading your fingers and straightening the back of your neck even sitting down. You will find that you can activate a similar feeling based on these much smaller cues, simply by tapping into the memory of how you felt when you stood strong. Sitting right back in a chair with your spine straight (and therefore a little away from the chair-back) is the position advocated for appearing confident in television interviews, and it has same effect elsewhere. So if you find yourself slumping, you can either switch to the open, more purposeful position, or really go for it and slump, no doubt making yourself – and anyone else in the vicinity – laugh. Nothing like a good moaning and groaning to get you going!

Rewards

A reward must be something you can really look forward to, to supplement but not replace the sense of achievement on completion. Bribes will help get you through the worst things – most of us have our price. The best rewards actively and positively enhance your sense of well-being and value. These are ones that make you want to go and finish something else! A holiday, time alone, flowers, cup of coffee or herb tea, great wine, some feedback, a night at the opera, a massage, new clothes or a haircut, an exchange with someone else for something they need to finish to please you – whatever seems to you to fit the effort expended on completing the task, and which will help reinforce your messages to yourself of a job well done.

Find an image of a reward or bribe that would work for you.
Is it physical, mental, emotional, practical, social or spiritual?
Does it involve you moving, talking, being alone or with others?
How much space and time does it take?
How will you feel when you receive it? Who would give it to you?

You can reward yourself, or ask someone else to reward you. The important thing is that you select something you really like, that you complete everything you've undertaken to do before you get the reward, and you find a giver who is reliable.

This might be you –
Enjoy keeping your promises to yourself.

Grief and Loss

If you want to change a habit, you need to come to terms with grief and loss. I believe that unless we address the feelings which emerge when we stop putting things off, then we may well repeat old patterns without really knowing why. So what are the connections?

Giving up an old familiar habit

The first connection is that our habit of procrastinating is like an old friend, one who did his or her best to help us when we needed them. Remember that you probably started procrastinating in order to avoid a difficult feeling, like feeling scared, anxious, upset, or hurt. Even if you now feel the Old Habit of procrastinating is holding you back, that it has become unproductive and limiting, at one time it was the best way you could find of managing your circumstances.

Now you're capable of developing new strategies which will bring you more satisfaction and happiness than you could have imagined back in the old days when you wrapped your dream of *What I'll Do Tomorrow* round you to keep you warm. So you need and probably want to say goodbye to the Old Habit, created to help you feel safe. But even if you're itching to get on the train (destination marked *To The Present!*) you need to say goodbye, with respect. You're not out to cut off a part of yourself, but to distance yourself from its impact on your life.

Old Habits don't give up putting in an appearance on our internal stage until "they" are extremely sure that we are able to manage on our own. And they may well re-appear at times of stress, tiredness, illness, hormonal changes, changes in life-style, when we start something new or under the mundane stress of day-to-day life once sparkly novelty has worn off. The Old Habit is purely coming back to check whether the New Habit is serving you properly. Don't panic. It's just a visit, intended to remind you to take care of yourself – it's not taking up residence again. Once genuinely re-assured, the Old Habit will depart.

Find an image of your Old Habit of procrastinating as a character which is extremely concerned for your well-being. Imagine you are getting on a train, and that you leaving your Old Habit on the platform. It's natural to feel sad saying good-bye to someone who had your best interest at heart. It can be eerily quiet and unfamiliar inside when they've gone. Getting to know your cartoon-cut-out Old Habit can help you befriend that part of yourself which procrastinates, and give it something better to do.

My Old Habit is an ancient crone, who worried incessantly about me getting hurt (mentally, physically or emotionally), or ending up as a bag lady. She could always see the positive in a situation but was much more aware of the potential negatives. She was acutely sensitive with hugely developed antennae, had a strong perfectionist streak, was highly judgmental and a drama queen par excellence. She criticised me and encouraged me to put things off, especially getting involved and completing, as her way of preventing me from getting hurt or smothered. Now she is an ally.

Mourning what you have missed

If you learnt to procrastinate to deal with significant gaps when you were a child, as you become more aware of yourself, your environment and other people, you may well find yourself longing for experiences you missed out on. These might include being held and cuddled, having company and support, being listened to and taken seriously, being encouraged to make your own choices, feeling safe enough to become absorbed, being comforted in letting something go, sharing celebration, and being enjoyed for who you are as well as what you do. Grieving for what was missed or lost is natural. Coming to terms with knowing that you are now fully responsible for those needs is the next stage. You have to give up dreams of being rescued, which can create storms of childlike-protest in any of us. It's especially hard to do this if you kept yourself going through difficult times by believing that rescue would arrive one day. You may feel frustrated, angry, resentful, frightened, sad – all of these are part of the process of acceptance.

Mourning what you lose

Thirdly, you may grieve because moving forward with your life means no longer holding onto the belief that it is possible to have everything. When you procrastinate, it's like staying at the crossroads, telling yourself that each and every road is open to you. But once you choose your path, and move forward, other paths will become unavailable, other doors close.. Ironically, the more you choose, the more you say goodbye to as well. You may have to say goodbye to roles, people, places, dreams. What you do choose, you experience more richly and deeply. What you give up, you need to grieve for.

> Hassan was a refugee who constantly put off making a new life for himself. Each evening, this formerly active, effective professional man told his wife he would go out of the house tomorrow, and each morning he refused to move. His family became increasingly anxious about him as he spent his days complaining about his present conditions and creating more and more unrealistic pictures of how wonderful life had been at home. Eventually his son persuaded him to see a counsellor, who had an understanding of the cultural and social challenges facing Hassan, the difficulties he was experiencing coming to terms with being a survivor when his parents had not escaped, and the pain of all his losses. Hassan saw the counsellor for many months. When the translator tentatively suggested Hassan might like to come to a community event planned to celebrate the next religious holiday, Hassan accepted, and went.

Mourning what will never be

Lastly, and perhaps most poignantly, as you begin to procrastinate less and enjoy life more, you will probably grieve as you are hit by the full impact of recognising that life is short, and that you are older than you were. As you become more effective and active, you will become acutely aware of how much time you have wasted. The opportunities you've missed. The letter you never sent, the conversation you didn't have, the dreams you never allowed yourselves to have, let alone fulfil. Because although, fortunately, there are some things that we can become or experience once we stop procrastinating, in some form or another, for other things it really is too late.

> *Too late to have a baby. Too late to visit your grandfather. Too late to send in the job application.Too late to stop drinking and driving. Too late to relish your children's childhood. Too late to start treating your partner better. Too late to vote this time. Too late to look after your teeth. Too late to help the homeless woman sleeping on your street. Too late to protest about torture. Too late to save the open countryside.*

This is the life unlived, the opportunities missed because you procrastinated. You may never get them back. This realisation can be extremely hard. And you may feel very sad, guilty, or full of regret. You may need to cry. You may feel very angry with yourself, that you hadn't recognised earlier that you were responsible and you could have made things different. It's OK. Cry . Be sad. Apologise where you can. Be gentle with yourself. Use the anger to clear your head to think about what can be learnt. Call a good friend who'll give you a hug and listen without judging, or find a lovely place where you can feel safe to let go alone.

And then ... after a little while ...

after a while you need to start recognising that a lot of time spent grieving is further detracting from whatever time you do have left on the planet. There is a difference between usefully acknowledging the past in order to honour it and learn from it, and dwelling on the past in ways which drain or sabotage your involvement with and contribution to your current life and relationships. Time spent regretting our past behaviour takes our energy away from all the possibilities in the present. Blaming yourself or other people or fate diminishes your energies. Difficult feelings give of their best when they are accepted and learnt from. And then you move on.

When you let yourself do this, you know that you have learnt, even if you still feel upset sometimes. I think there is probably a critical point that we all reach in this process, between being depressed by knowing that life is short and being energised by that realisation. It's extremely painful to go through, and you may always have moments of feeling sad that life hasn't been all you hoped, but you will find clarity of purpose, wisdom and peace of mind follow naturally. This is usually, not surprisingly, a spiral process; the more we allow ourselves to deeply feel grief at our waste of time, the more we free our energies to get fully involved in the glories, challenges and responsibilities of the present. But this time with a new lift, with an excitement about life, rather than having to drag and push ourselves through our days. Real feelings come in waves, they don't stay around constantly. When a wave of grief comes, allow it, feel it, breathe it. It will be followed by another wave of energy and excitement, and then another of something else. It's all part of the same process I have been describing throughout the book.

**When we feel blocked in going forward,
we need to locate what we need to let go of,
honour it, accept it, and move on.**

Part 4 **If Someone You Know Procrastinates**

Procrastination at Home

Procrastination at Work

Procrastination Out and About

"THINGS TO DO" LIST
1) WATCH TELLY
2) SLEEP
3) POTTER
4) HANG-OUT
5)

If Someone you know Procrastinates

If someone in your world procrastinates, you're probably all too aware of the effects this has on you, and partly aware of the effects it has on them. Depending on your relationship with that person, you've probably found ways to deal with it, and these strategies work best when you're rested, well and happy yourself. At other times, their procrastination drives you up the wall and round the bend. Even if you know that you procrastinate sometimes yourself, and you're working on that, it can help to think about specific strategies for self-protection and peace of mind.

Relationships are co-created; so if one person is procrastinating a lot, the behaviour has meaning for both of you. And both can be part of the solution.

Procrastination at home

If your partner procrastinates

It's likely that your partner procrastinate about some aspects of life, and you procrastinate about others, so that all-in-all, you complement each other. She is sure to get the family finances done, but you're the one who'll notice there's no washing powder left. He can get on with the decorating, but becomes agitated when it comes to buying new clothes, you're more than happy shopping but you put off any practical task around the home as long as possible. On the other hand, you both may have blocks over the same issues. You are both highly effective professionals, initiating, developing and completing projects, managing teams; at home, neither of you can focus on planning the holiday or even a weekend away.

Inevitably, procrastination in a relationship can be yet another way in which difficult feelings (resentment, anger, frustration, irritation and so on) get played out in a disguised fashion. So if you're living or having a close relationship with someone who procrastinates, you might first wish to tackle those areas of your life where you put things off yourself, to become clearer about what your own habits are telling you. Let your partner know what you're doing. Invite conversation about what works, what doesn't, what you both need and how to support each other in learning to get on and do what you want to do. Be sure not to tumble into a blaming or shaming stance - you're doing this bit for you, not to reform them! Become each other's allies wherever possible. Notice where you collude to over-emphasise difficulties in tasks you both hate, or assume the other should automatically take them on.

> Robert's elderly mother Claire, had a bad fall, and the family realised that she was becoming too frail to live in her own home. Wanting to solve the situation straightaway, Robert agreed with Susan, his wife, that they should clear out their spare bedroom and invite Claire to live with them. As Robert was away a lot on business, Susan said she would start packing up the room, but each time Robert came home Susan hadn't made a start. For one reason or another, she kept putting it off. The couple had a series of arguments about the situation, with Susan feeling pressurised and criticised and Robert feeling frustrated. Every time she thought about sorting out the room, Susan felt tearful and resentful; she was fond of her mother-in-law, and the feelings confused her. She continued to approach the task half-heartedly, or to avoid it altogether.
>
> Gradually the arguments escalated into heated rows, getting further away from the issue of Claire coming to stay and onto major issues about their relationship and who took (or didn't take) responsibility. The arguments finally ended when Susan yelled that she'd be better off living on her own. This shocked them both. Recognising that was not what she really wanted, Susan suggested they start the discussion again. Relieved that his wife was not about to leave him, Robert thought hard about his mother coming to live

> in their house, and realised that he was highly ambivalent. He had made the offer at the height of his anxiety, immediately after Claire's fall, but it wasn't necessarily what he, or Susan, or actually even Claire, wanted. By focusing on Susan's procrastination about clearing up the bedroom, he had been able to shelve his anxiety and ignore his own reluctance to discuss alternatives with Claire.

If procrastination is a small part of your partner's repertoire of behaviour, you probably know by now when to leave well alone! But what if your partner's habit has become quite a serious problem, or begins to cause difficulties on matters of significance? Sometimes procrastination as a real problem may not be apparent in the early stages of a relationship, fuelled as such times are by adrenaline and serotonin, the joy of new discovery, the rosy glow of being in love that gently plants wings in our heels and lets us feel like our best selves, capable of anything. But moving on from this glorious phase, it may become obvious that the person you love has got themselves seriously stuck in one or more areas of their life. This can be extremely hard to live with. It can seem as if the person you know and care about, and whom other people know, has disappeared, and you are left with someone you barely recognise. A person whose mystifying behaviour is causing you problems. A stranger around whom you feel frustrated, confused, angry, messed about, concerned, alarmed, unsupported, neglected, and sometimes very lonely.

So what works, and what isn't helpful, for you or your partner ?

1. When the Thing he or she is putting off doesn't particularly affect you

What may help:

- Addressing your own tendency to procrastinate
- Trusting the person to do what is right for them at their own pace

- Loving them even if they don't fulfil their own dreams
- Listening: asking what support they need
- Helping when asked, within limits that feel acceptable to you
- Offering a hug instead of getting involved with the person in a lot of *yes, but* ... ing
- Appreciating their concerns about the difficulty of the task
- Remembering their strengths and experiences of success, even when they have forgotten them.
- Expressing your appreciation and giving compliments as much for who your partner is as for what he or she does

What doesn't help:

> Ignoring or minimising your own tendency to procrastinate
> Calling the person a procrastinator, lazy, or becoming abusive
> Giving advice, unless asked for
> Helping a lot without being asked, "rescuing";
> Making comparisons between their behaviour and anyone else's, including your own
> Becoming involved in repetitive conversations about why the person procrastinating is not doing what they need to do
> Becoming very attached to the outcome of what he or she is trying to do
> Getting critical, or making threats
> Belittling or humiliating the person for finding the situation difficult
> Bribery
> Abandonment (or threats of this)
> Praising the person only when they achieve something you approve of
> Colluding with the person in pretending that they are not responsible for what they do, or that their behaviour is not damaging when it is
> Colluding with the person in their negative view of themselves, with generalised denigration of their abilities, or with the imagined awfulness and impossibility of the task etc. etc.
> Denying yourself pleasure until they have sorted themselves out

> Allowing all the pleasure of your relationship to become swallowed up by The Thing

2. When the thing he or she is putting off does affect you

What may help:

- Identifying and reducing your own tendency to procrastinate
- Paying attention to your own needs and notice how your partner's procrastination affects you.
- Noticing at what stage in the process of doing The Thing the person procrastinates, in order to be specific about the behaviour
- Explaining how the procrastination affects you, clearly and simply.
  Use phrases like –
  "*When you do xxxx, I feel yyyy*"
  or
  "*When you don't do xxxx, I feel yyyy.*"

Try to keep description of their behaviour as simple, objective and as un-emotionally-laden as possible. Don't generalise from one situation to another, or include *you always* – or *you never* – type comments – they are rarely likely to be true. Don't pack too many things you want changed into one comment.

So, for example –

"*Sometimes when you've been working you put everything away afterwards. But sometimes you leave piles of papers all over the table including unpaid bills and I feel irritated and anxious. That's not good for me.*"

rather than –

"*You keep leaving that b***** mess on the table, you never open any bank statements although I keep telling you you should, the garden shed is in chaos, you never call your mother and you're totally driving me crazy*"

- Asking for what you need, equally clearly, taking responsibility yourself where appropriate

so – *"I'd find it helpful if you tidied up when you finish your work and I'd like us to find a new way to sort out our financial paperwork. If I make supper, could you clear some space and we could look at the bills together afterwards?"*

This is much more effective than accusing and blaming. It gives the person the opportunity to see their behaviour, and its impact on you, in the context of your relationship. You are presenting a starting point for negotiation of behaviour which enables them to register their options and keep their dignity.

- If you find you are not being heard, set limits and boundaries and stick to them
- Locate other sources of support, relaxation and enjoyment for yourself and use them
- Ask your partner to go with you to talk things through with a third person whom both of you can trust to listen to both sides of the story
- If the procrastination is life threatening, be prepared, at the end of the day, to walk away (for example when someone promises but fails to stop drinking and driving)

What doesn't help:

> Ignoring your own tendency to procrastinate
> Ignoring or minimising your own needs, especially for safety and well-being
> Colluding with the person by pretending their behaviour is not their responsibility
> Pretending not to be hurt when you are
> Asking indirectly for what you need, dropping hints, sulking, sighing heavily; expecting the other person to intuitively "pick up" what you are thinking or need
> Getting abusive

> Setting limits and then not sticking to them, or alternatively making dramatic threats or revengeful gestures
> Blaming yourself for their behaviour
> Allowing their behaviour to take over your world
> Becoming a martyr

Living with someone who procrastinates a great deal can be a very isolating experience, especially if the person is productive in the areas of his or her life which are lived in the public domain. You may feel disloyal talking about what is happening to anyone else. You may feel angry that your partner is seen as organised and competent outside the home, but that you are exposed to their more chaotic and immature sides. You may wonder whether you are doing something unhelpful which is bringing out this behaviour. In the worst cases, you may begin to think it is your fault, especially if the mixed-up thinking of the person who procrastinates a lot is beginning to affect your own clarity of thought. Procrastination can be an irritant in an otherwise healthy and forward-moving life. But it can also be a sign of burn-out, that state beyond ordinary day-to-day stress, which can be a serious health hazard and require medical attention.

If you notice that procrastination seems to be a big problem for your partner, consider the following questions:

1. Does the person generally get on with addressing their needs and goals, but has a particular aspect of life in which they procrastinate (but eventually get the job done)?

2. Has the person recently started to procrastinate in an area in which they're usually relaxed and effective? Does the person seem more agitated and restless, listless or depressed, than usual? Is the person energised by new things, but is finding it hard to complete anything?

3. Does the person procrastinate as a way of life ?

If you're worried, look after your own needs and talk to your partner. If he or she cannot or will not make constructive changes, find someone else to share your concerns with. Far from being disloyal, letting your partner know that you need to talk to someone outside the relationship provides him or her with a model of someone saying *enough is enough* (frustration, worry, anxiety etc.). That may actually help break the procrastinatory loop your partner is stuck in.

If your child procrastinates

Given that procrastination is common to the majority of humans, it's highly likely that you will notice your children putting off all kinds of things. This is nothing to be alarmed about. It's a natural part of experimenting with action and passivity, cause and effect, control and power. Such behaviour would typically peak around the toddler years, (especially around potty-training time, see *The meaning of "Poo"*, below) and again at the mid-teens.

The time to deal with your child's habit of procrastination is if it starts to become habitual, problematic or dangerous. In Part 2, which addresses how we learn to do things and how procrastination develops, there are many suggestions for the kind of permissions and strategies which help children develop into effective, empathic individuals who confidently follow their own feeling-informed logic in the pursuit of a creative and joyful life. So if you notice your child putting things off in a significant way, you may like to re-read the sections which relate to that part of the **Action Spiral.**

What will work best with children is having an excellent role-model close to home – this means you! Find the aspect of their behaviour which irritates or worries you most and address it in yourself, and get support if you need to from your partner, a close friend or a professional counsellor or therapist.

A short digression on the Meaning of "Poo"

The complete body parallel for the process of going through the Action Spiral is *producing poo* (defecation). When we were tiny, we were mostly involved with taking things in, absorbing at all levels, and allowing what we didn't need to flow out. But gradually we become aware that once we take something in, hold it inside us for a while, something will be produced. As my brother said when his first son was very small, how this (*content of a few small jars of baby food*) gets to fill this (*huge box of disposable nappies*) is one of life's miracles. We keep the good bits of what we take in to grow stronger, and we get rid of what we don't need. We don't notice the day-to-day product of getting bigger and stronger that much, but we do eventually notice the poo.

Producing it is not just a passive process of letting go of something we don't need. It's also a muscular and creative act which produces a cleaned-out system and relaxed, satisfied feelings. Alongside the development of our teeth to cut up solid food, our digestive system is selecting, absorbing, processing and discarding what we don't need, and having to work much harder at it than when we just drank milk. As we grow and our muscles begin to come under our control, our adults (and other people we meet, like swimming pool attendants), begin to want us to control our sphincters too. People want us to be able to go through this particular loop of the **Action Spiral** in a certain way, time and place (*Look Mum, here's one I made earlier! My first act of creation – I would like to give it to you as a gift*). They may well praise us if we do, so our efforts are doubly rewarded. We can learn to complete our creative acts in ways that demonstrate our love for and co-operation with others. And we can learn to deal with our stuff ourselves, rather than dumping it on other people. Or we can withhold, refuse, resist, frustrate, and, having at last found something we can control, take revenge on our Adults.

Our adults may, (with apologies to Goldilocks), give us too much attention in the poo production department, or too little, or it may be just right, both parties gradually arriving at a satisfactory arrangement between them. Whatever happens around this time sets up all sorts of templates for our attitudes to our needs and those of others. The toddler years profoundly inform our attitude to action and control. Whether we feel that we are good (enough) or not, and that what we do is good (enough) or not, there are metaphors contained within our first creative process – the production of poo. The process teaches us about intake and production, give and take, generosity, withholding and negotiation. And it can also teach us about avoidance, unhealthy tension, agitation, and the lack of satisfaction or relief implicit in procrastination.

Have a look at these two descriptions, reflections from the smallest room. I recommend reading it both in relation to poo, and to how you feel about Things you procrastinate over. I'm not suggesting that small children actually think like this, although they may do, in images or in a general feeling-sense. As adults we may not think these thoughts exactly either, or we may do, in relation to what we are trying to do and how we feel about ourselves, our capacity to be productive, or lack of it, and the people around us. The point is that the **Action Spiral** is fundamentally interrupted and blocked by procrastination, and that much of how we negotiate the different stages of the spiral may be mirrored here. *And we can reverse our negative thoughts about any particular [illegible] of doing something by focusing on the relevant affirmation.*

Poo-speak

I am good The world is full of good things and people	*I am not good The world is bleak and demanding*
What comes out of me is good I can enjoy the process of allowing good things to come out of me	*What comes out of me is no good I can only force and strain to get the bad things out – I may be hurt in the process*
I like the feeling of having the good things inside me – but there does come a time to let go – there'll always be more good things to come	*Having the bad things inside me is all I've got and/or I just want to get the bad things out of me as quickly as possible*
The world will be glad for me when I allow my good things out. I know the world will welcome my things however they turn out.	*I will damage the world if I let the bad things inside me come out. I'm scared that will happen or I'm glad – I hate everyone*
I'm glad the world can enjoy what I have inside me I like the process of allowing the good things to come out of me: even when it takes effort, I enjoy the feeling of using my muscles. I breathe easily throughout	*Why should the world have what is inside me? What has the world ever done for me? Why should I have to suffer to produce something to please them? I stop myself breathing easily – I hold my breath*

I like thinking about the good things inside me – but I'd like to share them and then move onto new things – there's always more exciting things to be discovered

I'm afraid I'll feel empty if I let go of what's inside me – I feel like the bad things are all I've got and I feel ashamed. I feel uncomfortable and stale thinking about the same old things but at least they're familiar. I feel heavy and weary.

When I've allowed one of my good things out, I feel a satisfied and a bit tired in a nice way. Soon afterwards I feel refreshed, energetic and ready for the next thing. There's lots of good things outside me to be interested in as well

When I have forced out one of my bad things, I feel disappointed, empty, frustrated and sometimes angry. It's hard to move my attention to what's outside me. They aren't too wonderful either

My things aren't perfect but they are mine

My things are never perfect and I find that hard to bear

If someone doesn't like one of my things I don't mind too much.

If someone doesn't like one of my things I feel they don't like me; I feel criticised personally

Sometimes when I look back on my old things, I feel fondness for the me who produced them and an appreciation of how I have grown since then
My new things are different to my old things

When I look back on my things I feel self-critical, defensive and anxious that I still seem to be doing the same old stuff. I always think I should have done better. I never feel satisfied.

I'm excited to find out what new things will be inside me and outside me

It's hard to believe that new things will work out and not go bad inside me. It's difficult to feel excitement about anything

Carol's daughter had a dreadful problem with owning up. Carol was upset that Emma became very agitated and tormented about telling her when she'd done something wrong. The child put off talking about even trivial things until they were completely out of proportion. Emma had bad nightmares, but wouldn't tell Carol what they were about. Carol couldn't understand what was happening; she didn't like to think she was such a frightening parent, but she was irritated by the child's unwillingness to admit what she'd done. With the help of a child psychologist who talked with both of them, Carol came to realise that she set herself, and indirectly Emma, incredibly high standards. As a single mother, whose own mother had been extremely critical, Carol was very sensitive to being seen to be as a perfect mother, whose children wanted for nothing. She gave herself a bad time if she got anything wrong, for example if she didn't get them to class on time, or if she made a mistake filling in a school form. When the children did something wrong, she didn't shout as her mother had done, but became silent and withdrawn, feeling she had failed.

The psychologist speculated that this withdrawal might leave the children feeling they were still being punished. Carol's behaviour seemed to be a way of trying to protect both herself and her mother. The little girl had picked up that anything less than perfection upset her mother and made her anxious. She feared the shadow of her grandmother's demanding nature which was never far away from her mother's more controlled response when she did eventually confess her minor slips. Carol learnt to forgive herself for her own mistakes, to talk about them with friends in the children's hearing, and even laugh about what she'd done. As her mother relaxed, so

> did Emma; the nightmares stopped. Carol was delighted, and tearful, when Emma came straight out and told her mother she'd lost her purse, something previously she would have put off and covered up for weeks.

Notice your child's behaviour, and if it is causing problems, talk about it with him or her in a loving, constructive, and non-shaming way. Minimise confrontation over what is happening, and don't allow the Thing to become a battleground between you – children are just as capable as our partners of acting out other difficult feelings by putting things off. Don't allow atmospheres over bad behaviour to fester on in an un-ending kind of way, because this will be mirrored by the development of drawn-out procrastinatory habits which will become harder for your child to break.

Deal with issues directly, and briefly. Recognise examples of success, and promote the idea that the procrastinatory behaviour is the blip, rather than the other way round. Your child may have no idea why he puts things off, or he may surprise you. Involve her in identifying what she needs to help her make changes. Our children need to internalise models of adults who can break deadlocks, and who don't allow themselves to be dragged into unending, repetitive sagas of frustration. They need the security of adults who can survive being disliked, be imaginative, take tough decisions, follow through, be good-humoured – and have empathy for how hard it can be to be a toddler, child or teenager. Once you've really listened to each other, and what needs to be said has been said, make sure that your child recognises that life has moved on, that they are loved and valued and have many interesting things to be involved in and time to chill out.

We can have a major influence on how our children treat themselves.

What do you want that influence to be? Any positive changes you make for yourself will have a positive impact on what all our children inherit. And how you treat them will be absorbed at all levels, physically, mentally and emotionally, as part of the template for their "inner parent" which they are building to enable them to grow up and be loving, rounded, self-disciplined, independent adults. Their "internal conversations" will mirror the ways they were spoken to, and the permissions you offer will become their own. Think what a major range of permissions someone like Ellen MacArthur, the round-the-world yachtswoman, must have access to, for awareness, exploration, involvement, tenacity, ability to learn from mistakes, completion and celebration ... the list is endless. Her own amazing spirit and courage takes her forward and inspires millions, however different or mundane the circumstances. Procrastination is a habit which can be modelled and learnt, and so can the capacity for being happy, whole-hearted and effective. You can develop that capacity for yourself and your children.

Procrastination at work

If your employee procrastinates ....

If you employ or manage someone who procrastinates a lot, you need to watch carefully to see at which point within the process of carrying out a task the behaviour starts. It's unlikely to be across the board; if it is, and if this behaviour is strikingly different to their usually excellent performance, then you may have noticed a symptom of a much deeper issue (health problems, trouble at home, burn-out, or un-addressed conflicts about work) which needs to be addressed. But if it seems a more established part of the person's approach to working, once you've identified the stage at which they start stalling, notice how you manage this aspect of work yourself. You may need to do nothing more than get your own act together and model the kind of behaviour you want.

Next, notice exceptions to procrastinatory behaviour.

When does he or she –

- notice what is happening around him or her, rather than being blithely indifferent?

- arrive on time? Leap into action with energy and enthusiasm rather than dither?
- decide on a course of action, concentrate and remain absorbed in his or her tasks instead of being hugely distractible?
- complete on time and to budget, rather than endlessly extend with excuses and drama?
- admit to and learn from mistakes, enjoy rest and relaxation, celebrate successes – rather than avoid responsibility, repeat basic errors and/or never take a break?

Once you've noticed the exceptions, you can assess whether you've got a square peg in a round hole (for example a born "people-person" you've being trying to turn into an administrator, or an orderly, precise numbers-person into a salesman), and then move them to a more appropriate and more productive role. Alternatively you can begin discussions with the person along the lines discussed above –

> *describing behaviour specifically, including noting positive exceptions,*
> *saying what you need and want,*
> *finding out what they need and want,*
> *negotiating solutions together,*
> *agreeing how you'll both know the behaviour has changed for the better.*

If the person doesn't change, you need to set clear and firm limits. Procrastinatory behaviour doesn't usually go away of it's own accord, so it's best to act sooner rather than later, both to model effective action and to demonstrate the kind of standards you expect.

If your boss procrastinates

The behaviour of the people we work for can have a strong effect on our well-being. Addressing negative effects of an employer's behaviour can be difficult (and most people probably put it off!)

However if the behaviour is persistent, and is actually affecting your ability to do a good job, then sooner or later you'll need to say something.

As with anyone else, try to identify as precisely as possible exactly how the procrastination affects you. Does your boss ...

> Fail to notice or implement environmental changes that are needed for staff well-being? Appear to notice what you ask for but immediately forget? Fail to notice important changes in the market place which has direct impact on the strength of the business? Fail to open e-mail, letters or attend to bills?

> Come up with lots of new ideas, demands, comments, questions, which lead nowhere?
> Create far more openings and opportunities than the team can hope to chase up and fulfil?

> Interrupt other people's concentration or absorption with distractions?
> Have endless meetings that regularly wander off the agenda?
> Change and re-change tactics, so that direction is lost and work wasted?
> Leave a trail of incomplete paperwork for other people to sort out ?

> Create dramas around deadlines?
> Leave everything to the last minute, leaving you waiting around and having to work late to complete?
> Insist on perfection, or demand more and more improvements?

> Fail to learn from mistakes? Neglect to celebrate success?
> Fail to take time off, become increasingly exhausted, and fail to recognise anyone else's need for breaks?

I'm sure I've just described the boss from hell! – who wouldn't keep many employees for very long. Many employers will exhibit one or more of these behaviours, which doesn't mean he or she isn't a good manager overall. Recognise what affects you most in your own situation and start with something clear and identifiable. A good starting point is to use an approach based on very simply describing *what you need to help you perform better.* Suggest some options for ways forward which demonstrates that you have taken responsibility, wish to negotiate and which don't imply criticism. If time goes by with no change, you will of course need to increasingly set self-respecting limits, and find support from elsewhere in the organisation.

~

Procrastination out and about

What about if it's –

your son's teacher who forgets to talk to the Head about opportunities for the school choir?
your M.P. who never seems to have heard back from the council about your complaints?
your cousin who suggests marvellous places for you both to go but never makes a date?
your squash partner who's always in a tearing hurry and who repeatedly promises a better, more focused game, "next time"?
the insurance salesman who keeps sending you further questions about your claim?
Or any of the other people with whom you come into contact day-to-day, who have an impact on your life?

Understanding the stages through which things get done or put off will help you be specific when you are asking for what you need. It will enable you to be creative in offering support as an ally to the person who is putting things off, to help them get the job done, thus freeing you. We can't completely avoid the effects of other people's procrastination on our lives, but we can recognise it and co-operate with them to minimise the impact.

Part 5
A New Way of Living

YES!

A New Way of Living

What will life be like once you start doing things today rather than tomorrow? Procrastination slowed your system down to a heavy crawl, so you'll certainly gain a feeling of being lighter on your feet, and of being able to breathe more easily. But so, so, so much besides. The habit of putting things off took more than time, energy and resources. This may sound odd, but if you think about it, to procrastinate takes, amongst other qualities, the ability to –

- believe in a positive future
  (tomorrow would be a better day)
- use imagination
- use words to create convincing arguments
  (later would be better because ....)
- set high standards
  (I know just one more little change will improve things)
- tolerate delay
- make the best of life in less-than-exciting situations

You've been developing these abilities all the time you've been procrastinating! Once liberated from enabling you to avoid life, they all transform into extremely positive attributes which will underpin your ability to be tenacious in reaching for your goals and dreams. They form the flip-side of procrastination which you can use as strength. As you practice moving through each part of the **Action Spiral**, you un-block your system and get yourself un-stuck. You come out of the wings and onto the stage. You release your physical, mental and emotional energy and create openness to new relationships, ideas, plans, possibilities, opportunities - and the future. You free yourself to experience joy.

Without the old Thing hanging over you, the world is going to seem like a different place.

What you can expect

.......by allowing yourself to become aware

Over time you'll probably find life becoming a richer, deeper, more complex, brightly coloured, demanding, satisfying, frustrating, exciting, relaxing, painful and more loving place than previously (so you may need more sleep!). You'll re-experience a sense of wonder which you probably lost long ago. Do you know – or can you remember – the feeling of early morning on the first days of spring, the beauty and peace of soft, scented, April air? You'll have many moments like this again, at all times of the day and year, in a world made fresh and there for you to savour, all senses awake, your heart, body and mind open to new interest and experience.

If your new feelings are painful and distressing, talk to someone you can trust about what you are experiencing or remembering. If you are unused to noticing physical or emotional sensations, beginning to feel them again can be as uncomfortable as pins and needles, and as disconcerting as waking up in a new world. Let yourself slow down, take deep breaths from your stomach and let them out gently. You may start to notice you have a body for the first time in your life! – which can also bring some surprising and delightful results. So can becoming more aware of other people, their needs, desires, strengths and vulnerabilities. Your capacity for intimacy, and empathy will grow enormously. Don't expect it to be a one-way process, and don't rush yourself.

.......by allowing yourself to explore and experiment

If you practice allowing yourself to be open to new experiences and suggestions, over time your apprehension can turn to excitement and curiosity. You can also feel relief – you don't have to be in control all the time. Life really can support you as you try out new ways of doing things, and you'll develop resilience to the occasional and inevitable knocks you'll get in the process. Not every experiment will turn out perfectly – that's the point! – so you'll find your appreciation of other people's efforts, errors and success growing.

You'll probably find people in general becoming more

approachable and less enviable, and being with people who used to seem alarming will now appear challenging, exciting and stimulating. Being more willing to experiment can liberate your sense of imagination, creativity, fun and mischief, which has to be a good thing (your sex life will undoubtedly improve). You'll probably be and feel stronger and fitter. Expect more energy and more access to your "inner toddler", whose favourite question is *Why? (or why not?)*. In the short term, many of us also get in touch with a drive to be argumentative, careless, irritable, and those aspects of our nature which would like to be dare-devil or reckless. Keep yourself and other people safe.

.......by allowing yourself to choose and get involved

Trusting yourself to make good choices, and being able to stay with and get deeply involved in following through your decisions brings an enormous boost to your confidence and self-esteem. You build stamina, determination, discernment, sound judgement and resourcefulness. Your experience of whatever you choose to commit to will be deeper and more rewarding. It's a new state of maturity, so you may feel – or even become – taller. Some of us find our shoe sizes actually increases; good opportunity to experiment with new styles (and throw out the old)! You're back in the driving seat of your own life, rather than being a passenger, and the exhilaration of the ride is yours. Re-negotiating relationships may require tact and sensitivity.

But at times, many of us find ourselves wanting to use our rapidly sharpening "teeth" and ability to exclude by judging and teasing, or are tempted to be cutting, unkind, even cruel. These are simply feelings waking up; we need to protect other people with love and humour and use the feelings to further develop our powers of discernment and judgement of our own work and progress. And of course you'll inevitably continue to experience anxiety and even fear on occasion (but now you know you'll survive); you'll still have times of wanting someone else to make all your decisions for you. You have gained your independence, and you can still enjoy being dependant and *interdependent* sometimes as well. You may find yourself attracted to other independent people, and re-enthused by their commitment. You'll probably be asked to do more (effective people are always in demand) but you'll be able to be more discerning about your capacities and availability. Your capacity to sustain relationships will deepen considerably. *Your experience of time itself may change.*

.......by allowing yourself to complete

Experience of "good endings" and full completion releases tension and brings huge relaxation and relief. The more the effort expended, the longer and more intense the journey, the sweeter the feelings of release – just like the best orgasms (which you'll have more of). As you develop your ability to complete your involvements, not only is your experience of making love going to be enriched, but your general confidence, sense of meaning and purpose is likely to expand in leaps and bounds as well. People who find it hard to complete often feel a dull sense of apprehension, guilt and responsibility (like Eeyore the donkey), and shedding this can feel like losing 3 stone or 10 years – and you may look as though you have! You'll start to see the world again, having broken out of the chrysalis of your endeavours, and you can re-discover it's beauties afresh. You'll find your digestive system works better, and your appetite returns. Your house may seem bigger! (now that it's less cluttered).

All the time you've been involved you've been building a pool of experience to draw on, a memory bank of *doing what you said you'd do*, being committed, effective, and reliable, all of which leads to more faith in the future. If you've been living under a huge cloud, having the courage to say *enough* and walk away will give you enormous self-respect, and determination to make the most of life. But be careful not to throw babies out with the bathwater. Sometimes people get carried away with their new-found enthusiasm for completion, and walk away from relationships or situations which they later come to miss badly. If your new lease of liberated energy makes you impatient with other people, remember we all travel at our own pace. Learning how, when and what to let go of will bring you more joy and clarity, and it will enable you to hold what you value with a light hand.

.......by allowing yourself to pause

Allowing ourselves to pause is to become open to the unpredictable. Once our systems learn that we are deliberately creating space, all kinds of un-dealt-with emotional and mental stuff may surface, some of which may have nothing to do with the present circumstances. Have patience, take care of yourself and get support if you need to. Gradually the pleasure and value of pausing will become clear, and then you'll make sure to build it in as a necessity. You'll find your ability to listen to, learn from and appreciate your own wisdom, and that of other people, grows considerably. You'll save time, effort, physical, mental and emotional energy by not repeating the same old patterns and mistakes. You'll be much more aware that life is short, but it will be infinitely more satisfying and rewarding.

People who can look after themselves by taking rest properly are usually a pleasure to be around. They don't over-stretch themselves, they know how to say *no* whilst they've still got reserves, and they don't agitate other people with their exhaustion. Even in withdrawal, their confidence in their ability to replenish their energies makes them approachable, but they acknowledge their need for time by themselves with humour. If you are, or can become, one of these people, your freshness and enthusiasm, once recovered, is infectious and disarming because of its very physicality. If you can really rest, you can really, really exert yourself. When taking a break is as natural, sweet and deep for you as it is for a cat, you know that your capacity for effective action has fully recovered.

If you were someone like this,
what would you be saying to yourself right now?
Would you listen?

When any of us have spent years establishing procrastination as a habit, as a defensive strategy to cope with life, we may panic as we begin to realise that there are so many things we need to attend to, and that so much life has been wasted. We may feel trapped and want to change everything overnight. The fact is we cannot hope to be effective, productive, as aware and assured as we'd like to be, in an instant. *It takes time.* But if you begin now, there is all the time you need. Each tiny step further along the **Action Spiral** frees you to become as big as you are, as resilient, dynamic, loving and alive as you can be, following your natural inclinations to a radical transformation.

The spiral has always been a universal symbol of movement, growth and unfolding life. As you become increasingly capable of doing what you need and want to do, without unecessary delay, your world will expand beyond your hopes and imagination. And with the outer expansion will come an inner reward of quiet confidence, and strength.

So treat yourself with kindness, firmness and humour. Enjoy rest, find support along the way and welcome yourself to the richness of a new way of living.

Isn't it about time?

References and Further Reading

Self Help

For effective action –
Feel the Fear and Do it Anyway,
by Susan Jeffers, 1997, Rider, UK

The Seed Handbook
by Lynne Franks, 2000, Harper Collins, UK

The Work You Were Born to Do
by Nick Williams, 2000, Element Books, UK

For depression –
Depression: The way out of your prison
by Dorothy Rowe, 1999, Routledge, UK

For clearing clutter –
Clear Your Clutter with Feng Shui
by Karen Kingston, 1998, Piatkus Books, UK

For valuing time –
Women Who Run With the Wolves
by Clarissa Pinkola Estes, 1998, Rider

For creativity –
The Grace of Great Things
by Robert Grudin, 1991, Houghton Mifflin, US

The Artist's Way; a spiritual path to higher creativity
by Julia Cameron, 1992, Tarcher Putnam, US

For visualisation –
Life Choices, Life Changes
by Dina Glouberman, 1995, Thorsons, UK

Creative Visualisation
by Shakti Gawain, 1998, Bantam Books, US

Infant Development, Learning and Action

The Making and Breaking of Affectional Bonds
by John Bowlby, 1990, Routledge, UK

Growing Up Again *(Notes 1 and 2)*
by Jean Ilsley Clark and Connie Dawson, 1998, Hazelden Foundation, US

Gestalt Counselling in Action 2nd Edn.
by Petrushka Clarkson, 1999, Sage, UK

Our Need for Others and its Roots in Infancy
by Josephine Klein, 1992, Routledge, UK

Body Centred Psychotherapy: Hakomi Method
by Ron Kurtz, 1990, Life Rhythm, US

Becoming the way we are
by Pamela Levin, 1988, Health Communications Inc., US

The Drama of Being a Child
by Alice Miller, 1995, Virago Press, UK

Thou Shalt Not Be Aware
by Alice Miller, Lloyd de Mauss, 1998, Pluto Press, UK

Maturational Processes and the Facilitating Environment
by D.W. Winnicott, 1995, Karnac, UK

The Child, the Family and the Outside World
by D.W. Winnicott, 1991, Penguin, UK